MEDIEVAL SCANDINAVIA

From Conversion to Reformation, circa 800–1500

Birgit and Peter Sawyer

THE NORDIC SERIES, Volume 17

University of Minnesota Press
Minneapolis
London

Published by the University of Minnesota Press
111 Third Avenue South, Suite 290, Minneapolis, MN 55401-2520
http://www.upress.umn.edu
Printed in the United States of America on acid-free paper
Fifth Printing 2000

Library of Congress Cataloging-in-Publication Data

Sawyer, Birgit.
    Medieval Scandinavia : from conversion to Reformation, circa
800–1500 / Birgit and Peter Sawyer.
        p.   cm. — (The Nordic series : v. 17)
    Includes bibliographical references and index.
    ISBN 0-8166-1738-4 (acid-free paper). — ISBN 0-8166-1739-2 (pbk. :
acid-free paper)
    1. Scandinavia — History.   2. Civilization, Medieval.   I. Sawyer,
P. H.   II. Title.   III. Series.
DL61.S29   1993
948 — dc20   93-3511

Medieval Scandinavia

THE NORDIC SERIES

Contents

List of Illustrations

Preface

This book deals with the history of Scandinavia from the beginning of the ninth century, when Scandinavians came into closer and more regular contact with Christian Europe than ever before. Records of the activity of merchants, missionaries, Viking raiders, and royal embassies provide evidence that for the first time makes it possible to trace at least some features of developments in Scandinavia. The period we cover ends in the second and third decades of the sixteenth century, when there were two fundamental changes: first, the final collapse of the attempt to maintain a united Scandinavian kingdom, and second, the rejection by the rulers of Scandinavia of the authority of the bishop of Rome. When referring to periods longer than a century we have used three main subdivisions: the early Middle Ages (to c. 1100), which we sometimes call the Viking Age, the central Middle Ages (to c. 1300), and the late Middle Ages (to c. 1530).

The word "Scandinavia" does not appear to have been used in those centuries. It first occurs in Pliny's *Natural History* as a misspelling of *Scadinavia*, the name given to Skåne, which Pliny believed to be an island. The name Scandinavia was adopted in the eighteenth century as a convenient general term for the region in which Skåne lay. It has sometimes been used in a limited sense to describe the great peninsula now mainly shared between Norway and Sweden. This may make geographical sense but hardly does so historically; until 1658 a large part of what is now Sweden was in the Danish kingdom, and from 1380 to 1814 Norway was ruled by the king of the Danes. Scandinavia has consequently been used as a name for the three "Scandinavian" kingdoms, and that in turn has led to a great enlargement of meaning, for these kingdoms included, at various times, extensive territories elsewhere around the Baltic, in the British Isles, and in the Atlantic islands. The word has never been given such a wide meaning, however, and has normally been limited to the area in which Scandinavian speech has survived, notably the Faeroes, Iceland, and Finland, and it is with this wider "Scandinavia" that this book is concerned. Nevertheless, to avoid confusion the word will here be used for the central part of these kingdoms, that is, the "Scandinavian" peninsula and the peninsula of Jutland, with the associated islands.

As the extent of the kingdoms changed many times in the period, we have chosen to refer to modern countries when locating places or regions. Thus Skåne is in Sweden, although for most of the period it was part of Denmark, just as Finland was part of the Swedish kingdom from the thirteenth century to 1809. With a few exceptions we have adopted the form of place-names used in the 1967 edition of *The Times Atlas of the World*.

The first version of the Introduction and chapters 1, 8, 9, and 10 were written by Birgit, the others by Peter, but we have together rewritten them many times as the book took shape. The whole book has been extensively revised in the light of suggestions and criticisms made of the first version by Sverre Bagge, Knut Helle, Steinar Imsen, Niels Lund, and Thomas Lindkvist. We are deeply grateful to them for their encouragement and advice. They also pointed out mistakes and misunderstandings; those that remain are, of course, our responsibility. We have also profited from many discussions in various Scandinavian, U.S., Canadian, and British universities, in particular in the Medieval Seminar of Gothenburg University's History Institute. Thanks are due and are gladly given to the many other friends and colleagues who have given advice, made suggestions, or helped us to obtain pictures. We should especially like to thank Stig Jensen, Hans-Emil Lidén, Per Kristian Madsen, Else Roesdahl, Ragnar Sigsjö, Thorgunn Snædal, Erik Ulsig, Gun Westholm, and Ian Wood. And last, but by no means least, we should like to thank Gunilla Nilsson of Skara's Stadsinjenjörskontor for drawing the maps and tables.

Birgit and Peter Sawyer
Blombacka, Skara
Midsummer 1992

Introduction

The study of medieval Scandinavia has been and still is deeply influenced by the interpretation of its earliest history that was developed in the nineteenth century by political, legal, and literary historians and by archaeologists and anthropologists. Scandinavia figured prominently in discussions of early medieval Europe not only as the homeland of the Vikings but also as the region in which Germanic society remained uncontaminated by Christianity and other alien influences longer than anywhere else. Although most of the evidence for this supposedly pure Nordic stage is in texts written in the twelfth and thirteenth centuries, it was long believed that these provided reliable information about early Scandinavian history and society. It is mainly on the basis of medieval law-codes, Icelandic sagas, and Adam of Bremen's *History of the Archbishops of Hamburg-Bremen* that a picture of ancient Nordic society has been reconstructed, a picture that has answered different needs at different times and has been used for specific ideological purposes inside as well as outside Scandinavia (see chapter 10)—and that still influences the interpretation not only of early Scandinavian society, but also of its later medieval development.

The concept of an original Germanic cultural unity, combined with the idea of evolution, that the simple ("primitive") precedes the more complex ("developed") focused interest on Scandinavia. Because this part of Germanic Europe was the last to be Christianized and was thus the last to be affected by Roman and canon law, Scandinavian society was thought to have preserved primitive features that had once been common to all Germanic societies. A very important factor in shaping this approach was the development of social anthropology in the late nineteenth century. The ambition of early anthropologists was to order all human societies, institutions, and ideas in an evolutionary pattern, the theory being that the early stages, among historical peoples only preserved in a more or less weakened state, could be known by studying contemporary primitive peoples (Murray 1983, 28–29). This theory lies behind all the assumptions about Germanic tribes as aggregates of clans or lineages (either matrilineal or patrilineal) that still haunt discussions about kinship in early Scandinavia.

Although belief in a primitive Germanic law has now largely been abandoned, the legacy of nineteenth-century social anthropology and legal history still casts a shadow over medieval Scandinavia. Textbooks on history and legal history still claim that the earliest Scandinavian laws were based on customary law that was transmitted by word of mouth for centuries before being written down. Even though in the written versions this "old folk law" was reshaped under the influence of Roman and canon law, it is supposed to have left sufficiently clear traces to provide a secure basis for reconstructing prehistoric Scandinavian society. Research in the history of language and literature has similarly been rooted in nineteenth-century ideas, and the belief persists in some quarters that Icelandic poetry and sagas were written versions of purely native traditions that had been preserved orally for centuries. This view, once widely held, obviously gave these poems and sagas great value as sources for the early history of Scandinavia.

Traditional Interpretations

The interpretation of Scandinavia's early history has also been influenced by the theory of evolution. The assumption that the general trend has been one of "progress" from the simple to the complex has apparently made it possible to trace developments even when very few facts are known. The Middle Ages have, consequently, been seen as a time when clans, organized in tribes, were replaced by states; when local particularism gave way to national unity; and when kings, at first weak but later strong, gained control over societies that originally had no central authority. Many similar developments are supposed to have taken place: from an egalitarian to an increasingly stratified society, from custom to complex laws, from local barter to international trade, from pagan barbarity to Christian humanity and civilization. It has been generally supposed that development has been from the simple to the more complicated, often with the implication that the change has usually been for the better. Typological development, once greatly favored by archaeologists and still reflected in some museums, is a good example of this assumption of progress.

Such a theory of development poses many problems, not least as the changes are supposed to have taken place between A.D. 800 and 1500. In fact, in that period there were no clans in Scandinavia (see chapter 8, especially the conclusion), and at all times local particularism flourished alongside attempts to create larger political unions. There were different types of lordship and overlordship long before 800, and the royal power that eventually developed was also new and different and did not simply evolve from earlier overlordships. From the beginning of the period society was highly stratified, with slaves at the bottom, and the social evolution was toward equalization in that slaves were absorbed into the class of free tenants. Nothing is known about the hypothetical primitive law (see chapter 1, "Laws"), and as for the progress from barbarism to humanity, it should be noted that the later, not the early, laws prescribed the cruelest punishments. It is also impossible to claim that development in art and literature was from the simple to the complex; early skaldic poetry is far more complicated than later verse.

Other theoretical models have begun to play a much larger part in the interpretation of early Scandinavian history since it has become clear, at least to professional historians, that the colorful accounts of the distant past given by Saxo Grammaticus and Snorri Sturluson cannot be trusted. The void created by the rejection of these sources as a guide to the early history of Scandinavia has been filled with the help of other types of evidence, in particular the material remains that are studied by archaeologists and art historians. Attempts have been made to interpret this evidence in the light of what is known about "primitive" societies in other parts of the world with some success; anthropological models have contributed to a better understanding of the past. Unfortunately the Scandinavian evidence used in such comparisons, especially in discussions of religious history, has not always been well understood, and doubts about the reliability of many familiar sources are too often disregarded; even nowadays some archaeologists cite the Old English poem *Beowulf* as evidence for pre-Christian Scandinavia. It is therefore not surprising that many nonspecialists still accept as trustworthy the traditions found in the sagas and in Saxo's *Gesta Danorum*. It is perhaps more surprising that assumptions that are largely based on the evidence of such texts still figure prominently in discussions of early Scandinavian society, which is commonly made to appear an aggregation of extended families forming free peasant democracies that were guided by an innate sense of justice and in which all free men were equal and women were independent.

These ideas about early Scandinavia have obviously affected the interpretation of later developments, such as the process of Christianization, the development of ecclesiastical organization and of kingship and the machinery of government, the evolution of law, changes in social organization, family structure, and the emergence of an aristocracy. In our attempt to interpret medieval Scandinavia we have therefore paid particular attention to this early period, for it provides the basis for what follows. Moreover, ideas about the early centuries have been radically affected by recent discussions and studies that we have tried to take into account. In this book we have attempted to reexamine the evidence, relying as far as possible on contemporary sources rather than on the retrospective interpretations offered by medieval Scandinavians who had their own assumptions, and we have not attempted to trace developments before the ninth century. Later sources are of course not worthless; apart from providing valuable information about the time when they were written, they may also contain archaic elements (see chapter 1).

Source Problems

The written sources, discussed in chapter 1, pose problems that are familiar to historians of the medieval period in most parts of Europe. In the first place, they are generally concerned with relatively small sectors of society. With the exception of late medieval urban records, most of the people who figure in the sources belonged to the higher ranks of society—members of royal and aristocratic families and higher clergy. Almost everything was written by men, and their attitudes are normally reflected, a circumstance that calls for caution when considering the role of women. Most texts were, in fact, written by ecclesiastics, and their concerns and values are most prominent. The virtual monopoly of written culture by churchmen does not, however, mean that the church dominated daily life and oral culture to the same extent.

Even secular history was written by men who, if not active as clergy, had been educated in church schools. Their works are largely about the leaders of society, not the men and women who worked in fields and farms, markets and harbors. We read mostly about kings, bishops, and magnates and their disputes, about high politics and alliances, campaigns, victories, and defeats. It is true that in this man's world we also meet women, especially in the works of Icelanders and of the Dane Saxo Grammaticus, but these women, like the men who figure in these texts, are made to serve the underlying purposes of the authors. The history written in medieval Scandinavia has caused great problems for modern students of the period, a matter discussed more fully in chapter 10. One point that needs to be emphasized here is that historians wrote with a didactic purpose, to teach useful lessons from the past. Most historians had an Augustinian view of the past, which they saw as a fight between the kingdoms of God and the devil, between good and evil. Historians not only had a moral purpose; their works were expected to be effective propaganda to further the interests of the rulers, magnates, or bishops who commissioned them. One of their tasks was to glorify their patrons and their patron's ancestors. They were also expected to entertain. Medieval histories, in fact, had many purposes and tendencies, largely dictated by the circumstances when they were written. As a Swedish historian remarked, "contemporary circumstances are seen in the light of the past, and the past is interpreted in the light of the present" (Bolin 1931, 331).

Another consideration is that our sources are unevenly distributed in both space and time, and many have been lost. Most medieval diplomas, for example, have not survived, and estate surveys and accounts are so poorly preserved that it is virtually impossible to trace the history of any property or to study its management for more than a few years at most.

Some Conclusions

In this account of medieval Scandinavia we have had to omit many interesting and important topics, and we have not been able, in a book of this size, to provide a detailed narrative. We hope that the outline of political history in chapter 3 will serve as an adequate framework for the rest of the book, and that it, together with the topics that we have chosen to discuss at some length, will give a reasonably rounded and interesting impression not only of developments in Scandinavia in these centuries, but also of the ways in which we can know about them.

It is perhaps worth stating some of our main conclusions at this time. Scandinavia was in many ways much more like other parts of Europe than has been generally recognized, although there were some significant differences, for example, in the mechanisms of exchange and the law of inheritance. There were also great differences *within* Scandinavia. These have to some extent been obscured by the fact that all Scandinavians (except the Sami) spoke much the same language. The unity of the region has also been exaggerated by the tendency to assume that evidence from one part can be used to make good deficiencies elsewhere. This approach has been encouraged by the uneven distribution of different types of evidence at different periods. Eleventh-century runic inscriptions are common in eastern Sweden but rare in Norway. To balance that, many poems that were composed in Norway at that time have been preserved, but there are very few from Sweden. Numerous historical sagas were written in Iceland during the thirteenth century, but no texts of that kind were ever produced in medieval

Finland. Several histories of the Danes and Norwegians had been written before 1230, but after that date very little narrative history was written in either kingdom before the Reformation, although in Sweden several chronicles, some in verse, were produced in the fourteenth and fifteenth centuries. Such differences have naturally influenced the methods and aims of generations of scholars in different disciplines and in different parts of Scandinavia on whose work we have depended and to whom we are indebted. This variety of approach can make it difficult to achieve a satisfactory overall picture of the medieval history of the whole Scandinavian world. The problem is compounded by the very different historical and historiographical traditions in different parts of Scandinavia, discussed in chapter 10.

1

Sources

Compared with western Europe, Scandinavia is poorly provided with written evidence for its early medieval history. Before the eleventh century the only texts produced in Scandinavia were runic inscriptions and some coin legends; historians are therefore dependent on information gleaned from sources that were written elsewhere in Europe. The first known Scandinavian charter records a grant made by the Danish king in 1085, but it only survives as a copy. The earliest original, also Danish, is a fragment dated 1135; the earliest Swedish charter is thirty years after that. Many different kinds of texts were produced in the twelfth and thirteenth centuries, including saints' lives, histories, sagas, liturgical books, and collections of laws, both ecclesiastical and secular, and before 1200 some churches made lists of benefactors to be commemorated and surveys of their property. It was not until the second half of the thirteenth century, however, that the variety and volume of surviving evidence increases significantly, at first from the archives of monasteries, bishops, and royal government. Some laymen also kept records, and there are a few surveys and rentals of lay estates, mostly compiled after 1400. Charters, rentals, and surveys provide information about many places from time to time, but it was not until royal governments began keeping systematic taxation records in the sixteenth century that it is possible to obtain comprehensive information about the whole of Scandinavia, or to compare different regions and study changes in detail.

Many medieval records and manuscripts have been destroyed in the course of military campaigns in which some especially vulnerable areas, such as Västergötland and south Jutland, were repeatedly devastated. The Reformation was responsible for losses in all parts of Scandinavia. The only Swedish monastic library that was even partly preserved was Vadstena's; many of its manuscripts were given to Uppsala University. Most manu-

1

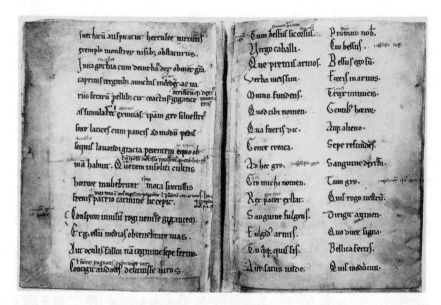

Figure 1.1. The Angers fragment of *Gesta Danorum*. Eight pages of Saxo's work were discovered in 1863, having been used to bind a fifteenth-century manuscript in the library of Angers in France. These pages were probably part of Saxo's working copy; the wide spacing left room for corrections and alterations. This is the only medieval manuscript of *Gesta Danorum*; for most of this text we depend on a printed version published in Paris in 1514. This fragment contains part of book 1, and these pages describe the encounter between a Danish hero, Bess, and Gro, a Swedish princess. Their exchanges, in verse, begin at the bottom of the left-hand page in the figure and continue on the next page. Peter Fisher's translation of this passage (p. 13) reads as follows: "Then Bess spoke 'You, maiden, who ride upon the steed's back, exchanging words with me, tell us your name, and from what lineage you take your birth.' " Photograph from Det Kongelige Biblioteket, Copenhagen.

scripts were dismembered for the sake of the parchment, which was used for many different purposes, even as wrapping for butter. Some leaves have survived because they were used as protective covers for administrative records of the sixteenth and seventeenth centuries, mostly now kept in national archives. They are tantalizing evidence of what has been lost. There are, for example, leaves from many fine liturgical books of the twelfth century, and some older than that (Gjerløw). Accidental fires, medieval as well as modern, have also taken their toll of records and manuscripts. The early archives of Stockholm were lost when the town's Rådhus burned in 1419, and many medieval records disappeared in the fires that destroyed Stock-

holm Castle in 1697 and Copenhagen University Library in 1728. Fortunately transcripts or excerpts of some archival materials were made in the
sixteenth and seventeenth centuries by historians, antiquaries, and lawyers.

Other types of evidence compensate for the paucity of conventional historical sources. Material recovered by archaeological excavation or by
chance discovery, buildings that still stand, coins, works of art—both
simple and sophisticated—and place-names have all contributed to a fuller
understanding of Scandinavian history and society than can be obtained
from the surviving texts, not just in the early period but throughout the
Middle Ages. Archaeological investigations can, indeed, yield information
about such topics as technology and diet on which texts cast little or no
light, even in richly documented parts of Europe.

Three groups of sources have recently been the subject of much discussion and reevaluation: Icelandic sagas, provincial law-codes, and runic inscriptions. The sagas and laws, together with the first accounts of Scandinavian history discussed in chapter 10, have played a large role in shaping
the traditional interpretation of early Scandinavian history, some aspects of
which are questioned in this book. Runic inscriptions have, on the contrary, been neglected by historians. A few are well known and often illustrate books and articles about the Vikings, but the potential of this remarkable epigraphic material as a whole has only recently been recognized.

Foreign Sources

Paradoxically, foreign sources cast more light on Scandinavia in the ninth
century than in the tenth. The Franks, having completed their conquest of
the Saxons by about 800, were then neighbors of the Danes, in whom they
took a keen interest for a while. Frankish sources consequently furnish
some information about Danish kings for the first half of the ninth century
(see "Ninth Century" in chapter 3). Chronicles and other works written by
the victims of the Vikings in ninth-century Europe, although biased, provide early evidence about Scandinavian armies; the *Anglo-Saxon Chronicle*,
for example, clearly distinguished between armies led by jarls and those led
by kings in the ninth century. Only two texts explicitly described conditions at that time in Scandinavia: *Vita Anskarii* (the Life of Anskar) and the
Old English version of Orosius.

The *Vita Anskarii*, written in about 875 by Rimbert, Anskar's successor
as archbishop of Hamburg-Bremen, has perhaps been accepted too readily
as a reliable and straightforward account of the missionary's life and activities. Comparison with earlier evidence suggests that Rimbert sometimes

adjusted facts to suit his main purpose, which was to justify and defend the union of the sees of Hamburg and Bremen. He was also concerned to emphasize the need for constancy in faith; many of the anecdotes he relates were intended to reinforce that message. The *Vita Anskarii* is nevertheless valuable as a source of information, which can sometimes be confirmed by other evidence, about various topics such as lot casting, assemblies, the function of kings, and pagan beliefs (Rimbert [hereafter *VA*]; Wood).

The English version of Orosius complements the Frankish sources. Orosius did not mention Scandinavia, a region that was obviously of great interest to the English in the ninth century. The translator was able to add some information obtained from various sources (Lund). One was Wulfstan, probably an Englishman, who described a voyage in the Baltic. Another was a Norwegian, Ottar, who visited the English king, Alfred, in the last years of the ninth century and gave an account of two major voyages he had made, one around North Cape into the White Sea, the other from his home in north Norway south to Hedeby. Some information about Ottar's home circumstances and the tribute he exacted from the Sami is also included.

Western sources are less helpful for the tenth century; the only information given about the Danes by Widukind in his *Saxon Chronicle*, completed in 968, is about the conversion of King Harald Bluetooth (see chapter 5). The next major source of information, and misinformation, about Scandinavia is Adam of Bremen's *Gesta* (see chapter 10).

Foreign sources continue throughout the Middle Ages to provide information about Scandinavia that would otherwise be unobtainable. Only the most important categories can be noted here. Chronicles produced in other parts of Europe, especially in Germany and the British Isles, supplement the meager Scandinavian annals, and many European archives contain records of diplomatic and other contacts with Scandinavia. The records of the papacy are the most voluminous and comprehensive source. Papal registers contain hundreds of letters to Scandinavian rulers and churchmen, and there are also records of papal taxation. There is a register of the letters of Gregory VII (1073–85), but the continuous registration of papal letters began with Innocent III (1189–1216). Many originals or copies from other periods were kept in church archives as evidence of privileges granted by popes, and decretals in which popes laid down the law were copied in collections made by canon lawyers. The value of such collections as a source is well illustrated by the letter concerning Knut Eriksson's marital problem, which only survives in a collection of decretals compiled in Spain in the seventeenth century. For the later Middle Ages the records of Lübeck and other Hanseatic towns are a major source of information that, combined with the English customs accounts of the fourteenth and fifteenth centuries, make it possible to discover a great deal about Scandinavia's overseas trade at that time.

Archaeological Evidence

In recent decades there have been remarkable, even dramatic, advances in Scandinavian archaeology. Surprising discoveries have been made not only by excavation but also by new methods of analyzing the material remains that have been found. There have been excavations in most towns with medieval origins, generally made possible and necessary by rebuilding; many rural settlements, or at least their cemeteries, have been investigated, and some Danish villages have been completely uncovered.

Excavations have not, of course, been limited to settlements and graves. Investigations of areas in which iron was produced have yielded a great deal of information about the methods used and can provide the basis for reasonable estimates of the quantity produced in some districts from time to time (Clarke; Martens). Marine archaeology has greatly enlarged knowledge of medieval shipping and harbors (Crumlin-Pedersen and Hansen).

Archaeologists are often tempted to compile distribution maps, but these can be misleading. Arguments from silence are particularly hazardous. Much has been destroyed by centuries of cultivation or by modern developments. The fact that in Skåne there are only 0.7 prehistoric remains per square kilometer although the equivalent figure for Uppland is 11 does not prove that Uppland was more densely occupied in prehistoric times than Skåne. The explanation is that Skåne has been more intensively cultivated than the Mälar region, where prehistoric remains tend to be in rocky areas that have not been disturbed by plowing. Differences in the distribution of artifacts may also reflect differences in the activity of archaeologists, developers, or people using metal detectors. Distribution maps are not entirely worthless, however; the discovery, in dated contexts, of objects such as whetstones or millstones far from the places they originally came from can provide clues to the way goods were distributed (Resi). Workshops, tools, and objects make it possible to discover how things were made and increase our respect for the skills of medieval craftsmen. Archaeology can even contribute to a better understanding of the organization of some crafts. The fact that the design of combs produced throughout the Scandinavian world, from Staraja Ladoga to Dublin, changed in much the same way in the early Middle Ages suggests that they were made by itinerant craftsmen whose zones of activity overlapped (K. Ambrosiani). Permanent and independent workshops would have tended to develop different, local designs, as happened later. There have been great advances recently in environmental archaeology, which now provides information about diet and vegetation that is unobtainable in any other way. Much else can be learned from the study of the bones of birds, beasts, and fish as well as of humans.

Perhaps the most significant developments in archaeological science are the improved methods of dating that are now available, best of all by dendrochronology, the dating of timber by the pattern of annual growth rings. This is proving to be a crucially important technique that has already yielded some surprising results. It has, for example, been possible to show that the timbers used in making the chamber in which the Danish king Gorm was buried came from trees that were felled in 958. Dendrochronology is especially useful in dating churches and other buildings, but care has to be taken to recognize which timbers have been replaced, and that requires knowledge of the history of building technology. The contents of medieval buildings, their furnishings, sculptures in wood and stone, and wall paintings are a quarry of information about such matters as the cults of saints, patrons, and cultural influences. Wall paintings are often used to illustrate aspects of medieval life, but they can mislead, for some were based on and closely copy illustrations in manuscripts or woodcuts from other parts of Europe. If, however, the source is known, the way in which the Scandinavian artist adapted it can be instructive.

Coin Evidence

The value of coins and coin-hoards as evidence for Scandinavian history in the early Middle Ages has long been recognized, and there is now growing awareness of their potential as sources of information about later developments, political as well as economic. Coins were first made in Scandinavia in about 825, probably at Hedeby. To judge by those that have survived, very few were produced there. It was not until the last years of the tenth century that relatively large numbers of coins were produced, and then at mints in Sigtuna and somewhere in south Scandinavia, probably Lund. In those two centuries hundreds of thousands of Islamic coins were imported into Scandinavia from Russia and east Europe. The flow of these eastern coins diminished toward the end of the tenth century and ended by 1013. That source was replaced by imports of English and German coins. Some 250,000 Islamic, English, and German coins have been found in Scandinavia, most of them in hoards deposited before the mid-twelfth century.

Figure 1.2. Paintings in Södra Råda Church, Sweden. The roof and walls of the nave of the wooden church at Södra Råda, on the boundary of Västergötland, east of Lake Vänern, were covered in 1494 with paintings by an artist called Amund, who also decorated several other churches in Skara diocese. There are several themes, including the parable of the prodigal son, which is illustrated and elaborated in twenty scenes, eight of which are reproduced here. The upper row shows the son being entertained by ladies of easy virtue, and the lower pictures show him reduced to working as a swineherd, being beaten for eating the pig's food, and welcomed home after the intervention of an angel (Ullén 1979). Photograph by Marianne Bratt. © Antikvariska-topografiska arkivet, Stockholm.

Many of these hoards also contain unminted silver. Some of this wealth may have been acquired peacefully, as gifts or in the course of trade, but most was plunder or tribute, or pay earned by Scandinavian warriors who served rulers in western or eastern Europe (Blackburn and Metcalf; Jonsson and Malmer).

Regular coinages began to be issued by Danish and Norwegian kings in the eleventh century, but not in Sweden, apart from the short-lived Sigtuna mint, until about 1150, a delay that reflects the late unification of that kingdom and the weakness of its rulers. Coins are, indeed, one indication of the effectiveness of government in medieval Scandinavia; Danish coinage virtually ceased for a while after 1330, when the kingdom appeared to be on the verge of dissolution. Many Scandinavian coins, even at the best of times, were very light; some weighed less than 0.2 gram and were so thin that they could only be struck on one side and are technically known as bracteates. Early medieval coins were mainly silver, but later issues tended to be debased. In Norway, for example, after a century in which coins, although light, generally had a high proportion of silver, debasement began soon after 1200, and by the end of the century coins only contained 30 percent or less of the metal. Early in the fifteenth century Eric of Pomerania's coins were almost pure copper (Bendixen 1967; Lagerqvist 1970).

Such coins were of little value internationally, and this debasement naturally had inflationary consequences within Scandinavia. Coins therefore tended to be used for small purchases; major payments and rents were often made in kind, or in foreign coin that began once again to be imported in large quantities in the later Middle Ages, especially to Denmark and the neighboring parts of Sweden. Many Danish hoards contain a large proportion of German coins; the largest hoard, from Kirial in Djursland and deposited in about 1365, contained 81,000 German coins and weighed 33.5 kilograms. There were also accidental accumulations; the largest have been found in monasteries and churches. Hoards and accidental accumulations are especially instructive, for they show what coins were in circulation from time to time in different regions and illuminate the contacts within Scandinavia and with the outside world (Malmer; Klackenberg).

Place-names

Place-names can provide much information about medieval Scandinavia, although their interpretation does pose problems. Most were first recorded in the fifteenth or sixteenth centuries, long after they were coined and when their original meaning had been forgotten. Many of the words used to form names survive only in dialects or are unknown. Some that appear familiar had different meanings when they were used to name places or had different meanings in different regions. The word *by*, for example, which is closely related to the verb *bö*, "to dwell," and was used to name thousands of places in Scandinavia, meant "village" in Denmark and "single farm" in Norway, and in both countries now means "town," although in Sweden it still means "village." In interpreting names account must be taken of such changes of meaning and of other ways in which they may have been affected by linguistic changes (Christensen and Sørensen; Dalberg and Sørensen).

Despite such uncertainties place-names can cast light on a wide range of topics, including the development of language, pre-Christian religion, changes in the landscape, boundaries, and communications. Their main value for medieval history has been as evidence for the development of settlement. They provide more comprehensive information than can possibly be gained by archaeological investigations. The contribution of place-names to settlement history is limited, however, by the uncertainty about the date of many of them; it is rarely possible to determine the currency of a particular type of name more closely than within three or four centuries, and some were in use for much longer periods. Nevertheless, the thousands of names describing clearings, for example, dramatically reflect the extensive colonization of forest in many parts of Scandinavia between the tenth and fourteenth centuries. In the more fertile parts of Denmark and southern Sweden that were already fairly well populated in the Iron Age, place-names are a less satisfactory guide to settlement history. In such areas archaeologists have discovered traces of many settlements that were occupied sometime during the first millennium A.D. Some are deserted with no known name (although a few field names like Gamleby, "Old *by*," can be clues to their existence). Others are in or very close to settlements with names that are unlikely to be so early; those with Christian names such as the Danish Pederstrup, "Peter's thorp," cannot be older than the eleventh century. Many earlier settlements, of course, may have been abandoned and their sites reoccupied later, but in such cases the names give a misleading impression of the development of settlement (Grøngaard-Jeppesen).

The abandonment of a site does not necessarily mean that the settlement was deserted. In many parts of Scandinavia, during the first millennium A.D. settlements were moved a few hundred yards at intervals of a century or more and only acquired a permanent location in the eleventh or twelfth centuries. It is likely that at that stage many were given the name by which they were later known. It is also likely that in Scandinavia, as in England, many early settlements were treated as part of estates or districts and were only given separate, permanent names when the large territory broke up or was reorganized. Some names that can, on good grounds, be dated to the Iron Age, although later associated with particular settlements, originally may have described extensive districts in which there were many settlements.

Runic Inscriptions

Runes were known in Sweden at least as early as the third century and continued to be used there throughout the Middle Ages, after the conversion in parallel with the Latin alphabet. A total of about five thousand runic inscriptions are known in Scandinavia. Most of them are on stone monuments—memorials or gravestones—but they are also found on wooden, metal, and bone objects, such as tools, weapons, coins, and church bells, and on baptismal fonts. The monumental inscriptions, which tend to be better preserved, larger, and more imposing than others, can give the misleading impression that the script was prestigious and particularly associated with people of high status. That runes consist exclusively of vertical and diagonal lines shows that they were originally designed to be cut across the grain of wood—horizontal lines would tend to be lost in it. A knife and a piece of wood were all that was needed to carve an inscription. There is therefore no reason to doubt that they were used in daily life at an early stage. A stick found in Hedeby has an obscure inscription, probably of the ninth century, that may refer to a contract of sale. Excavations in other places where wood is well preserved, notably Bergen and Lödöse, have unearthed a great variety of inscriptions showing that runes were used for personal, even amorous, messages as well as for business, political, or legal purposes. Some inscriptions with personal names found at Bergen appear to have been used to identify the owners of goods, probably wool-packs, and a twelfth-century calendar has been found at Lödöse.

The best-known inscriptions are the Danish, Norwegian, and Swedish rune-stones. The custom of erecting stone monuments with runic inscriptions began in the migration period but flourished most vigorously from the end of the tenth century to the beginning of the twelfth.[1] The approximately two thousand inscriptions known from that period are very different from earlier or later runic monuments and show that there was then a common and distinctive monumental fashion throughout Scandinavia. These inscriptions are mostly clear and factual, and almost all are remarkably similar in language, formulas, and content. The earlier inscriptions are a striking contrast; many are exceedingly obscure, their contents vary greatly, and some have magic formulas.

Most rune-stones of the tenth and eleventh centuries were erected in honor of dead people, and almost all inscriptions begin with a memorial formula, telling us first who sponsored the monument, then in whose memory it was done, and in 90 percent of the cases how the sponsors and deceased were related. Sometimes additional information about the sponsor or the dead person (or both) follows—for example, their social status, titles, voyages abroad, military achievements, causes and places of death. Magical spells and invocations of pagan gods are very rare; they occur in Denmark but are exceptional in Sweden where, instead, Christian crosses and prayers are common, especially in Uppland. Many inscriptions end by naming the rune carver.

Although many rune-stones have disappeared and new discoveries are made from time to time, there is no good reason to suppose that the original distribution was very different from that known today. About 50 are known in Norway, about 200 in the medieval Danish area (including what are now the Swedish provinces of Halland, Blekinge, and Skåne), and at least 1,800 in the territory of medieval Sweden, more than half of them in Uppland. The dating of individual inscriptions is most uncertain, but it is generally accepted that the Danish (except those from Bornholm) are from the late tenth and early eleventh centuries. The inscriptions in Västergötland and Östergötland are considered to be more or less contemporary with the Danish, those in other parts of Sweden somewhat younger; in Uppland (and on Bornholm) rune-stones were not erected until some decades into the eleventh century, and in some places they were apparently still being put up well into the following century. The uneven distribution of the inscriptions and the short period in which they were erected have been much discussed.

Rune-stones have been used in many disciplines as a source of knowledge about the Viking Age; they can throw light on such varied matters as language and orthography, art and poetry, place-names and personal names, kinship, settlement, communications, Viking expeditions, and, not least, the spread of Christianity, for most stones are Christian. Many of these topics have been investigated or are currently being studied, but much remains to be done, above all within a framework that is both inter-Nordic and interdisciplinary. Most discussions have been regional or limited to the inscriptions in one country, and there has been a tendency to concentrate on one aspect, such as the language, the form of the runes, the layout, or the ornament. As a result some regional characteristics have not been recognized or thought to be significant, and the value of the stones as evidence for the period has not been fully appreciated. Historians, for example, have tended to pay most attention to the rune-stones that commemorate men who died abroad, which may give the impression that such inscriptions are typical, when, in fact, they amount to less than 10 percent of the whole material. Most monuments were for people who lived and died at home and constitute a corpus of contemporary evidence for the period that has been largely untapped, at least by historians. It is true that the inscriptions seldom provide information about events or identifiable persons, and it might justly be asked what historical knowledge could be gained from the large number that only tell us that someone about whom nothing else is known has raised a stone (which is obvious) in memory of an equally obscure person. The answer must be: not much, if only single stones are considered, but *studied as a whole*, the corpus of rune-stones is a most rewarding source for the social, economic, and political history of Scandinavia at the time.[2]

In order to use the rune-stones as a source we must try to understand why they were erected. There is general agreement that this fashion met certain needs, but there is little agreement on what those needs were. Earlier attempts to explain the sudden explosion of runic inscriptions as a result of Viking activity or change of faith are not satisfactory. It is true that Viking raids are a possible explanation for the stones erected in honor of men who died abroad, but because such stones constitute only a small minority, they clearly cannot explain the fashion. Many handbooks and general works nevertheless refer to the rune-stones of the period as "Viking monuments," probably because that was the view of such eminent experts as Erik Moltke and Sven B. F. Jansson. The latter goes so far as to say that "when the great expeditions were over, the old trade routes closed, and the Viking ships no longer made ready each spring for voyages to east and west, then that meant the end of the carving and setting up of rune-stones in the proper sense of the term. They may be called the monuments of the Viking voyages, and the sensitive reader may catch in many of their inscriptions the Viking's love of adventure and exploits of boisterous daring" (Jansson, 38). Even if it is argued that the voyage stones were the proper rune-stones, having set the style and fashion for all the others, it remains to be explained why suddenly toward the end of the Viking Age seagoing relatives were honored in this special way in so many different parts of Scandinavia. Scandinavians had voyaged abroad for centuries and erected monuments of various kinds, but not like those of the tenth and eleventh centuries. Other factors, therefore, must be sought to explain the fashion and its uneven spread.

The process of Christianization is certainly one factor, for the fashion reflected the transition from pagan to Christian burial customs. Some scholars argue that the erection of rune-stones answered emotional needs among the newly converted who, having buried their relatives in new ways and places—that is, in churchyards—nevertheless wanted to honor their relatives in traditional places, at home, by a road, or at a place of assembly. That may have been the reason some memorials were erected, but many rune-stones were moved at an early date from their original sites to stand in churchyards or to be built into the fabric of churches; others may even from the outset have been placed in or close to a church. This suggests that it was the *lack of churchyards* that created the need to erect a Christian rune-stone. In Uppland the building of churches and the consecration of cemeteries was apparently delayed for a long time, and in this province many rune-stones seem to have functioned as Christian gravestones in pagan cemeteries (Gräslund). It is therefore likely that this type of monument compensated for the abandonment of grave goods; the new and simple Christian burial habits must have been perceived as an enormous breach with the old custom that had not only honored the dead but also displayed the wealth and status of his or her family. In a transitional period, before churches and churchyards became the natural places for memorials, ostentatious rune-stones in public places could have served those purposes.

The transition to Christian forms of burial cannot, however, be the only reason for the appearance of rune-stones; it explains neither the uneven distribution of the stones, nor why so few women were honored in this way (in only 7 percent of all inscriptions, half of them together with men). The much higher proportion of richly furnished women's graves in the Iron Age suggests that religious change and new burial customs cannot be the whole explanation for the new fashion. Moreover, the distribution of rune-stones suggests that in some parts of Scandinavia they were not needed, either because circumstances were different or because the functions elsewhere served by rune-stones were fulfilled in some other way.

Any attempt to discover what those functions were must first take into account that rune-stones were memorials not only to the dead but also to the people who raised them; sponsors are almost always named first. Another characteristic feature of virtually all inscriptions is that the relationship of the sponsor and the deceased is stated, implying that this was significant in the context. A systematic study of the whole material has revealed that there were indeed certain principles determining who commemorated whom, with some significant regional variations. Because the general principle was that people were commemorated by their closest relatives or companions (comrades-in-arms, business or marriage partners) it can reasonably be assumed that the sponsors had some interest in what the dead had owned or been entitled to. That interest was commonly a claim, personally or on behalf of minors, to inherit land, goods, or status (such as the rank or title of thegn); some sponsors had a right to a share of what had been owned jointly in marriage or a partnership.

Whatever the function of these memorials, they can be expected to *reflect*, at least partly, the inheritance customs of the people who commissioned them. There is much to indicate that it was the new conditions—of responsibility and ownership—following the death of a relative or partner that determined not only who commemorated whom but also the order in which sponsors were named and the care with which their different relationships with the dead were specified.

There are, in fact, two main patterns, one prevailing in Uppland, the other in Denmark; other regions show traces of both in varying degrees (B. Sawyer 1988, 1991a). The Uppland pattern is of multiple sponsors, including numerous women, and the Danish is of individual sponsors, few of them women. This raises the question of whether the patterns reflect different systems of inheritance among the stone erectors, predominantly partible in Uppland and impartible in Denmark (as well as in Norway and in Götaland). Partible inheritance was the normal rule later, but we should not exclude the possibility that some earlier inheritances were not divided. At the time the rune-stones were being put up, the Danes were ruled by exceptionally powerful kings who could perhaps have prevented the partition of land they gave to their leading followers. An alternative explanation is that multiple sponsors included all those with a claim to inherit, while individual sponsors had a claim to something that could not or should not be divided, such as a position as royal agent or the main residence of a landowner, which was generally reserved for the eldest son. Whatever the explanation for these different patterns, the main questions raised by the rune-stones are why, at just that time, such an abundance of information about inheritance and ownership is monumentally displayed, what need was met by erecting these memorials, and why they are so remarkably similar.

Rune-Stones as a Crisis Symptom: A Hypothesis

The rune-stone fashion of the late tenth and eleventh centuries was probably initiated by King Harald Bluetooth's huge memorial to his parents at Jelling. The inscription on that stone, although long and elaborate, seems to have set the pattern. Harald had very great prestige throughout Scandinavia, and it is hardly surprising that the monument he erected proved so influential. The Jelling stone is, moreover, a symbol not only of the transition from paganism to Christianity but also of the development of a new form of government (chapter 4). These religious and political developments, together with the consequent social and economic changes, seem to have been directly responsible for the proliferation of runic inscriptions on the pattern set at Jelling. The fact that most Danish rune-stones are in areas that were brought under direct royal control by Harald Bluetooth and his son Sven suggests that the rune-stones were a response to that development. There are relatively few in south Jutland and the island of Fyn, areas that were the heart of the Danish kingdom long before Harald "won all Denmark." There are even fewer in Halland and south Norway, regions where Danish kings were still only overlords in the early eleventh century. It was in Sjælland and Skåne that people found it desirable to erect stones to assert claims, old or new, in the manner that Harald had done. As already suggested, the association of the inscriptions with growing royal power in Denmark may explain why most had single sponsors.

In Götaland, where a new type of royal authority was being established, rune-stones are similarly rare in areas that were most closely associated with kings, in which bishoprics and royal monasteries were founded later. Kings were even more closely associated with Svealand, in particular with Uppsala, but they had less authority there than in Götaland. The rune-stone fashion took root in that region largely for religious reasons. Many families erected monuments to show their acceptance of Christianity. Missionaries may indeed have actively encouraged converts to erect rune-stones as evidence of their success. It is likely that by publicly registering the claims of Christian heirs and potential benefactors in this way, clergy were able to compensate for any difficulties caused by the public assemblies' (in which heirs were recognized) remaining pagan. Christianity was not generally accepted in Uppland until the end of the eleventh century, and as long as there was what has been called a free-church system, rune-stones seem to have served as memorials to church benefactors, including sponsors.

A religious motive for sponsoring runic inscriptions does not exclude a political one; they could also be a response to attempts made in the eleventh century to increase royal authority in the Mälar region. It is significant that the densest concentration of inscriptions in Uppland is in the area around Sigtuna, a royal town founded in about 975. What is more, the inscriptions immediately west of Sigtuna are very different from those in other parts of Uppland; many of them are, indeed, more like those in Denmark and Götaland, with a high proportion of individual claims and few explicitly Christian inscriptions (B. Sawyer 199a, 109). Where, as in Denmark, conversion was effected by a powerful king, there was no need for individuals or families to proclaim adherence to the new faith—declarations of *paganism* marked defiance of the accepted norm. There are about twenty pagan inscriptions in Denmark, but only six in Sweden, three of them in Västergötland and the others in Södermanland. Conversely, that most rune-stones in Uppland are ostentatiously Christian indicates that there the *Christian* belief was a breach with tradition that needed to be marked. In the area west of Sigtuna, however, the Christian faith was apparently not an issue, and it is also in this area that the lionstones occur—that is, rune-stones with decoration including the very stylized four-legged animal that is thought to have been inspired by the great Jelling stone. Of the fifty-five such lionstones in Uppland almost 80 percent are in southwest Uppland. If, as seems likely, this figure was a symbol of royal power, its frequent occurrence in that area is one of several indications that Sigtuna and the district west of it was a bridgehead for the establishment in Svealand of a new type of royal authority developed in Denmark. The political and religious changes that, it is argued here, led to the erection of rune-stones happened much more slowly in Svealand than in Denmark or Götaland, which explains why they were erected over a much longer period and are far more numerous in Svealand than elsewhere.

Whether or not this interpretation of the runic inscriptions as a symptom of dramatic change is accepted, they undoubtedly cast much light on social and economic conditions of the time (see chapter 8).

The Role of Oral Tradition

Although runes were used much more widely than has sometimes been supposed, this use was mainly for memorial inscriptions, short messages, and occasional poems: they did not give rise to a written culture. Knowledge about most things—customs, social relations, kinship, craftsmanship, history, the art of living, and ideas about life and death, creation, and doomsday—was passed on by word of mouth. This oral culture flourished alongside the written culture that was introduced by the church, each influencing the other. Consequently, it is uncertain how far the early written versions of laws, sagas, and history produced in Scandinavia were based on oral traditions, and to what extent those traditions were affected by being put into writing.

For an earlier generation of scholars this was no problem; it was generally believed that records of past events, beliefs, and customs were preserved in sagas, poems, and legal formulas that were passed by word of mouth unchanged for centuries before they were written down in the twelfth century and later.

Few if any scholars nowadays believe that the relationship between past reality and the ways it was represented in oral tradition and texts is so simple. In the first place, modern studies of the development and transmission of traditions have demonstrated that tradition and historicity are very different. Oral traditions, whether preserved in stories, poems, or rules of law, are modified from time to time to suit changing circumstances, and when they are ultimately put in writing, the versions that are then current, not their distant and forgotten sources, are drawn on. In medieval Scandinavia traditions were not recorded mechanically; authors were not passive mediators but adapters. They also had written sources, including laws and literary works from other parts of Europe, that greatly influenced the form as well as the content of the texts produced in Scandinavia.

There are very different opinions, however, about the possibility of tracing native traditions in Scandinavian texts. For many scholars the pendulum has swung so far that they treat sagas and laws exclusively as products of the time they were written and consider that traditional elements in them are undetectable or nonexistent. According to that view, sagas and laws can be used only as sources for the ideas, values, and attitudes of the thirteenth and fourteenth centuries. Some students of the sagas have, however, not given up hope of finding criteria to identify traditional elements in them. Legal historians, in contrast, appear to be increasingly pessimistic about such a possibility. Indeed, some have gone so far as to deny that the medieval laws contain any native element.

Laws

Many medieval Scandinavian law collections have been preserved.[3] There are provincial laws and church legislation, as well as the later general law-codes for rural communities in Norway and Sweden known as landlaws (Swedish *landslagar*, singular *landslag*); medieval Denmark had no such general law-code. Norway and Sweden also had comprehensive urban law-codes, supplementing the landlaws. The Norwegian landlaws and town laws were issued in the 1270s by Magnus Håkonsson, who consequently earned the epithet "Law-mender" (Lagaböte). In 1271, after the Icelanders acknowledged the Norwegian king, he issued new laws for them, *Jarnsiða*, but these were replaced ten years later by *Jónsbók*, in which earlier Icelandic law was combined with the new landlaw. In Sweden similar comprehensive codes for the whole kingdom were produced in the 1350s under Magnus Eriksson. A revision was authorized in 1442 by King Christopher, but it is doubtful if it was used before the sixteenth century.

Of the eighteen surviving provincial laws, only three were authorized by kings; the law of Jutland by Valdemar II in 1241, the Uppland law by Birger Magnusson in 1296, and the Södermanland law in 1327 by Magnus Eriksson (or his regents). The date of the others (three Danish, four Norwegian, and eight Swedish) and of the equivalent Icelandic collection known as *Grágás*, is uncertain, and little or nothing is known about the circumstances of their compilation. Their status is also obscure and has been much discussed. An early view, originating with Germanists, was that they were private compilations (Swedish *rättsböcker*, German *Rechtsbücher*) in contrast to the official law-codes (Swedish *lagböcker*, German *Gesetzbücher*), a significant distinction in assessing their value as sources. It was believed that, as private compilations combining legislation, decisions made by courts in particular cases, and orally preserved customary law, they could be made to yield information both about archaic Scandinavian law and the way in which it had been changed over centuries, thus casting remarkable light on the development of Scandinavian (and therefore of Germanic) society from prehistoric times.[4]

The claim that the provincial laws were private compilations in which different stages of legal development were gathered was supported by arguments based on their content and on their language and style. They are unsystematic, with repetitions and contradictions; they include laws that were out of date; and they sometimes explicitly contrast old and new laws. A good example is the older Västergötland law on inheritance: "On his deathbed a man must not give anything away from his heir [to the church] unless the heir himself agrees. Learned men say that according to the law of God, the heir must not disagree" (Äldre Västgötalagen, 77 [Ab 10]). The Norwegian Gulating Law juxtaposed old and new law in a remarkable way. The version attributed to Saint Olav was revised in about 1163 by or for Magnus Erlingsson, and both versions are given in parallel in the manuscripts; the oldest surviving manuscript is a fragment from about 1180. The contradictions in the laws may partly result from the fact that new laws did not come into force immediately. Until they were adopted by appropriate assemblies, they were no more than proposals. The Swedish landlaw, for example, was adopted in Västergötland about forty years after it was first issued. In such circumstances it was sensible to include both old and new rules in any collection designed to be used in court.

It has been claimed that characteristic features of the early customary element in the laws are narrative style and the detailed description of particular cases; for example, "A farmer who lives in a village where he owns land and house, is forced to sell" (Dalalagen, 47 [Bb 1]). Other distinguishing features such as alliteration ("Land shall be built with law"), rhythmic constructions, and quasi-proverbial formulas have been interpreted as aids in memorizing the laws before they were written down. Anthropologists and students of modern folklore have shown that these are, in fact, not very effective mnemonic devices, and other recent studies have cast serious doubt on the value of such features as proofs of great age. There is, for example, more alliteration in church law and other manifestly new laws than in those that are older. Alliteration appears to reflect the influence of Latin literature and, like the other purportedly archaic features, seems to have been deliberately used to give an impression of antiquity. Any orally preserved customs that were incorporated in the laws were, as already noted, unlikely to have been much more than a generation old.

The distinction between official codes as statements of current law, and private compilations containing a mixture of old and new laws, cannot be maintained. It was not recognized by contemporaries, and the unofficial texts were produced to be used in legal proceedings. The compilers of the anonymous provincial laws were not impartial gatherers of miscellaneous laws; they had their own purposes, and these affected what they chose to include. In fact the provincial laws have a very limited range and concentrate on a few topics, mainly church organization and church law, marriage and inheritance, landownership and tenancies, and the organization of rural communities. Most space is devoted to fixing penalties for various misdeeds.

The authors of the provincial laws were in contact with lawyers elsewhere, and their compilations need to be seen in the context of general European legal development. As the extent of the influence of canon, Roman, and other foreign law in Scandinavia is recognized, it is becoming increasingly difficult to be certain what is native. Some laws are explicitly said to be old custom, but such assertions do not inspire confidence. They are most common in codes authorized by kings, and there are grounds for suspecting that they were intended to make new laws more acceptable. Some scholars deny that it is possible to identify the native element, but others consider that the contradictions and different principles in the Scandinavian laws reflect differences between early native law and innovations from abroad—from canon law, for example. One scholar, Elsa Sjöholm (1988), has argued that the Danish and east Swedish laws have no native element whatsoever but are entirely derived from foreign sources, mediated by clergy. Most commentators have rejected that view as too extreme. Much was undoubtedly borrowed, but it would not have taken root in completely barren soil. Some new laws may have been adopted because they served the legislator's purpose, but others were probably accepted as good formulations of familiar rules.[5]

It is generally accepted that the laws do contain some native rules and procedures, difficult though it may be to identify them. They certainly cannot be regarded as relics of primitive Germanic law; at best they provide evidence for the period immediately before conversion. Antiquarian curiosity may explain why some out-of-date laws were included, but others were retained because they served a contemporary purpose. Obsolete laws about slaves, for example, were included long after slavery was abolished because they offered a convenient explanation for, and justification of, the control some men exercised over others by suggesting that a large section of society was descended from slaves and consequently had no, or a very limited, right to inherit free land.

That the earliest, and sometimes the only, manuscript of many of the provincial laws of Norway and Sweden, and the Icelandic *Grágás*, were produced in the decades immediately before the royal codes were issued suggests that comprehensive royal legislation was preceded by a period, earlier in Norway than in Sweden, in which the provincial aristocracies were eager to define the law observed in their assemblies. In doing so there were conflicts of interest and disagreements, most obviously between bishops and lay aristocrats, and the outcome varied, depending on the relative power of the different groups and individuals at the time. Some texts may even have been produced to provide the men drafting the royal codes with information about the law observed in the provinces. Until the royal codes were accepted by the provincial assemblies, a long-drawn-out process in Sweden, these texts were useful for the men who used them to conduct proceedings. As they decided what rules to apply, conflicting rules in the texts mattered little.

The decisions of courts, commissions, judges, and arbitrators began to be recorded in the late thirteenth century, and little is known about the observance of laws before then. Town records, mostly of the fifteenth century, show how urban laws functioned in practice in some places, including Stockholm and Kalmar. Diplomas show that the provisions of the Norwegian landlaw were generally observed, but as diplomas were occasionally drawn up to legalize exceptional inheritance arrangements, some may give a misleading impression (Imsen). This practice seems to have been

common in Sweden, where, in any case, laws tended to be treated as rec-
ommendations to be taken into account rather than as rules to be obeyed
(Gunneng).

Icelandic Sagas

The Old Norse word *saga* (plural *sögur*, cognate with the verb *segja*, "to
say") originally meant "what is said," but it came to be used for the narratives written in Iceland and Norway from the twelfth century to the fourteenth. The earliest were about Norwegian kings. The first of these were
written before 1150, but most were produced between 1190 and about
1230, a period in which sagas also began to be written about the bishops
and leading families of Iceland. The sagas about bishops, a few of whom
were treated as saints, covered the period from the eleventh century to
1340. Sagas in which Icelandic laymen were the leading characters were
originally called *Islendingasögur*, but that term and its English equivalent,
"Icelandic Family Sagas," is now restricted to those dealing with the period
between settlement and the early eleventh century. A similar term, *Islen-
dinga saga*, is, confusingly, used for sagas written in the thirteenth century
about contemporary or recent events in Iceland. This group is sometimes
referred to by the title of the longest of them, *Sturlunga Saga*, and that name
will be used here. Many of the bishops' sagas can also be considered contemporary, and so can three about Norwegian kings: Sverri, written for
the king by Abbot Karl Jonsson; Håkon Håkonsson, written after the
king's death, partly on the basis of documents, by Snorri Sturluson's
nephew, Sturla Thorðasson; and Sturla Thorðasson's saga about Håkon's
son and successor, Magnus, of which only a fragment survives.

There are also mythic-heroic sagas (*Fornaldarsögur*) about the period before the settlement of Iceland. These were the last to be produced, between
about 1250 and 1400. Some may have been written to give leading Icelandic
families a prehistory, as had been done earlier for the Norwegian kings.
They are extremely varied but are all more fantastic than the other sagas
mentioned here, and it has proved difficult to draw a clear line between
them and the romances that were produced at the same time (Kalinke,
326–27).

There has been prolonged debate about the origins and sources of the
sagas. For some time this debate was between proponents of what have
been labeled the freeprose and bookprose theories. The former claimed that
the distinctive character of the sagas shows them to be purely native, com-

posed and preserved orally before being written down. According to that interpretation, they were free of foreign influence, so comparison with other European literature was pointless. Bookprose theory was that the sagas were the work of thirteenth-century Icelanders who, although influenced by tradition, relied mainly on written models and their own imagination; the sagas should therefore be treated as literary products, not historical sources.

Discussion of origins and sources continues now, but not in such polarized terms.[6] It is generally recognized that one theory minimized, while the other exaggerated, the contribution made by saga authors. The form and content of the sagas shows that authors did not have a free hand. As Theodore Andersson has pointed out, their form is "too elaborate to have been invented in a vacuum at the beginning of the thirteenth century. There must have been an artistic continuity between preliterary and literary periods and the written saga must have derived much of its form and technique from the oral stories that went before" (20). It is no less significant that the family sagas are consistent in the way they represent Icelandic society, its ideals, beliefs, values, and conventions. This can hardly be an invention, for that would presuppose a virtual conspiracy among many writers. The sagas must, therefore, reflect in some degree a tradition with some basis in reality (Ólason, 38).

A lively discussion about the respective contributions of authors and of oral tradition continues as efforts are made to recognize what is distinctively Icelandic or Scandinavian, and what is due to influences from other parts of Europe. For this purpose the sagas need to be studied individually, for they were written in different circumstances and probably for different reasons. There is also a need to determine criteria and methods to distinguish tradition from invention. It is a complication that oral tradition continued to flourish and develop at the same time that sagas were being written; during a long transitional period each influenced the other. Similarly, eddic and skaldic poetry, although Scandinavian, was much influenced by contact with the British Isles, where, by the ninth century, influences from English, Welsh, Irish, Continental, and Scandinavian quarters met. Roberta Frank has suggested that in the reign of Knut, "London was probably *the* center in the North for the production and distribution of skaldic poetry" (1985, 179).

The problems posed by the sagas have led many historians to treat those dealing with past events, in particular the family sagas, as literature that can only be used as evidence for the period in which they were written, but to accept the contemporary sagas as historically reliable. Such a division of the sagas into historical and literary is unfortunate. The contemporary sagas are no less literary products than the others, and their historical superiority is questionable. In the first place, some are less contemporary than others; several were written up to a hundred years after the events they describe. In any case, contemporaneity is no guarantee of truth. Authors had their own purposes and made omissions and deliberate distortions for tactical or other reasons. Some apparently deliberate omissions are revealed by comparison with other contemporary texts. For example, the contemporary sagas do not mention the exposure of children, as the family sagas do, and there is good evidence in the Christian laws that this happened in the thirteenth century. They are similarly silent about accusations of homosexuality, known as *nið*, which do appear in the family sagas and were undoubtedly a common cause of dispute in thirteenth-century Iceland (Sørensen 1980, 100). It is clear that the authors of the sagas were deliberately silent about some current practices and customs when they wrote about their own time but not when they wrote about the pagan past. This double standard particularly affected their treatment of women.

Sagas about Icelandic families before the conversion and about early Norwegian kings cannot be dismissed as fiction. Their reliability as sources for the details of political or military events, individual careers, and even family history is doubtful, but the generally consistent picture they give of social structure, conduct, beliefs, and values must have some basis in reality, although not that of any one time. As scholars have been made aware of the ways in which traditions are gradually changed to suit changing circumstances, many have responded by trying to understand what significance the traditional element in the sagas had for both authors and their audiences. The ambition of many students now is not to look for evidence of historical events or individuals, but rather to see what can be discovered about social values from the themes, tendencies, patterns, structures, and contradictions in the texts (Clover 1985, 256). This approach does not mean that all hope of identifying early patterns and values has been abandoned, but the search is likely to be beraviled by subjective judgments. So far, very different conclusions have been reached, but it is generally agreed that the best hope of finding traditional elements is in the sagas that were written earliest.

The task of recognizing traditional elements is no simple matter. Three methods are being used. One is to identify features that are also characteristic of other European cultures. The weakness of this approach is that common characteristics may not have been the result of borrowing but were in fact common to both cultures. Another technique is to look for the distinguishing features of oral transmission. This has not led to any general consensus, but many agree that oral and written narratives are structured differently and that repetitions are a feature of the former. A third method is to compare the sagas with other evidence for Icelandic society.

Any traditional elements that can be identified in the sagas are, of course, no older than the texts, but some certainly had roots in the distant past and may perhaps open a window into pre-Christian Scandinavia. This prospect makes the Icelandic sagas exciting sources for medieval historians.

The Oral Texts: Eddic and Skaldic Poetry

It has long been claimed that poetry is the best evidence for the pre-Christian culture of Scandinavia. The two main types of poetry are eddic and skaldic. The eddic verse is preserved in a thirteenth-century manuscript known as the *Poetic*, or *Elder Edda*, to distinguish it from the *Prose Edda*, in which Snorri Sturluson surveyed and systematized Norse mythology and legend, with many quotations of poetry, mostly in short extracts.

Eddic poems are anonymous and deal with, among other things, gods and prehistoric heroes. They have obviously been altered in transmission, despite their metrical form, and it is therefore impossible to determine when they were first composed. Features such as archaisms, metrical irregularity, and dramatic episodes that have been taken as signs of great antiquity may well have been characteristics of the genre. As Preben Meulengracht Sørensen has pointed out, "One cannot claim with any certainty that an eddic poem such as *Völuspá* was written about the year 1000 in the form we now have it. There are, however, grounds for thinking that poems dealing with the same subject, namely creation and the end of the world, were being composed from the tenth century to the thirteenth" (1977, 90).

Skaldic poetry is very different. The names of the poets and the circumstances in which poems were composed (for example, to celebrate a victory or to praise or blame a prince, dead or alive) are often known. Skaldic poetry is likely to have been better preserved than eddic, because it was essentially allusive, the poets rejoiced in obscurity, and the verse forms are complicated. It had to be remembered correctly if at all; verses could be, and sometimes were, slightly altered, but major changes are unlikely. This poetry has therefore been considered very reliable evidence for the Viking Age, despite its difficulty. Its value has been enhanced by its content: most poems deal with people the poets knew and with events that had happened in the recent past, often with the poet as participant. Another reason for trusting these poems as reliable evidence is that they were composed for an audience familiar with the circumstances. This argument was advanced by Snorri Sturluson himself in the preface to *Heimskringla*:

> We regard as true what is said in those poems that were declaimed in front of princes themselves or their sons. We accept as true all that those poems tell about their travels and battles. For it is the practice of skalds to praise most the man whose presence they are in, and nobody would dare to tell the man himself about deeds which everybody who heard—even the man himself—knew to be lies and deceit. That would be scorn, not praise.[7]

Apart from the likelihood that eulogies exaggerate the virtues of their subject, there are other reasons for caution in using this poetry as a historical source. Some verses were certainly composed in the thirteenth century and attributed to early poets by authors to authenticate their prose narratives. The authenticity of many other verses has been doubted. The historical value of the poems is further limited because, in the words of Alistair Campbell, "the poets aimed at the artistic decoration of facts known to their hearers rather than at giving factual information" (66).

A more fundamental problem is that all but one of the skaldic poems composed before the twelfth century are only preserved in texts of the thirteenth century or later, in which verses are cited separately, not as poems.[8] They are not necessarily quoted in the original order of the poem. At times this can be worked out with the help of internal evidence, but when that is not possible, a poem is a poor guide to the sequence of events mentioned in it (Fidjestøl). Historians and others have sometimes had too much trust in the order in which verses have been arranged by editors. Roberta Frank has concluded, rightly, that "history may help us to understand Norse court poetry, but skaldic verse can tell us little about history that we did not already know" (1985, 174).

To complicate matters, skaldic verse has sometimes been completely misunderstood, even by experts. This was already happening in thirteenth-century Iceland. Snorri Sturluson, for example, interpreted some words for drink as the names of gods (Frank 1981). Occasionally the meaning of a whole verse was misunderstood. A good example is Snorri's treatment of a verse describing an attack on London Bridge by Olav Haraldsson. It is clear that Olav was fighting against the English, but Snorri, believing that he never did so, took the verse to mean that Olav was helping the English king to recover London from the Danes (Campbell, 76–82). Another misunderstanding has led historians from Saxo to the present day to believe that the Vikings practiced what is known as the blood-eagle sacrifice. The details vary, from simply cutting the shape of an eagle into the back of the victim to the more lurid practice of opening the rib cage to form "wings."

The source is a verse describing an eagle, the carrion bird, slashing the backs of men killed in battle (Frank 1990a).

The first known skalds were Norwegians, but it was not long before most of these poets came from Iceland. They had an important role in the royal and princely courts of Scandinavia, but little is known about them or the way they were recruited, and it is uncertain whether their poetry was, in Roberta Frank's words, "propaganda for the ruling class, a formal announcement of public discontent, or a codification of patterns of heroism and deceit." The skalds certainly had a dual role, to criticize as well as to praise, and they were therefore dangerous; "princes were probably as eager to gain power over poetry as to be entertained by it" (Frank 1985, 182).

The varied functions of the skald—shaper of opinion, critic, genealogist, entertainer—were eventually taken over by the historians, who not only preserved much of the poetry but also continued to use artistry and ambiguity in order to achieve their ends, as the skalds had in very different ways done earlier.

2
Lands and People

Scandinavia is a large region. The distance from Vardö, east of North Cape, where the Norwegian king Håkon V built a fort in the early fourteenth century, to the southern boundary of medieval Denmark, the river Eider, is over 1,200 miles (2,000 km); Bordeaux and Warsaw are not so far apart. The region has a great variety of landscapes, one of the greatest contrasts being between Norway, a quarter of which is more than 3,200 feet (1,000 m) above sea level, and Denmark, where the highest point is 574 feet (175 m) and the sea is never more than 46 miles (75 km) away. The western part of the great Scandinavian peninsula is a region of mountains, much of it over 4,000 feet (1,200 m) high. One chain of mountains, known as the Keel, forms the boundary between Norway and Sweden north of Trondheim Fjord. Along much of the west coast the mountains reach the sea to form a deeply indented coastline with many fjords, some of them over 60 miles (100 km) long. In the north the mountains extend into the sea to form many islands, one group of which, Lofoten, stretches more than 125 miles (200 km) from the mainland. The highest summits, almost 8,000 feet (2,500 m), are toward the south, but heights of over 6,500 feet (2,000 m) are reached in the far north.[1]

The central region is lower, and the mountains can be most easily crossed there; east of Trondheim Fjord there are passes under 1,600 feet (500 m). To the east of the mountains there is a wide, uneven plateau with extensive plains, scattered mountains, and hills traversed by rivers that generally flow southeast into the Gulf of Bothnia. This area now forms the northern part of Sweden. The southern part of Sweden, between the Kattegat and the Baltic, is generally low-lying but with scattered hills, a higher central region rising to almost 1,300 feet (400 m), and many lakes, including Vänern, which, with a surface area of over 2,000 square miles (5,500 km²), is the third largest in Europe.

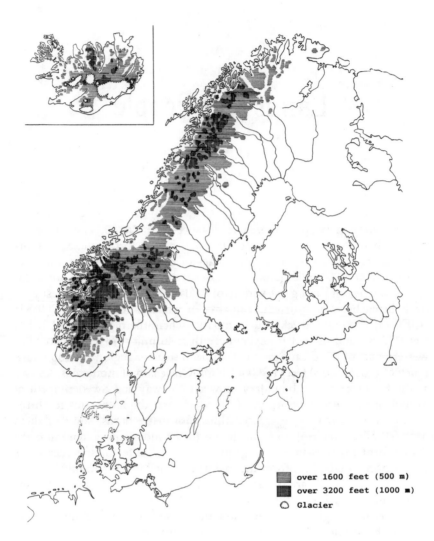

over 1600 feet (500 m)
over 3200 feet (1000 m)
Glacier

Figure 2.1. Scandinavia, Finland, and Iceland: The main physical features.

There are also many islands. Apart from those along the coast of north and west Norway, the largest are Bornholm, Öland, and Gotland, and Sjælland and Fyn in the Danish archipelago. Another archipelago, Åland, lies in the entrance of the Gulf of Bothnia. To the east of that gulf, in what is now Finland, there is a low coastal plain with a slightly raised inland plateau on which there are extensive lakes.

Changing Coastlines

The main structure of the Scandinavian landscape has remained virtually unchanged for millennia, although the extent of lakes and marshland has been greatly reduced by modern drainage, and natural processes have altered much of the coastline. Since the end of the Ice Age the sea level has risen, but in a large part of Scandinavia the land has risen faster. As a result, along most of the coasts of Norway and Sweden the relative sea level has dropped, but in Denmark it has risen; the whole region has, in effect, tilted along an axis that crosses north Jutland and the southern tip of Skåne. The change has not been continuous or regular; differences in the underlying geological structure have caused local variations, and in some parts of Sweden it can be shown that there have been short periods when the relative sea level rose. The overall effect has been greatest in the northern part of the Gulf of Bothnia, where the level is still dropping at a rate of about 2.5 feet (80 cm) a century. In the Stockholm region and around Oslo the rate is about half that. The effect is hardly noticeable on precipitous coasts, but where shores shelve gently, as they do around the Gulf of Bothnia and in many parts of eastern Sweden, the extent of dry land has gradually grown, increasing the resources of those fortunate enough to control coastal areas. The change has also affected channels and made some harbors inaccessible. The harbor of Teljä, for example, in the Finnish river Kumo had to be moved about 18 miles (30 km) to Ulviva in the thirteenth century and three hundred years later another 3 miles (5 km) to Pori. Many harbors on the west side of the Gulf of Bothnia, including Sundsvall, Piteå, and Luleå, have similarly had to be moved. Another consequence is that some sea inlets have been converted into inland lakes. The most significant example is the lake Mälaren, which was finally cut off from the sea in the thirteenth century after a period in which the passage into it became increasingly difficult. When ships could no longer sail directly to various points around Mälaren, one of the islands in its entrance, called Stockholm, became the major center for trade in the region.

In most parts of Denmark the sea level is now more or less the same as it was a thousand years ago, but few, if any, parts of the coast have remained unchanged since then. Storms have moved sand dunes, opened or closed channels, and blocked streams, while the less dramatic processes of erosion and silting caused by tides and currents have also changed the coastal regions in ways that cannot now be discovered. Some islands off the west coast of Jutland were apparently larger in the Middle Ages than they are now, and there are good reasons for thinking that Limfjord was open to the west until the eleventh century. In south Jutland the land has sunk by as much as three feet since the ninth century, but the change has been concealed, at least on the west, by the build-up of the coastal marshes.

Climate

The variety of landscapes is matched by the range of climates. The most significant contrast is between the west and north coasts of Norway, where the sea never freezes, and the adjacent mountain region, where the average temperature remains below freezing for over half the year. There are in fact several glaciers, some of them so close to the coast that they are visible from the shore. Apart from the coast west of North Cape, the whole of the northern part of the peninsula has an arctic climate; in some places along the shore of the Gulf of Bothnia there is normally firm ice for well over four months each year. Southern Scandinavia does not have such harsh winters; in Denmark the temperature rarely remains below freezing for more than a month. The Norwegian coast is kept ice free by the warmer water brought by the North Atlantic Drift, but in the summer the ocean has a cooling effect. The areas east of the mountains have very cold winters and warm summers. Long-term changes in weather patterns have caused changes in average temperature and in the amount of rain at different seasons of the year, but such variations mattered less to the inhabitants of medieval Scandinavia than the extremes that could occur from time to time. Exceptionally severe winters, dry springs, or wet summers could occur even in periods when the climate appears in general to have been favorable. A succession of years when the harvest was ruined and the hay crop spoiled could, of course, lead to the abandonment of some farms, but the dramatic reduction of the population and the wholesale desertion of farms in late medieval Scandinavia was caused not by the deterioration of the climate but by the plague that spread to Scandinavia in 1349.

Even in periods of fair weather very large amounts of rain and snow fall on the Norwegian mountains, mostly brought by winds from the Atlantic; in many areas, including Bergen, the annual total is the equivalent of 80 inches (2 m) of rain, and some places have much more than that. In the more sheltered areas to the east the normal average is about 20 inches. The southern part of the Norwegian mountain region is mainly drained by rivers that flow into Oslo Fjord or into Vänern, which is itself drained by Göta Älv. The main drainage of the mountain region north of Trondheim Fjord is by rivers that flow southeast into the Gulf of Bothnia. In their natural state, before being regulated to generate electricity, these rivers carried a huge volume of water during the spring and early summer, when snow and ice thawed. At the mouth of Indalsälven, for example, the flow was about 7,000 cubic feet/second (200 m³/second) in the winter months but rose to 52,000 cubic feet/second (1,500 m³/second) in June. Where drainage is poor, swamps have developed, for in most parts of Scandinavia water does not evaporate as fast as it accumulates; in the north some 30 percent of the surface is covered by bogs that are not worth draining. Farther south, before modern drainage works, there were extensive tracts of waterlogged ground.

Flora and Fauna

In most of Scandinavia, days are long in the summer and short in the winter. North of the Arctic Circle there are 24 hours of daylight at midsummer, and even as far south as Bergen, Oslo, Uppsala, and Helsinki, all of which lie close to latitude 60°N, there are 22 hours of daylight, including twilight, at midsummer, but less than 8 hours at midwinter. The natural vegetation south of the arctic tundra is woodland, much of it on relatively infertile soils. There are extensive areas of barren rock along the coasts of Norway and Sweden as well as in the mountains, but trees grow where they can. Spruce, pine, and birch are predominant in the north, while Denmark and the neighboring coasts of the Scandinavian peninsula have deciduous trees, notably oak and beech. Between these two regions there is a zone of mixed forest, very narrow along the coasts of Norway and south Finland but expanding to form a broad belt across the lowlands of southern and central Sweden. The northern boundary of the mixed forest is a significant ecological frontier, the Swedish section of which has been called the *limes norrlandicus* by geographers.

To the north of that frontier very large areas, especially in the mountains and the arctic, are uninhabitable, formerly visited occasionally only by hunters, now by tourists. In the ninth century there were also vast stretches of forest without permanent settlement, even south of the *limes norrlandicus*. By then, however, farms or villages, some of them long established, were located in many of the places where good soils and a supply of fresh water provided favorable conditions. The families who lived in these settlements largely depended on what they could themselves grow, gather, or catch. Woodland provided edible fungi as well as fuel and building materials. Animals could graze in marshland and some forests, there were natural water meadows along watercourses, and fish could be caught in many places. Most of the land that was cultivated, and much of the pasture, had once been wooded. The first stage in clearing woodland was to burn the trees and undergrowth. Numerous place-names refer to burning and include such words as the verbs *brenna* or *sviða*. Many such names are modern, and some may refer to the effect of natural fires, but others certainly reflect early clearances. Some are even more specific; over a hundred place-names in Norway include the noun *vål*, meaning "trunks or roots of burnt trees, stumps in burned ground." Stumps and stones would have to be removed before plowing could be done efficiently. This was a laborious undertaking and must normally have been a cooperative effort. Where soils were sufficiently fertile, clearings could be kept as arable, but many became pasture after a while. In some the woodland was allowed to recover, but overgrazing, especially by sheep and goats, could prevent that, and in some circumstances heathland resulted. During the Middle Ages the area of heathland in Denmark, southwestern Sweden, and along the west coast of Norway was greatly enlarged.

Where the soil was relatively infertile, it was nevertheless possible to burn the trees and undergrowth and grow a crop, commonly of rye, in the ash. In those circumstances plowing was not necessary, and the stumps and stones could be left in place. Clearings of that kind were normally cultivated for three years, the later crops usually being turnips or cabbages. They might then be grazed for a while before being allowed to revert to woodland. After a couple of decades the process could be repeated. This system of recurrent clearance, known in Swedish as *svedjebruk* (from the verb *sviða*, "to burn"), was widespread in Finland and eastern Sweden in the Middle Ages but was uncommon in other parts of Scandinavia before the seventeenth century (*Kulturhistorisk Leksikon for nordisk middelalder*, s.v. "bleka" and "Svedjebruk," hereafter *KHL*).

Forest fires are easily started and are often caused naturally by lightning, but random burning that might leave some partly burned trees standing or cluttering the ground could not be relied on to clear woodland effectively. A better result was achieved by more careful planning. If deciduous trees are felled in the early summer, the leaves continue to draw sap, leaving the trunk and branches drier and more easily consumed by fire. This does not happen with conifers, and in coniferous forest the ground is generally covered with an infertile and often damp layer that does not readily burn. It is consequently easier to clear deciduous than coniferous woodland. It is also more rewarding, for the soils tend to be more fertile and the climate milder. The most extensive early clearances therefore tended to be in southern Scandinavia, south of the ecological frontier of the *limes norrlandicus*.

North of that frontier, although the forests were predominantly coniferous, birches also flourished and in the far north were almost the only trees. After a forest fire the new growth tends to be deciduous trees, mainly birch but also alder and aspen, and it is likely that many of the early clearances in the coniferous region were made in such patches of deciduous trees that could be more easily cleared.

By the twelfth century a technique for clearing coniferous woodland was developed in north Russia, in the region of Novgorod. It was discovered that if a complete ring of bark was stripped from a pine or spruce the tree stopped growing but continued to draw sap from the roots, thus drying them and the surrounding ground. After eight to fifteen years forest prepared in this way, and its floor, could be more effectively burnt. The ash was for a short while very fertile, and high yields of rye could be obtained in the first year, but the fertility was soon exhausted, and a new clearing had to be used. The trees that recolonized the old clearing tended to be birch and alder, which, being deciduous, could be cleared more easily after twenty years or so. This technique soon spread into Karelia and eastern Finland, making a more extensive exploitation of that region possible. It was not adopted in Sweden until the sixteenth century, when Finnish immigrants were encouraged by Gustav Vasa to help clear the vast forests.

Resources

Already by the ninth century there was some arable cultivation in most parts of Scandinavia where it was possible. Cereals could even be grown north of the Arctic Circle, where long hours of daylight and relatively high temperatures in the summer compensate for the short growing season. Farther south, cereals could be grown with more confidence, but the area of arable cultivation was slight until the eleventh century, when it began to be increased dramatically. By the thirteenth century there were large areas of arable in many parts of Denmark, Skåne, and the plains of Götaland (now the provinces of Väster- and Östergötland), as well as around the lakes Mälaren in middle Sweden and Mjösa in eastern Norway. Perhaps the most remarkable concentration of arable was around Trondheim Fjord, less than 180 miles (300 km) from the Arctic Circle.

In the early Middle Ages most Scandinavians depended largely on pastoral farming; marshes and woodland provided extensive grazing, and one of the most important activities in the farming year was the gathering of hay for winter feed. Some people could supplement their diet with nuts, berries, edible fungi, and even honey, but fish was the most important additional food. Few inland settlements were far away from a lake, river, or stream in which fish or eels could be caught, and people who lived near the sea could hope at some seasons to eat seabirds and their eggs. As fish migrated in search of feeding or breeding grounds, they were at times remarkably abundant in some coastal waters. In winter large quantities of cod could be caught near Lofoten, and shoals of herring came close to various stretches of the Scandinavian coasts at different times of the year. The most famous center for herring fishing was in Öresund where, in late summer, they were so numerous that Saxo Grammaticus, writing in about 1200, could claim that "the whole sound contains such plentiful shoals that sometimes boats striking them have difficulty in rowing clear and no fishing-gear but the hands is needed to take them" (Saxo, Preface, ii). There were various methods of preserving fish to provide food at other times of the year, or for people who lived far away from the fishing grounds. Preserved fish was, indeed, the most important Scandinavian export in the later Middle Ages (chapter 7).

In the early Middle Ages Scandinavians could not only feed themselves, they could also obtain the raw materials they needed within the region. Some things, such as wood, bones, and hides, were easily available almost everywhere, but other important materials, such as iron and whetstones, were not. Iron ores occur in many places, often in marshes as bog iron or on the beds of lakes, and by the ninth century some districts with especially rich deposits, and with abundant wood to provide the fuel and charcoal needed to make the metal, specialized in producing it to supply other regions. Iron was, for example, not made in Denmark as it had been earlier, and the Danes obtained what they needed from Norway and Sweden. The rich deposits of copper in Sweden were not exploited on any scale before the thirteenth century. In several parts of Norway and Sweden there are rocks from which very good whetstones and millstones can be made; by the tenth century, and probably much earlier, these were being widely distributed throughout Scandinavia and even exported. There were also outcrops of steatite, a rock that is quite soft and easily worked when quarried but that hardens in the air. It is known as soapstone and was used to make a variety of things, including cooking pots that were especially useful before high quality and durable pottery vessels were available. A soapstone bowl could also be used as a hearth on a boat.

The forests, the mountains, and even the arctic tundra had a varied animal population, which was exploited by the ninth century. Many animals were valued for their fur pelts. Scandinavia was already known as a source of fine furs in sixth-century Byzantium, and the export continued. In the later Middle Ages furs were a relatively unimportant export, but in the ninth and tenth centuries the export of furs allowed Scandinavians to obtain luxuries, such as glass beakers, fine cloth, and weapons, with which the rich and powerful could mark their superiority. Scandinavians also hunted walrus in arctic waters and by the ninth century had begun to export their tusks, which were prized as a source of ivory.

In the early Middle Ages there were markets throughout Scandinavia in which the produce of different regions was exchanged. Thus the people making iron in Telemark could obtain grain and other necessities that were not available locally. Those who gained most from this traffic in the specialized produce of different regions were the people who controlled the routes by which such products were taken to other parts of Scandinavia or exported. It was no accident that the dynasty that eventually created the kingdom of Norway had controlled the southern part of the west coast (fig. 3.3) and had been able to profit from the valuable produce, furs, ivory, and fish that were shipped along that coast from the north. Similarly, the power of the Danish kings was in part a result of their control of the entrance to the Baltic. In much the same way, but on a smaller scale, those who controlled the routes from inland districts that produced anything of value were able to benefit. Skien was a center of this kind, through which most of Telemark's iron was exported, and there can be little doubt that this was the basis of the wealth and power of the family based at Brattsberg nearby. An earlier center was at Kaupang at the mouth of the Numedal valley. At some of the key centers for interregional trading, towns developed. A few were exceptionally early, notably Hedeby, but the main urban development did not begin until the eleventh century.

Peoples

The northernmost part of Scandinavia was inhabited by a distinct people often called Lapps, but who called themselves Sami, the name that will be used in this book (Ruong). In the ninth century they occupied the arctic and subarctic region, from Nordland in Norway to the Kola peninsula, as well as the central part of the Scandinavian peninsula as far south as Dalarna. Their territory had earlier been even more extensive, including the whole of modern Finland and the north shore of the Gulf of Bothnia. Blood groups show that they are ethnically distinct from other inhabitants of Scandinavia, although there has by now been much intermarriage with neighboring peoples (Beckman). It is not known what language they spoke originally, but at a very early date they adopted a form of Finnish, a non-Indo-European group of languages that was by about A.D. 500 spoken over a very wide region from the Baltic to the Urals. They lived by fishing and hunting, mostly reindeer, which supplied meat, skins for clothing, tents, and boats, and horn with which various implements and ornaments could be made. In the Middle Ages they had some tame reindeer that were used as draft beasts or as decoys in hunting; it was only in the sixteenth and seventeenth centuries that Scandinavian governments forced the Sami to herd reindeer. Only those who lived in Russia preserved their original way of life until this century. Sami settled along the coast of north Norway were mainly fishermen and are known as the Sea Sami.

Most of the other inhabitants of Scandinavia spoke a language known as Old Nordic. Place-names suggest that many of the regional differences in vocabulary and pronunciation that are first recorded in modern times already existed in the Middle Ages. Language is, of course, an unsatisfactory guide to ethnic origins. Blood groups, which reveal the Sami as very different, suggest that most Scandinavians belonged to one ethnic group, but there are some significant local variations that may derive from earlier populations. A few place-names, especially names of lakes, may preserve traces of earlier languages that perhaps also affected some dialects.

In the eleventh century this language was called the Danish tongue even in Iceland, which suggests that its domination in Scandinavia was a result of Danish influence; if so, it must have been exerted long before the ninth century. The Scandinavians who settled in the British Isles and in Iceland in the ninth century all spoke some form of Nordic. That the Sami borrowed a number of Nordic words in primitive forms shows that they were in contact with people who spoke Nordic at a very early stage of its development, long before the emigrations of the ninth century.

In the ninth century foreigners distinguished three main groups in Scandinavia: Norwegians or Northmen (a description that was occasionally used for all Scandinavians), Danes, and Sueones or, in Old English, Sweon, a name commonly but misleadingly translated as "Swedes"; we shall call them Svear. A fourth group, the Götar, occupied Götaland, but they were rarely encountered by foreign merchants or missionaries in the ninth century and are therefore not mentioned in most of the earliest texts. These peoples were particularly associated with separate regions of Scandinavia. The whole of modern Denmark, together with the west coast of Sweden and southeast Norway, was considered Danish territory in the ninth century. It was a well-defined region, united by water and surrounded by forest. Beyond the forest to the east were the Götar. The larger belt of forest called Tiveden and Kolmården separated the Götar from the Svear, who occupied the region around Mälaren and a large section of the east coast. The Norwegians lived along the North Way, a coastal region separated from the rest of Scandinavia by mountains.

Communications

These collective group names give a misleading impression of unity. In fact each group comprised numerous communities that were separated by natural boundaries. The most effective communications barrier was forest. In 1177, for example, a party of Norwegians took seventy-one days to travel through the forest from Malung in Dalarna to Storsjön in Jämtland, a distance of about 170 miles (280 km) in a direct line. It is true that the journey was made in the spring, when the thaw made conditions even more difficult, but forests were never easily traversed. The two main components of medieval Sweden, Svealand and Götaland, were separated by a wide band of forest through which a road was made for the first time in the twelfth century. Throughout the Middle Ages these two districts could be distinguished as Nordanskog, "north of the wood," and Sunnanskog, "south of the wood." It is not surprising that the word *mark*, originally meaning a boundary and used in that sense in England for the Welsh and Scottish marches, was used in Scandinavia for forest regions and thus acquired the meaning "wood." It occurs in many place- and district names combining both meanings.

Marshes and swamps could also hinder communications, especially in the summer, but they were no obstacle when frozen. It was generally possible to travel much faster over snow and ice than over bare ground, even when it was dry. A reasonable rate in winter was 50 miles (80 km) a day, but in summer a normal day's journey was only half that. It was possible to travel faster on horseback on routes that were well provided with bridges and causeways, but horses need to be fed and rested; for long journeys a system of replacement or post horses would have been needed. In summer 25 miles (40 km) a day seems to have been a normal rate of travel. In northern and central Scandinavia, winter was the best time to travel; many markets or fairs were held then, and military campaigns were often undertaken at that time of year, despite the shortage of fodder.

Some of the most important routes were along glacial eskers, gravel ridges left by the retreating ice, some of them continuous for great distances. They were especially valuable in marshy districts. Mountain routes could be even better; travel was relatively easy above the tree line, where wintry conditions persisted for over half the year. In the eleventh century special shelters for travelers were built on the main routes, and medieval laws regulated their use and maintenance. Both archaeological and linguistic evidence, however, shows that long before such facilities were provided, people living near the head of some Norwegian valleys had closer contact with coastal settlements on the far side of the mountains than with people living along the lower reaches of those valleys. The dialect of Valdres, for example, is West, not East, Norwegian, and the district lay in the diocese of Stavanger, not Oslo.

The difficulty of inland travel meant that the best means of communication, especially over long distances, was by water. In the eleventh century it took four weeks to travel by land from Skåne to Mälaren but only five days by sea (Adam of Bremen, 3:28).[2] The contrast was vividly illustrated by the experience of Pietro Querini, who in 1432 traveled by sea from the island of Röst in Lofoten to Trondheim in 15 days and took twice as long to cover about the same distance on foot to reach Vadstena in Sweden. The name Norway, meaning literally "the north way," underlines the vital importance of that coastal route.

Overlords

Many of the early medieval communities that had developed within the natural regions of Scandinavia were in large measure independent and regulated their own affairs. Later evidence suggests that this was done in assemblies that were as much social and religious as legal and political occasions. In all parts of Scandinavia, except perhaps among the Sami, society was hierarchical. In the early Middle Ages some men and women were unfree, and at all times there were various grades of freemen, ranging from those who had been freed to men of superior status who had lordship not only over their own households, as all freemen had, but also over other freemen. There were also rulers, and these too were ranged in hierarchies in which some were acknowledged as overlords by others. Such overlordships were inherently unstable and could be ended by the defeat or the death of an overlord; few lasted more than a couple of generations.

The earliest reliable, direct evidence for such overlordships in Scandinavia is from the early ninth century, but there can be no doubt that they were a normal phenomenon long before that, as they were in most other parts of Europe. Conflicts between communities and their leaders must have created a succession of overlordships among the Scandinavians. Some exceptionally powerful, or lucky, rulers probably claimed exceptionally extensive overlordships, and these may have been responsible for at least some of the cultural contacts revealed by archaeological and linguistic evidence.

Overlordships were more easily established and maintained where there were good communications. It is therefore not surprising that the earliest known overlords in Scandinavia were Danish kings who, in the early ninth century, thanks to their fleet, could control not only the Danish archipelago but also the surrounding coastlands. It is even possible that their distant superiority was sometimes acknowledged by men living far to the north along the North Way.

External Colonization

The power of Scandinavian rulers and other lords depended on the loyalty of warriors, who had to be rewarded. Few lords had sufficient resources to keep a resident band of retainers, but all had a following of sworn men who could be called upon when necessary and who would, in return for their support, expect support for themselves as well as enhanced prestige and a share in the plunder and tribute won in successful expeditions. Until the ninth century such expeditions were within Scandinavia and the Baltic region, but shortly before the year 800 Scandinavians discovered that there were rewarding opportunities further afield; they were known in western Europe as Vikings and in eastern Europe as Varangians.[3] Some leaders, having won fame, a fortune, and an enlarged following, returned to Scandinavia to compete for power there. Others were content to stay abroad. Several Russian princely dynasties were founded by Scandinavian adventurers of the ninth and tenth centuries whose sons or grandsons adopted the language and customs of the local population. Other Scandinavians took over or created lordships in the British Isles and the neighboring parts of the continent. Like their eastern contemporaries, most were soon assimilated and adopted the language and religion of the people they had conquered, and by the year 1000 they had all, in varying degrees, been absorbed into the political structures that were then being shaped. Others who settled in Orkney, Shetland, and the more remote, hitherto largely uninhabited islands of the Faeroes and Iceland, preserved their own speech, and their descendants maintained close contact with their Scandinavian homeland. These islands thus became, in effect, an extension of the Scandinavian world, which was further enlarged toward the end of the tenth century by the discovery and colonization of the habitable fjords of southwest Greenland. It was not long before a few intrepid Greenlanders ventured to North America, where they established at least one temporary base in northern Newfoundland, but they soon abandoned it.

Iceland, the largest of these colonies, has a special place in Scandinavian history thanks to the role of the Icelanders in producing and preserving the vernacular literature on which much of our knowledge of Scandinavian history and culture depends. The relatively well documented society established by the colonists in Iceland also provides some of the most valuable clues to the character of the Scandinavian society they had left.

Very little of Iceland is habitable; a tenth is covered by glaciers and most of the interior is desert. Even below the 1,300-foot (400 m) contour there is a huge area bare of vegetation. The habitable areas are along the coast and in some valleys. Erosion and volcanic activity in the past thousand years has greatly reduced the area of useful land. Lava flows have destroyed some settlements, but more extensive damage has been caused by volcanic ash. Many early settlements west and north of the volcano called Hekla were abandoned for that reason soon after 1200 following an eruption. The eruption of Katla in 1357 and of Öræfajökull in 1362 devastated two densely populated districts in southern Iceland, and an eruption of a volcano in the northwest of the glacier Vatnjökull, probably in 1477, deposited huge quantities of ash on eastern Iceland (Rafnsson). Poisonous gases that are sometimes emitted can be even more devastating. In 1783 a huge explosion that created a crater 7 miles (11 km) long killed half the horses and three-quarters of the sheep in Iceland. Many people were poisoned too, and it has been estimated that in the following two years at least 10,000 Icelanders died from starvation as a direct consequence of the eruption. Iceland also suffers from erosion, made worse by the removal of most of the natural wood that existed when the settlement began, and some coastal settlements have had to be abandoned because the sea level has risen.

Demography

It has been claimed that Scandinavians emigrated in the ninth and tenth centuries because resources in their homelands were inadequate. That may be true of the coastal districts of western Norway, where potential arable land was scarce, but emigrants were attracted to Iceland, and later to Greenland, by the good opportunities they offered for stock farming. Elsewhere in Scandinavia there were large areas available for internal colonization. The evidence of pagan cemeteries suggests that in the Mälar region the population doubled in the Viking Age to a total of about forty thousand, living on about four thousand farms, but there were still good opportunities for further expansion that were exploited later (B. Ambrosiani). A similar increase may have occurred in other parts of Scandinavia, but not in all. There is no evidence for any such increase in Denmark at that time. The extent of Danish arable and woodland did not change significantly during the Viking Age. Despite the enormous quantities of oak used in buildings, bridges, ships, and even fences, forest oaks did not become scarce in Denmark until the twelfth century, which suggests that the woodlands were carefully managed. In the eleventh century arable cultivation began to increase dramatically at the expense of woodland (P. Sawyer 1988a, 31). The population of Denmark and other parts of Scandinavia then began to increase rapidly. There was a similar increase in many other areas of Europe at the same time, but no agreed explanation for it. It seems likely that in normal times there was a tendency for populations to increase, with a cumulative effect that was countered by war, disease, and emigration; the emigration of Scandinavians in the ninth and tenth centuries must have reduced the rate of growth. The general improvement of the climate in the eleventh and twelfth centuries must have been an important factor, increasing yields and making some marginal land more attractive. There were, of course, regional differences; harsh winters and wet summers could occur even in so-called climatic optima, but the overall improvement made it possible to produce more food. The supply was also increased by the shift from pastoral to arable farming, but whether that was a cause or an effect of the population increase is uncertain.

Before their conversion to Christianity Scandinavians attempted to restrict or control population growth by exposing or neglecting infants (Clover 1988). As in many other societies it is likely that girls were more vulnerable than boys. The church opposed the practice, but when the Icelanders formally accepted Christianity, they kept the old law concerning the exposure of infants, at least for a while. That is better evidence for the custom than the episodes of exposure in sagas about pagan times that were written in the thirteenth or fourteenth centuries. The fact that the exposure of children was prohibited in some Scandinavian laws compiled in the twelfth and thirteenth centuries implies that it had not been completely stopped; indeed, some laws permitted exposure when a baby was deformed. The degree of deformity required for the legal exposure of a baby is carefully defined in some laws, but the definition was, of course, open to interpretation.

The evidence of skeletons suggests that the conditions for many women improved after the Viking Age (Sellevold 1989a, b). The stature of men remained much the same from that time throughout the Middle Ages, but the average height of *all* women in medieval cemeteries was greater than of women in pagan graves, most of whom were of high status and who, to judge by the Danish evidence, tended to live longer than men.

That does not mean that all women were well looked after. More women than men died between twenty and thirty-five years old, but in the next age group, thirty-five to fifty, men were more vulnerable. The high mortality of young women has been blamed on complications in pregnancies and childbirth, but that appears to be an oversimplification. Calvin

Wells has argued that high mortality connected with childbearing is a modern phenomenon, largely due to infections and complications that were rare or unknown in Europe before the nineteenth century (cited by Sellevold 1989a, n. 6). It may be that girls were not as well cared for as boys in childhood and were ill prepared for the strain of childbirth, but the survivors had a good chance of outliving their male contemporaries. Although the ratio of the sexes in Scandinavia is not known, after the Viking period there does seem to have been some increase in the number of women old enough to bear children, which must have contributed to the population increase that began then.

The total size of the population at any time in the medieval period can only be estimated, and the estimates vary greatly. It does, however, seem likely that in the early fourteenth century, when the medieval population was greatest, there were rather more than two million people in Scandinavia, half of them in the medieval Danish kingdom. Estimates for Norway vary from 300,000 to 500,000, but they were certainly unevenly distributed with some relatively dense concentrations and very large uninhabited areas.

Settlements

There is no doubt that the population increase resulted in the expansion of many established farms and villages and in the creation of many new farms. This was also the period of urban growth. Ribe and Århus, together with Schleswig, if that is considered a continuation of Hedeby, are the only Scandinavian towns whose origins can be traced much earlier than the year 1000, but many others were founded at that time, including Viborg, Odense, Roskilde, Lund, Oslo, Trondheim, and Sigtuna; a century later all the major medieval towns of Denmark and Norway had been firmly established. These towns were important as political, economic, and cultural centers, but they were small; Bergen and Stockholm were the largest towns in medieval Scandinavia, each with at most 7,000 inhabitants in about 1300. Most of the population increase that began in the eleventh century was absorbed in rural settlements.

It is difficult to generalize about the expansion of existing settlements, but there is no doubt that thousands of new ones were created throughout Scandinavia, most of them with distinctive names. In Denmark and Sweden many were called *thorp*, now familiar in such place-names as Kålltorp, Kastrup, or Kirkerup. The word spread to Scandinavia from Germany by the eighth century, but most of the Danish *thorps* were probably established between A.D. 1000 and 1200, a period that also saw a rapid reduction in the extent of woodland. Many of the Swedish *thorps* were combined with Christian names—for example, Perstorp (Per is a form of Peter)—showing that these place-names were given in or after the eleventh century. In Norway many of the new settlements were in the mountains but more were in woodland, and in both Norway and Sweden thousands were given names such as Konnerud or Fagered, appropriately incorporating the word *rud*, meaning "clearing." Most of these places remained small settlements with limited resources, and many were abandoned in the fourteenth century. In the territory of medieval Denmark some 3,500 places called *thorp* are known but it has been estimated that a similar number have vanished.

This medieval colonization created many separate, isolated farms. That also appears to have been the normal pattern of earlier settlement in Norway and in other regions that were predominantly forest and mountain. It was reproduced in Iceland by the Norwegian colonists and can be studied there more easily than in Norway, thanks to volcanic activity. Many farms in the vicinity of the volcano Hekla were smothered by volcanic ash when it erupted in the twelfth century. The disaster was not so sudden that the inhabitants could not remove their belongings and the most valuable building materials, including the main timbers, but enough was left, and has been preserved by the ash, to make it possible to study these settlements in some detail (fig. 2.2).

In Sweden, especially where there were relatively large expanses of plain, there were many villages and hamlets in the thirteenth century. Their earlier history is uncertain. Some may have been formed by the subdivision of older farms. This happened even in western Norway, where subdivision produced very compact, even congested, settlements in which the several buildings of the different holdings were irregularly interspersed, with little space between them (fig. 2.3). Each holding had its own parcels of arable and meadow scattered in the neighboring fields. This type of settlement seems to have been determined by the topography; in confined valleys there were few sites suitable for new settlements. In eastern Norway, where conditions were less cramped and sites for new settlements were more readily available, some farms were divided, but rarely into more than two holdings. It is therefore unlikely that subdivision alone can account for the formation of the larger, regular villages of the Viking Age and earlier that have been uncovered by Danish archaeologists and that are implied by the earliest Danish and Swedish laws.

Rural settlements have been excavated on a large scale only in Denmark, and even there only a handful have been completely uncovered. There is, however, no doubt that there were regular villages as well as single farms in Den-

Figure 2.2. Reconstruction of the house at Stöng, Iceland. The excavated remains of a farm at Stöng have made it possible to build this reconstruction some distance away from the site. Turf walls lined with timber rest on a stone base. Both of the two main rooms have hearths; the larger room is a hall about forty feet long. A dairy and a lavatory extend from the back of the house. Photograph by Rafn Hafnfjörð.

mark long before the ninth century, and one of them, Vorbasse in central Jutland, about 15 miles (25 km) southwest of Jelling, has been traced through successive stages back to the the first century B.C. (Hvass 1983, 1984).

Most, perhaps all, Danish villages had some arable, but until the eleventh century the economy was predominantly pastoral. Many farms had byres, either as part of the dwelling house or in a separate building, and as horses were far less common than cattle, it seems likely that the byres were mainly intended to shelter cows and oxen. Two of the houses in Vorbasse in the ninth century each had twenty-two such stalls, and in the eleventh century several farms could house at least fifty animals. Although they were much smaller than their modern successors, there were surprisingly many of them in Viking-Age Vorbasse. Few were needed as draft animals—there was little arable—and they must have produced far more milk, cheese, butter, meat, and skins than the farmers and their households needed. It therefore seems likely that some cattle produce was sold, even exported.

Figure 2.3. The farm of Mölster, in Voss, west Norway. Although not medieval, this farm is a good illustration of a typical rural settlement in west Norway. It was divided into two holdings, each with eight buildings serving different functions, including a dwelling, stable, barn, and wood-store. Photograph from Riksantikvaren, Oslo.

Excavations in many parts of Denmark have shown that in the first millennium A.D. most settlements were moved a few hundred yards at intervals varying from about one to three centuries. Vorbasse had seven or eight sites before it was permanently established in its present location. Such moves offered an opportunity to cultivate the fertilized ground where the cattle had been housed; traces of cultivation have been found on the site of one of the abandoned farms at Vorbasse. The several sites of that village all lay within about half a square mile, with good access to low-lying water meadows where cattle could graze and winter feed could be harvested. In the twelfth century the village was moved for the last time to a new site a little over half a mile away, close to the best land for arable cultivation in the vicinity. Vorbasse seems to be typical in this respect; most Danish settlements were permanently established in the eleventh or twelfth centuries on sites that had not previously been occupied and that seem to have been chosen to be close to land suitable for arable farming. There was certainly a great increase in the area of plowed ground and in the amount of cereal produced during the eleventh and twelfth centuries. This increase was partly a result of the creation of many new settlements, but changes like that observed at Vorbasse also contributed. In Norway, in contrast, pastoral farming was always important, and there are indications that in the west it increased in the thirteenth century, as it did in many parts of Scandinavia as a consequence of the Black Death (chapter 7) (Sølvberg).

The most remarkable feature of Vorbasse is its regularity. The number of farms remained the same—seven—in all three stages from the eighth century to the twelfth. With one exception in the eleventh century, at each stage the farm enclosures were all much the same size and so were the dwelling houses. This suggests that the inhabitants were not free and independent landowners but tenants of a lord who, directly or indirectly through a steward, regulated the individual holdings. This is consistent with other indications that there were in Viking-Age Scandinavia not only kings and chieftains but also magnates or nobles who dominated their regions and who, like their successors in the twelfth century, must have owned large areas of land, some of which was held by tenants who paid part of their surplus as rent.

Village communities that could reallocate fields from time to time, as they did, could perhaps have agreed on a regular plan for their farm buildings, but where a lord owned all or a large part of a settlement, he or his agent would have had a decisive say in any arrangements that were made. Some, perhaps many villages were therefore probably shaped not by natural growth, but by the influence of lords.

Little attention has been paid to the possible role of lordship in the evolution of Scandinavian settlement because it has commonly been assumed that Scandinavian society was originally dominated by free and independent but mostly small-scale landowners, with few lords other than kings. It is significant that the regions in which large, regular villages were most common are those where, in the twelfth and thirteenth centuries, large estates were held not only by kings and lay lords, but also, thanks to the generosity of earlier benefactors, by bishops and monasteries. This was no accident; larger villages could most readily develop in areas with relatively open plains that were able to support a denser population than the less fertile regions of forest and mountain. They also had more potential arable. Arable cultivation required more labor than pastoral farming but yielded more food, thus making larger settlements both possible and desirable; villages in which neighbors could provide the labor, equipment, and draft animals needed for arable farming had advantages over isolated farms. Those regions, moreover, could be most easily controlled by lords whose power in large measure depended on their ability to exact a share of the produce. The increase in arable cultivation in the eleventh and twelfth centuries may in part have been a response to increased demand and higher prices, but it was especially in the interest of landlords, clerical as well as lay, to increase yields and so make it possible to exact higher rents. It also increased the value of tithes, to the profit of church patrons (see chapter 5). It is therefore likely that landlords who were eager to obtain more rent and tithe and to increase the yield of their own farms encouraged the relocation of settlements near land that would make the best arable fields.

The Black Death

Many of the farms newly established between the eleventh century and the thirteenth were on marginal land near the upper limit of cultivation or on poor or poorly drained land, and they were therefore especially vulnerable when the climate began to deteriorate, as it apparently did in many areas in the thirteenth century. Some settlements may have been abandoned then, but the large-scale desertion of settlements was caused not by the weather but by the bubonic plague that reached Scandinavia in 1349, or possibly in the previous autumn, brought by ship from England (Benedictow 1990; Ulsig 1991). The disease reached southern France late in 1347, and by the time the epidemic had run its course in 1352, it had affected most of Europe and in many areas had killed a third or more of the population. It was spread by fleas that were active in warm weather; in northern Europe it spread fastest in the summer and appeared to die out in the winter months. Its progress was fairly slow across land but much faster by ship. It reached Oslo first and in 1349 spread up the valleys that converge on Oslo Fjord, along the coast, and to the Danish islands. It reached Bergen directly from England in the same year and was carried by ship to Trondheim, where the archbishop died of it on 17 October. The plague reached Jutland from Germany in 1350 and then spread through the south Baltic and into southern Sweden. It did not spread north of Uppland or to Finland. Iceland was also spared this first epidemic but was badly affected in 1402–4 by a new outbreak, also brought from England. There was a second plague in Iceland at the end of the century.

In many parts of Europe this first plague epidemic, despite the dramatic reduction of population that it caused, did not leave many farms vacant because there was a large reservoir of landless people. This seems to have been the situation in many parts of Scandinavia. The later recurrences of the plague, at intervals of about a decade for the rest of the century and then less frequently, were responsible for the desertions of a very large

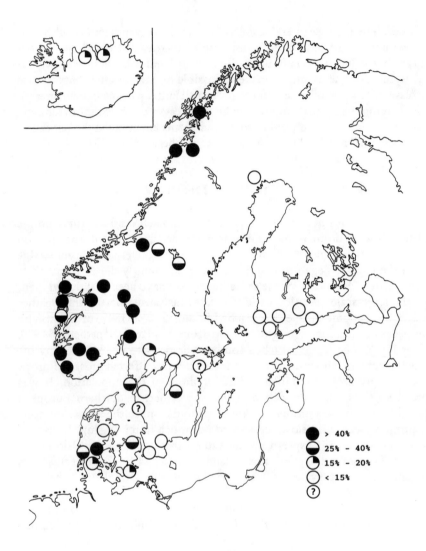

Figure 2.4. The proportion of farms deserted between 1350 and 1500 in various districts (Gissel et al. 1981).

number of farms by 1400 (fig. 2.4). Norway appears to have suffered most, but that may be because its single farms were more vulnerable than the villages of Denmark and Sweden, many of which survived, although greatly reduced in size.

3
Political History: An Outline

The earliest historians of Scandinavia, writing in the twelfth and thirteenth centuries, believed that, although the Danish kingdom had existed since time immemorial, the kingdoms of Norway and Sweden were relatively recent creations, formed in the tenth and eleventh centuries by the unification of many small kingdoms. Earlier sources confirm that the Danish kingdom was well established and powerful by the end of the eighth century, but there is no contemporary evidence for a multitude of small kingdoms in other parts of Scandinavia at that time. Apart from the small island of Bornholm, which was said to have its own king, the only kingdoms mentioned in ninth-century texts were those of the Danes and the Svear. There may have been others, but in many parts of Scandinavia power did not lie in the hands of a single ruler but was shared between a number of lords or chieftains, each with his own men or retainers. This was the pattern of government that Norwegian emigrants took to Iceland in the ninth century, and two centuries later power in that Scandinavian colony was still divided between some three dozen chieftains called *goðar* (sing. *goði*), a title that also occurs on three tenth-century runic inscriptions on the Danish island of Fyn. A *goði* was originally a lord of men, not of territory, and his authority was publicly exercised in assemblies, or *things*, where he was supported by his *thingmen*. The lordship exercised by a *goði* was known as his *goðorð*. The number of *goðar* was gradually reduced by conquest or more peacefully by marriage alliances, and by 1220 five families controlled all the *goðorð* in Iceland. So, for example, the three *goðorð* around Skagafjörður (fig. 8.1) were held by one family in 1118 and by one member of that family at the end of the century. This naturally led to a territorialization of power. A chieftain began to claim authority over

Figure 3.1. General map of Scandinavia, Finland, and Iceland.

all who lived in his district, which could be called a *ríki* or even a *stor ríki*, a large *ríki*, if it was big enough (Sigurðsson). By the ninth century some kingdoms that are unmentioned in contemporary sources may have been formed by a similar process in Scandinavia, but in many regions the old structure with multiple lords survived until the thirteenth century, as it did in Iceland.

Figure 3.2. Southern Scandinavia.

The Ninth Century

In the early ninth century many of these rulers and chieftains, especially in south Scandinavia, acknowledged Danish kings as their overlords. The heart of the Danish kingdom was at that time in south and central Jutland and the neighboring islands, but the Danish empire included not only the whole Danish archipelago but also the surrounding coastlands. The west coast of Sweden was so effectively under Danish influence that it was known in the ninth century as "Denmark," meaning the frontier region of the Danes. The Danish kings, as overlords of "Denmark," had indirect influence over the people living in Västergötland whose routes to the sea were along Göta Älv or the rivers that flowed through Halland. Similarly, Danish influence was felt far up the valleys that converge on Oslo Fjord. Most of this Danish empire was within easy reach of the sea; the authority of Danish kings depended on naval power as well as on an army. With their fleet they could control and profit from the trade between the Baltic and western Europe that increased greatly in the eighth century. This was not only a valuable source of income, it also gave Danish rulers some influence over peoples living around the Baltic whose produce had to pass through Danish territory to reach western European markets.

Our knowledge of the Danish kingdom in the ninth century largely depends on Frankish sources. These make it possible to follow the succession of Danish kings in some detail for sixty years after 804 (P. Sawyer, 1991a). All of them, and all those who are known to have claimed Danish kingship, belonged to one family, which split into two segments sometime in the eighth century. The monopoly of kingship implies that this family had great prestige, which must have derived from an ancestor about whom we can only hope to have distorted hints in legends that were first recorded centuries later. The kingship could be divided or shared between two or more brothers, but the Franks seem to have thought of the Danish kingdom as a unity, like their own. There seems to have been no fixed rule of succession. When a choice had to be made, this was done by leading men, sometimes after violent conflict. Claimants who failed to gain recognition, and survived, must normally have gone into exile. After Godfred's death his sons found refuge with the Svear for three years before returning to oust their rivals. By then Scandinavians had discovered that they could gather great wealth in western Europe by plundering, exacting tribute or ransoms, or demanding protection money. For the rest of the century any members of the Danish royal family who were excluded from power at home could win fame, fortune, and a larger following as leaders of Viking armies in western Europe.

Frankish sources also give some information about Danish activity among the Slavs and Frisians, but they provide little information about parts of the Danish empire that were more remote from the Frankish frontier. An entry in the Frankish royal annals for 813 is a remarkable exception. In that year Frankish envoys were unable to meet the Danish kings (there were then two, reigning jointly), who were campaigning in Vestfold, the region west of Oslo Fjord, because, following a Danish dynastic dispute, the "princes and people" of that district had refused to submit to them. Vestfold was then not a kingdom but a distinct district with a people and *principes*, chieftains or leaders.

Among the Svear effective authority was similarly in the hands of chieftains.[1] They had a king, who was closely associated with the cult celebrated at Uppsala, but he was little more than a figurehead, providing a focus of unity that was needed to maintain the peace on which the prosperity of the region depended. Royal ancestry was not as necessary for kings of the Svear as it was in the Danish kingdom; from the tenth century to the thirteenth, many of them were not even natives of Svealand; several were Götar, and at least two were members of the Danish royal family. The succession sometimes passed to the son (or sons) of a king, but on several occasions an outsider seized the kingship not by conquering the Svear but by killing the incumbent king and gaining recognition by the Svea chieftains, who apparently preferred to acknowledge an outsider rather than to promote one of themselves.

In the ninth century the Svear, who occupied most of the east coast of Sweden, were gathering tribute in Finland and north Russia. The king of the Svear took part in some expeditions across the Baltic, but most of this activity was undertaken by the chieftains. They and their followers were sometimes collectively known as Svíthjóð, "the Svea-thjóð or people," and that name was also used for the territory from which they extorted tribute and in which many of them settled. As a result north Russia could later be called Great or Cold Svithjóð, in contrast to Little Svithjóð, the name sometimes given to Svealand.

Many of the Scandinavians who lost contests for power, such as deposed kings or members of royal families, who were considered dangerous rivals by their more successful kinsmen, sought safety in exile, as did some men who were unwilling to submit to an overlord. Refuge could be found in other parts of Scandinavia, with Slavs, Saxons, or even Franks, but by the ninth century it was alternatively possible to make exile profitable by raiding in western Europe or gathering tribute in Russia. The remarkable success of the Danes in dominating the coastlands around Kattegat and Skagerrak, and possibly more distant parts of Scandinavia, before and after the year 800 must have driven many local rulers in the region and their kinsmen to seek their fortune overseas. The fact that in the ninth century the English called Scandinavian pirates "Vikings" may be significant in this connection. The most satisfactory of the many explanations that have been offered for the original meaning of that word is "inhabitant of, or man from, Viken (that is, the region of Oslo Fjord)," implying that men from that district were prominent as raiders in England (Hellberg 1980; Hødnebø). If so, it is reasonable to assume that some of them were escaping the Danes, who were eager to control that part of Norway, especially the western part, Vestfold, in order to secure a supply of the iron that was then being produced in Telemark.

Some Scandinavian exiles stayed abroad, having conquered or created lordships in western Europe or Russia, but some returned home in the hope of gaining, or regaining, power. By the middle of the ninth century returning Vikings were causing trouble for the Danish king, Horik, and in 854 he and most members of his family were killed in battle against his nephew, who, having been excluded from power, had spent years as a Viking. The dynasty survived for a while, but by the end of the century Danish power had declined, and in 934 the Danes suffered the humiliation of having to pay tribute to the German king.

The Tenth Century

The collapse of the Danish empire gave Harald Finehair, a prince or king who ruled in southwest Norway, the chance to make himself overlord over a large part of Norway. As a result he was remembered as the founder of the Norwegian kingdom. In fact, his family only retained the kingship for two generations after his death in about 930. Disputes among his sons and the opposition of rival chieftains undermined that native Norwegian overlordship, allowing the Danes to regain their lost superiority. The revival of Danish power probably began under King Gorm, who died in 958—at least that is the date of his first burial chamber. Gorm's son and successor, Harald, later known as "Bluetooth," enlarged Danish royal authority even more. On the great runic monument near his father's grave at Jelling Harald Bluetooth claimed that he had won all "Denmark." The extent and effectiveness of Harald's authority are confirmed by the forts constructed in north Jutland (Fyrkat and Aggersborg), Fyn (Nonnebakken in Odense), and Sjælland (Trelleborg). Fyrkat and Trelleborg in Sjælland were constructed in the years 979–81. The remarkably close similarity between them and the other forts suggests that they were all built at much the same time on the orders of Harald, who was king until 987. A fort that has recently been discovered in Trelleborg in Skåne is in many respects similar, but the differences suggest that Harald had influence in that area but did not control it as directly as he did the islands west of Öresund. These forts probably served several purposes: to overawe the local populations and to secure

Figure 3.3. The main royal estates in southwest Norway. Several places are named in connection with Harald Finehair and his son Håkon in early poetry or in saga traditions. Harald stayed on Utstein after his victory at Hafrsfjord; Håkon was on Fitjar when he was attacked by his nephews and died of his wounds on his way to Alrekstad (now Årstad), the royal residence preceding Bergen; Håkon was buried on Seim (Helle 1991, 28).

Harald's control of the different regions; they may also have served as bases for defense against attack. Whatever their purpose, they required a great deal of manpower and huge amounts of timber, showing that Harald could command large resources in most parts of the medieval kingdom. They also suggest that he was no longer content to be an overlord over local chieftains but had begun to exercise direct control through his own agents (Roesdahl 1982, 147–55).[2]

Harald's monument at Jelling also claims that he won Norway. There is some support for this in poetry that shows he supported one faction in the Norwegian royal family (*KHL*, s.v. "Vellekla"). In the interregnum after the death of Harald Grey-cloak, in about 970, Håkon, jarl of Lade, who was himself overlord of sixteen jarls in Norway, acknowledged the Danish king as his superior. Håkon fought for Harald in Jutland, probably against the Germans either in 974 when they invaded south Jutland, or nine years later when they were driven out. Harald's success in recovering his territory was made possible by the defeat of a German army by the Saracens in Calabria in 982. In that battle many Saxon lords were killed, giving Harald and his Slav allies the opportunity to revenge themselves on their Saxon neighbors. In 983 Harald regained control of Hedeby, and the Slavs devastated Holstein and burned Hamburg. For at least a generation the Danes were free of any threat of German interference. Four years after that success, Harald was driven into exile by a rebellion and replaced by his son Sven, who was by 1140 known as "Forkbeard." The circumstances of the rebellion are not known, but it is a reasonable guess that Harald had burdened the Danes too heavily; that is at least consistent with the fact that the forts built toward the end of his reign, and the bridge across the Vejle River at Ravninge Enge that was built at the same time, were allowed to decay. The extension of direct royal control east of Store Bælt was continued by Sven, who began to integrate Skåne, and perhaps Halland, in the kingdom, thus gaining control of Öresund. Lund and Roskilde now began to be the main centers of Danish royal power, thus shifting the center of the kingdom from Jutland to what had formerly been "Denmark."

Toward the end of the tenth century there was a renewal of Viking attacks on western Europe. One reason for this was the extension of Danish domination in Scandinavia by Sven Forkbeard (P. Sawyer 1991c). He sought to escape Horik's fate by leading several large-scale and profitable expeditions against England, thus ensuring that he was well placed to counter any challenge by a rival. He did have to face such a challenge in Norway. In 995 Olav Tryggvason, a Norwegian with a successful career as a Viking behind him, was recognized as king in western Norway, seized control of the area around Trondheim Fjord that had been ruled by the jarl of Lade, and conquered eastern Norway, including Viken. His success was short-lived. In 999 he was killed in the battle of Svold against Sven, who thus restored the Danish overlordship of Norway.

The revival of Danish power also provoked opposition elsewhere. In or soon after 992 Erik, king of the Svear, formed an alliance with the Polish ruler Boleslav, whose sister he married, and they launched a joint attack on the Danes. Later writers who were hostile to Sven claimed that he was soundly defeated and driven into a prolonged exile. If the allies were indeed successful, it can only have been for a short while. Sven was secure enough at home to lead raids on England in 991 and 994, and soon after the second one he married the widow of King Erik.[3] Erik was succeeded as king of the Svear by his son Olof, whose actions after Sven's death suggest that he acknowledged the Danish king as his overlord. It was apparently as a tributary that he assisted Sven in the battle against the Norwegian king Olav Tryggvason. His subordinate status may have given rise to his nickname, "Skötkonung," which seems originally to have meant "tributary-king," although different explanations were offered in the thirteenth century when it is first recorded.

The Eleventh Century

During the first decade of the eleventh century Sven Forkbeard was overlord of the greater part of Scandinavia, and in 1013 he conquered England, but when he died in February 1014, his empire disintegrated. His son Knut, who had taken part in the English campaign, was elected king by the army, but the English refused to accept him, and he was forced to return to Denmark. Knut apparently expected to be recognized as king by the Danes, for he had some coin dies giving him that title made by English craftsmen (Blackburn). The Danes had, however, chosen Sven's other son, Harald, as their king. In 1015, Knut returned to England, and by the end of 1016 he had reconquered it. It was therefore as king of the English that, after the death of his brother, he was recognized as king by the Danes, probably in 1019.

By then another Viking adventurer, Olav Haraldsson, had been recognized as king by the Norwegians, who once again rejected Danish authority. It was not until 1028 that Knut was able to make good his claim to be king of the Norwegians. The Swedish king Olof Skötkonung also rebelled, marking his defiance by giving one of his daughters in marriage to the Norwegian king. When Knut finally succeeded in driving Olav Haraldsson into exile, he planned to revive the custom of ruling through a native jarl. Håkon, grandson of the jarl of Lade who had submitted to Harald Bluetooth, was the ideal choice, but he was drowned in 1029. Olav Haraldsson seized the opportunity to return from exile in Russia. He traveled through the territory of his Swedish ally Anund, Olof Skötkonung's son, but as he approached Trondheim Fjord he was met by his enemies and killed in battle at Stiklestad in 1030. Knut then made the mistake of attempting to impose his own son Sven as king of Norway, under the tutelage of the boy's English mother, Ælfgifu. This move was unpopular, and the short period of Ælfgifu's rule was remembered as a time of harsh and unjust exactions. The Norwegians rebelled and expelled Sven and Ælfgifu, perhaps even before Knut died in 1035. Olav Haraldsson was soon and widely recognized

as a martyr. His son Magnus was brought from exile in Russia and acknowledged as king. Norway had at last escaped Danish control, and it
remained independent for over three hundred years. By the middle of the
eleventh century all the lands around Oslo Fjord were under Norwegian
control, although the Danes later made several attempts to regain a foothold there. The boundary between the kingdoms was then Göta Älv. That
river divides into two branches as it approaches the sea, and by 1100 the
Norwegians had established a royal residence and base on the northern
branch, at Konghelle, but they claimed that their territory extended to the
southern one. It was not until the thirteenth century that the Götar, by then
united with the Svear in the Swedish kingdom, gained control of the southern estuary of the river (Olsson). Until then the Danes and Norwegians
could theoretically have denied them access to the sea, but in practice they
did not. The port of Lödöse, founded in the eleventh century on the east—
Swedish—bank of the river, some 25 miles (40 km) inland, had a flourishing overseas trade long before the estuary was controlled by the Swedes.

The Kingdom of Sweden

Sweden was the last of the Scandinavian kingdoms to be firmly established
(P. Sawyer 1991b). Because in the eleventh and twelfth centuries many
kings of the Svear were Götar, links existed between the two regions, but
these areas were separated by a wide band of forest, through which a road
was not made until the late twelfth century. Religious disunity was a more
serious obstacle to political unity. An overlordship did not depend on religious uniformity—in the tenth century a pagan jarl of Lade acknowledged
the Christian king of the Danes as his lord—but the unity of a kingdom
required the formal acceptance of the same religion, at least by its leading
men. It was not until the pagan cult of Uppsala was finally suppressed toward the end of the eleventh century that Christian kings could begin to
claim direct authority in the whole of Svealand, but in the early twelfth
century, as in the eleventh, kings in Sweden had direct control over only
part of the country; elsewhere they were little more than overlords, largely
dependent on local rulers called jarls or, in Latin, *duces*.

Apart from the kings mentioned by Rimbert, Olof Skötkonung is the
first Swedish king who can be firmly associated with particular regions of
Sweden. He began to issue coins from Sigtuna as "king of the Svear" in
about 995, and he was also closely associated with Götaland, especially
Västergötland. He laid the foundations for the first Swedish bishopric in
Västergötland, and a contemporary poet called him ruler of the Götar

Figure 3.4. Bohus Castle on the Göta Älv. In 1308 the Norwegian king Håkon V began to build this stronghold to control traffic along Göta Älv. It stands at the point where the river divides into two branches. Konghelle stood on the northern arm, which is seen here behind the castle. It was originally built of timber, with a ditch and rampart as outer defense, but in the fifteenth century it began to be rebuilt in stone, and some walls are up to nine yards thick. When completed in the sixteenth century, it was Scandinavia's largest and strongest castle. Photograph by Curt Nyström.

("*dögling Gauta*") as well as of the Svear ("*Svía gramr*"). Sigtuna was founded in about 975, apparently as a bridgehead for a new type of royal power. The runic inscriptions immediately to the west of the town are in many respects unlike those in other parts of Uppland and have some features reminiscent of those in Denmark and Götaland. This difference suggests the possibility that Sigtuna was founded by Olof's father, Erik, and that he, like some later kings of the Svear, came from Götaland. If so, it is likely that recognition as kings of the Svear enhanced their status in Götaland, whatever it had been earlier, and may even have led to their acknowledgment there as kings. The first certain reference to a kingdom of the Götar is in a letter of Pope Adrian IV, who had been in Sweden, in which he refers to Karl Sverkersson as ruling *regnum Gothorum* in or shortly before 1159, several years before he was recognized as king of the Svear. He was also the first Swedish ruler to be addressed by the papacy as king of the Svear and Götar, but the first known to have acted as king throughout the developing kingdom was Knut Eriksson, a member of the rival dynasty, who gained recognition as king throughout Sweden by 1172 and reigned for twenty-three years. He is the first king known to have granted land and privileges in all parts of the country and the first to have coins struck in his name in both Götaland and Svealand.

Christian Kings

Conversion to Christianity was the key factor in the formation of all three Scandinavian kingdoms. In Denmark and Norway the kings who shaped the medieval kingdoms were those who were closely linked with the conversion, a connection that was made explicit in the runic inscription on the monument that Harald Bluetooth erected at Jelling, claiming that he had "won all Denmark and Norway for himself, and made the Danes Christian." In Norway, Olav Tryggvason and Olav Haraldsson were remembered as the missionary kings who completed the conversion of the Norwegians, and, although both were defeated by the Danes, their role in laying the foundations of an independent and united Norway was regarded as crucial by later generations. In Sweden too, it was Olof Skötkonung, the first Christian king, who, by successfully defying the Danish supremacy, began the process that eventually united the Götar and Svear to form the medieval kingdom.

Christianity brought many benefits, including a new ideology and a literate clergy with wide experience, members of an international organization based on written law and with a relatively elaborate machinery to implement it. What is more, the church played an important part in determining the limits of the kingdoms. The archiepiscopal provinces were in effect precursors of the medieval Norwegian and Swedish kingdoms. An independent Norwegian archbishopric was created in 1153 (or 1152) with a province that included Iceland, Greenland, and other Atlantic islands that had been colonized by Norwegians, although a century passed before Iceland and Greenland were incorporated in the Norwegian kingdom. Similarly, the Swedish archbishopric of Uppsala, founded in 1164, included the bishopric of Åbo some decades before that diocese was incorporated in the Swedish kingdom. The province of Uppsala, by joining the two Götaland sees with the three in Svealand, was an important factor in the unification of these two original components of the medieval Swedish kingdom. The provincial councils summoned by archbishops or papal legates were, indeed, the first national councils in both Sweden and Norway.

Royal Succession

By the end of the twelfth century all three kingdoms were firmly established. The accepted rule in each of them was that only members of the royal families could become kings. All Danish kings after Sven Estridsen were his descendants, and he himself was (through his mother, Knut's sister) a descendant of Gorm, as all Danish kings but one had been since the mid-tenth century. It has been claimed that the hereditary principle was accepted even earlier in Norway and that all Norwegian kings were descendants of Harald Finehair. That is, however, a fiction. The founder of the Norwegian royal dynasty was Harald Hard-ruler, who died in 1066. His own claim was as half-brother of Olav Haraldsson. Harald Finehair's dynasty ended with the death of Harald Grey-cloak in about 970, and neither Olav Tryggvason nor Olav Haraldsson was his descendant (Krag).

In Sweden, kings did not have to be members of a royal family until the latter part of the twelfth century. Before that the Svear elected, or recognized, several kings who were not of royal descent, including Sverker, who was king from about 1132 to his assassination in 1156, and his successor, Erik, who was killed at Uppsala in 1160 and soon thereafter, like Olav Haraldsson, recognized as a saint. Association with earlier kings by marriage was considered an advantage, although not essential. In the mid-eleventh century Stenkil was recognized as king of the Svear. He was not of royal descent but married the daughter of the previous king, Emund. Their son Inge, who reigned for over twenty years, was the link through which all later kings except Sverker sought dynastic legitimacy. Sverker married two widows of Danish royalty, but his son Karl married a descendant of Inge I. Erik, who was king of the Svear after Sverker, also married a descendant of Inge. For a hundred years all Swedish kings were descendants of either Erik or Sverker, but that competition ended in 1250, when Valdemar was chosen. His father, Birger Jarl, was a descendant of Sverker, and his mother, Ingeborg, a descendant of Erik. Valdemar was deposed in

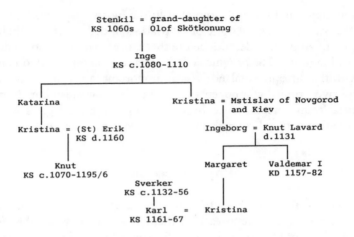

Figure 3.5. Some marriages of Swedish kings in the eleventh and twelfth centuries (KS = King of Sweden).

1275 in favor of his brother Magnus, who was the ancestor of all Swedish kings until the early fifteenth century (see fig. 3.10).

The limitation of kingship to members of the royal families did not eliminate the need to make a choice. Leading men normally did the choosing, sometimes after a fight, but the successful claimant had to be recognized in public assemblies. Different assemblies at times chose different candidates; on numerous occasions in all three kingdoms joint kings were chosen, either by agreement or in rivalry. They were normally brothers, but occasionally the division was between more distant kinsmen. There was no tradition of primogeniture, so all the sons of a king might claim an equal right to succeed. After the death of Sven Estridsen in 1074 some of his numerous sons thought they should jointly rule the Danish kingdom. That did not happen, and five of them succeeded in turn. In the next generation the succession was more violently disputed by the sons of the last two, Erik and Niels. For a short while there were three kings, but the conflict was ended in 1157 when Erik's grandson, Valdemar, emerged as the victor. He was succeeded in turn by his two legitimate sons, but soon after the death of the younger, Valdemar II, in 1241, Valdemar II's three sons vied for the kingship. The conflicts between them and their heirs that frequently disrupted the Danish kingdom during the next hundred years were largely responsible for the decline of Danish power that culminated in 1332, when for eight years the Danes had no king.

Norway was far more extensive than Denmark and had a much shorter tradition of unity. After Harald Hard-ruler the normal pattern was for the sons of the last king to rule jointly. They apparently did so in relative peace until the death of King Sigurd "the Crusader" in 1130. Civil war then broke out and continued, with intervals, until 1208 (Bagge 1975, 1986). During one of the intervals the archbishopric of Nidaros was created in 1152 or 1153, but soon afterward conflict began again. In the 1160s the faction led by Erling Skakke gained the upper hand for a while. His wife was King Sigurd's daughter, and their young son Magnus was elected king in 1161. Two years later an attempt was made to regulate the order of succession, but these rules were not respected, and kings continued to be chosen by different assemblies for the next sixty years.

Magnus was opposed by several rivals who claimed to be the sons of previous kings, but most were defeated by his father. The most serious challenger was Sverri, who arrived in 1177 from the Faeroes claiming to be a great-grandson of Sigurd the Crusader. He was soon recognized as king in Tröndelag, and by 1184, supported by his band of retainers known as the Birchlegs, he had defeated and killed both Erling and Magnus. Many Norwegians nevertheless would not recognize him as their king, and Øystein, archbishop of Nidaros, refused to crown him. Instead, Bishop Nicholas of Oslo did so in 1194, but shortly afterward Nicholas joined and became one of the leaders of a newly formed opposition group known as the Baglings (Croziers). Conflict between the two factions continued after Sverri's death in 1202, and not until 1217 was Sverri's grandson, Håkon, recognized as king throughout Norway. He was supported by and shared power with a distant relative, Skule Jarl, who in 1239 unsuccessfully attempted to overthrow him. After that date Håkon's rule was unchallenged, and in 1260 a law determining the order of succession was agreed upon. It was revised in 1273 and was modified again in 1302 when King Håkon V's two daughters, his only children, were betrothed. The acceptance of a rule of succession in advance was a stabilizing factor, but the main reason Norway did not suffer succession disputes of the kind that disrupted the other kingdoms was that between 1227 and 1387 only one Norwegian king died leaving more than one legitimate son.

1250–1350

By the middle of the thirteenth century Norway had emerged from the prolonged period of civil wars as the most stable of the Scandinavian kingdoms. This state of affairs was partly a result of the wars; after a century of conflict many Norwegians, clergy as well as laymen, were disposed to accept a strengthened monarchy as the best guarantor of peace. The *King's Mirror*, a Norwegian treatise on kingship written in the 1250s, reflects a political ideology that may be described as almost absolutist, with the king ruling by divine right as God's representative, chosen not by human electors but by inheritance (Bagge 1987). This view of kingship seems to have been shared by many influential Norwegians. Norwegian magnates were, moreover, relatively poor and lacked the resources that would have enabled them to challenge the king or to give effective support to rival claimants. Their best hope of increased wealth and prestige was by becoming king's men and serving as royal agents, thus further strengthening royal authority.

By the beginning of the twelfth century Norwegian kings already controlled the whole coast as far north as Lofoten, and they had begun to make their authority effective in eastern Norway. The consolidation of the kingdom was, of course, hindered by the civil wars, but soon after they were over the king's writ ran far to the north of Lofoten and in most settled areas inland south of Finnmark, which remained a tributary region in which Norwegian claims were disputed by Swedes and Russians. The final stage in the shaping of the kingdom was reached in the 1260s with the incorporation of Iceland and Greenland. This move was some compensation for Håkon Håkonsson's failure to assert his claim to overlordship over some of the British islands that had also been colonized by Norwegians in the ninth and tenth centuries. Håkon died in 1263, a year after being defeated by the Scottish king at Largs, and three years later his son and successor, Magnus, agreed in the Treaty of Perth to surrender the Isle of Man and the Hebrides to the Scottish king in return for a large cash payment, an annual tribute, and recognition of Norwegian sovereignty over Orkney and Shetland. In Håkon's reign Norwegians had begun to take a more active interest in what had been "Denmark." Marstrand was founded to strengthen Norwegian control of the Bohuslän coast, where there were at that time lucrative herring fisheries. Norwegians also began trying to extend their territory south of Göta Älv at the expense of the Danes. This effort was partly a response to the internal difficulties of the Danish kings, but a more positive attraction was the Skåne market, which grew rapidly in the thirteenth century to become one of the major fairs of medieval Europe. They were briefly successful when Magnus Eriksson, as king of both Norway and Sweden, held Halland and Skåne from 1332 until 1360 when those provinces were recovered by the Danes. One result of this Norwegian interest in Kattegat was the increasing importance of Oslo, which under Håkon V (1299–1319) replaced Bergen as the main center of royal government.

By the end of the thirteenth century the other Scandinavian kingdoms had also been greatly enlarged. The best opportunities for Danish expan-

Figure 3.6. Model of Holmen, Bergen. This model (in the Rosencrantz Tower, Bergen) shows Holmen as it was in about 1300 and is here seen from the east. This center of royal and ecclesiastical government commanded the approach to Bergen from the sea. In the middle of the fortified royal residence stands the original royal chapel and behind it the great hall built by Håkon Håkonsson between 1247 and 1261. A new chapel, consecrated in 1302, is being built in the foreground. The large church in the background is the cathedral, with the Dominican friary in the upper-right corner, beyond the bishop's residence. Photograph by Ole Egil Eide. © Alvheim & Eide, Bergen.

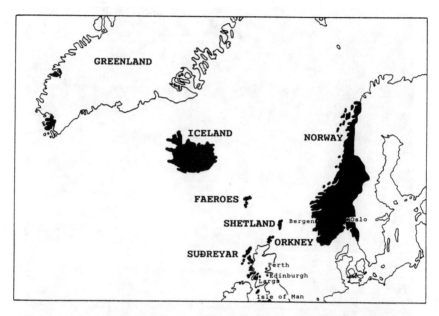

Figure 3.7. The kingdom of Norway in 1265 (based on Helle 1990, 143).

sion were in the Slav territory between Jutland and the river Vistula, but the Danes faced vigorous opposition from the Saxons, who by the 1160s had the upper hand in the western part of that region. The Danes therefore concentrated their efforts farther east. By 1169 Valdemar I had conquered Rügen, and in 1185 the prince of the Pomeranians submitted to Valdemar's son, Knut. Knut was well placed to take advantage of the dispute over the imperial succession that broke out in 1197, and for a while the Danes were the dominant power in the western Baltic. In 1201 even Lübeck, which had been founded by Henry the Lion in 1158, acknowledged Knut as its protector and lord. Valdemar II, who succeeded his brother in 1202, recognized Frederik II as emperor and was rewarded by a Golden Bull granting him all the territory that the Danes had won from the Elbe to the Oder; he then adopted the title "king of the Danes and the Slavs."

After 1185 the way was open for expansion farther east. Livonia and Prussia were conquered by Germans; Scandinavians were more interested in the Gulf of Finland, which commanded the approaches to the region of the lakes Ladoga and Onega, the main source of high-quality furs. Ever since the eighth century Scandinavians had gathered tribute in that region, but by the twelfth century it was controlled by the prince of Novgorod and his boyars. Scandinavians and Germans were welcome as merchants in

Novgorod—to buy furs, not to gather them as plunder or tribute in the territory. Scandinavians could, however, hope to profit from Novgorod's trade either by plundering merchants on their way to or from the city or, better still, by establishing strongholds to control the routes to it. Several raids of a traditional kind on the coasts of the Gulf of Finland by Danes, Norwegians, and Swedes occurred in the twelfth century, but it was not until 1218 that the Danish king Valdemar II gained a permanent foothold in the region by establishing a fort close to the best harbor on the Estonian coast, where an important trading place had been established earlier. The new settlement was called Tallinn, "the fort of the Danes," by the natives, and Reval by the Danes. A community of traders, craftsmen, and clergy, mostly Germans, grew under its protection, and the archiepiscopal province of Lund was extended by the creation of a bishopric there. Valdemar II and his successors claimed the whole of Estonia, but in reality they controlled little more than Tallinn, and in 1346 the Danes surrendered their claim to the Teutonic Order in return for 10,000 marks.

Swedes concentrated their efforts on Finland, which lay outside the zone of Novgorod's control, although it was liable to raids by Karelians, who were Novgorod's tributaries. In the eleventh century colonists from the Mälar region had begun to settle alongside Finns in the coastal region known as Finland Proper, where the bishopric of Åbo was established by 1220, and in Satakunta. During the thirteenth century the papacy encouraged the Swedes to crusade not only against pagan Finns but also against the orthodox Christians of Novgorod. The first serious attack on Novgorod was defeated by Alexander Nevsky in 1240, but nine years later Birger Jarl was more successful in a campaign directed against the Finns of Tavastia, and as a result the unpopulated south coast region was opened to Swedish colonists and came to be called Nyland, "New Land." Another crusade, led by Torgils Knutsson in 1292, enabled the Swedes to build a fortress at Viborg. For thirty years the Swedes attempted to extend their territory at the expense of Novgorod and even tried to gain control of the River Neva, but Novgorod, with the support of the princes of Moscow, successfully resisted. In 1323 the Treaty of Nöteborg was agreed and defined the boundary between them, which remained much the same until the end of the fifteenth century (fig. 3.8).

Two versions of the treaty were made. The Swedes received one in Russian with a Latin translation, the version held by Novgorod was in Swedish. The boundary on the Karelian isthmus was carefully defined by numerous points (along the thick solid line in fig. 3.8). In the Lake Region the treaty names four places that can be identified, key points in the navigation system (the large dots in the figure). The treaty did not mark a

Figure 3.8. The Treaty of Nöteborg, 1323. For key see pp. 67–68.

boundary here but allowed both parties to have access to the routes through the Lake Region. Further north two boundaries (dotted lines in the figure) enclosed a huge area that both Swedes and Novgorodians could exploit. In the Swedish version held by Novgorod, the boundary that the Swedes were not supposed to cross followed the watershed north to end at *nor i haffuit*, "north in the sea," that is, the White Sea (**N** in the figure). The Russian version ended at *Kajano more*, "the Kainuu-sea"—an early name for the northernmost part of the Gulf of Bothnia (**K** in the figure). A treaty made in 1326 in the name of Magnus Eriksson as king of Norway with Novgorod similarly marked the limit for the Russians at Lyngstuen, while the Norwegians had access to the whole of the Kola peninsula as far as Trianæma, and along the coast of the White Sea (Gandvik) as far as Veleaga. The Russians called the north coast the Northmen's coast, hence the name Murmansk (Murman = Norrmen).[4]

The Treaty of Nöteborg was made in the name of Magnus Eriksson, who, at the age of three, had become king of both Norway and Sweden in

1319. He was the son of Duke Erik, brother and leading opponent of Birger Magnusson, king of Sweden from 1280 to 1318. In 1318 Erik and his brother were imprisoned by the king, and they both died in captivity. In 1312 Erik had married Ingeborg, daughter of the Norwegian king Håkon V, and under Norwegian law their son Magnus automatically succeeded Håkon in 1319. In Sweden Birger, who intended that his own son should be his successor, gained no advantage by the death of his brothers, for the Swedish magnates drove him into exile, executed his son, and elected Magnus Eriksson as king, thus creating a personal union; the kingdoms remained entirely separate with their own councils and laws. One consideration in the Swedish choice of Magnus Eriksson was that a long minority would give the magnates the opportunity to consolidate their own privileges. Their aims were well expressed in the charter of liberties drawn up soon after the election.

During the first years of his minority Magnus was under the guardianship of his mother, who in 1321 arranged to marry the king's sister Eufemia to a German prince, Albrekt of Mecklenburg, a match that proved to be of great significance, for their son, also called Albrekt, was elected king in opposition to Magnus in 1364. Ingeborg's influence was not welcomed by the councils of either kingdom, and in 1322–23 she was deprived of her guardianship in favor of men who were, in effect, regents. In 1331, when Magnus took over personal responsibility for the government of his kingdoms, his position seemed secure. The councils of regency, despite many disputes, had succeeded in preserving the integrity of both kingdoms.

The situation in Denmark was very different. Magnus Eriksson's minority coincided with the reign of Christopher II, who had been forced by financial necessity to grant virtually all his resources—lands, castles, and revenues—to magnates, mostly Germans, as security for loans. He was king in little more than name, and upon his death in 1332 no successor was chosen. The interregnum lasted for eight years, during which real power was in the hands of Gerhard and Johan, two counts of Holstein, who between them controlled most of Denmark. Christopher's brother and predecessor, Erik Menved, who reigned from 1286 to 1319, has been given much of the blame for this remarkable situation; his bold interventions in north German and Swedish politics were costly, and he died leaving the financial resources of the kingdom exhausted. Christopher contributed to his own difficulties, however, by openly challenging his brother in the last years of his reign. He was supported by Ludvig of Brandenburg, an alliance that was reinforced by the marriage of Christopher's daughter to Ludvig. The promised dowry was 10,000 marks, which Christopher could not afford. Ludvig's determination to have this debt paid was an important factor in the decision to make Valdemar, Christopher's younger son, king in 1340; he obtained the money by surrendering Estonia to the Teutonic Knights.

The relative weakness of the Danish kingdom after the death of Valdemar II in 1241 was a temptation to its Scandinavian as well as its German neighbors. In the thirteenth century the Norwegians had already tried to encroach on Danish territory, and in 1287 they gave refuge to the men accused of murdering the Danish king Erik Glipping in the previous year. These rebels were encouraged by the Norwegians to build castles at Varberg and Hunehals in north Halland and on the island of Hjelm on the other side of Kattegat, which the Danes were forced to recognize for a while as Norwegian, but these castles were in Danish hands by 1306. The great prize was the Skåne market, and in 1289 the Norwegians apparently made an unsuccessful attempt to seize control of it. Magnus Eriksson, who was able to draw on the resources of both Sweden and Norway, was more fortunate. In 1332 he gained control of Skåne and its market and retained it for almost thirty years. The Scanians, including the archbishop of Lund, resented being ruled and taxed by the Germans and welcomed his intervention, and Count Johan was prepared to surrender his claim in return for 34,000 silver marks. Magnus also attempted to extend his territory in the east and in 1348 resumed hostilities against Novgorod, but without success. Military failure was one of the various reasons he faced growing opposition after 1350. To pay for the purchase of Skåne and for costly military undertakings, he raised taxes. Tax increases were never popular, but after the devastation caused by the plague such extra demands were unacceptable. He even angered the church by attempting to tax its property and earned papal disapproval by failing to repay a loan he had been granted from a tax imposed by the papacy to pay for the crusade against the Russians. Another cause of complaint was that he broke the terms of the 1319 charter by giving fiefs and castles to foreigners, one of the main beneficiaries being his brother-in-law Albrekt of Mecklenburg. In 1356 there was open rebellion against Magnus in favor of his son Erik, whose younger brother Håkon had become king of Norway the year before. In 1357 Sweden was divided between Erik and his father, but two years later Erik died.

Magnus Eriksson's difficulties were made worse by the revival of Danish power under Valdemar IV, who was elected in 1340. One reason for ending the interregnum was that a king was needed to legitimize the possession of fiefs. Another was the fear that Magnus, as king of both Norway and Sweden, might seek to claim the Danish kingship; his acquisition of Skåne as a fief could be seen as a step in that direction. Valdemar IV exploited the unpopularity of the Germans, recovering many of the fiefs and castles that they had acquired, and he was also able to take advantage of the overextension of Magnus Eriksson and the internal conflicts in Sweden. He co-operated with the papacy, which at this time of schism was eager for support, and with the pope's help he filled many sees with the bishops he wanted. He abandoned Estonia but seized Gotland after reconquering Skåne in 1360.

These setbacks further weakened Magnus Eriksson's position in Sweden. In 1362 he was deposed, and for a short while his son Håkon was recognized as king, but father and son soon joined forces and, most remarkably, early in 1363 came to terms with the Danish king, a reconciliation that was marked by the marriage of Håkon to Valdemar's daughter Margaret. Some Swedish magnates reacted by electing the young Albrekt of Mecklenburg as their king. Magnus and Håkon continued to oppose Albrekt, but in 1371 a settlement was reached. Magnus died three years later.

The alliance between the three Scandinavian kings in 1363 was partly motivated by fear of Lübeck and its Hanseatic partners. This was justified, for the German merchants were prepared to fight to protect their trade. In 1370, after two wars, the Danes were forced to renew the towns' privileges in the Peace of Stralsund and to grant them the castles of Falsterbo, Helsingborg, Malmö, and Skanör for fifteen years, with the right to collect two-thirds of their revenues.

The Kalmar Union

After the death of Valdemar's only son in 1363 the Danish succession depended on his two daughters. The elder, Ingeborg, married Henrik of Mecklenburg (brother of the Swedish king). Their expectation that their son, another Albrekt, would be chosen to succeed Valdemar was frustrated by the rapid reaction of Margaret and Håkon after Valdemar's death in 1375. They persuaded the Danish electors to choose their son Olav, then age four. When, in 1380, Olav succeeded his father as king of Norway, a new personal union was created, and it was later claimed on his behalf that he was the rightful heir to Sweden. In 1380 Olav was still a child; real authority lay with his mother, Margaret, even after he was declared to be of full age in 1385. When he died in 1387, Margaret was invited by some influential Swedes, who were discontent with the rule of their German king, to lead the opposition against him. A year later she gained a decisive advantage by acquiring the greater part of the castles and property that had been held by Sweden's greatest landowner, Bo Jonsson (Grip), who died in 1386 (fig. 3.9). (A "grip" or griffin was a mythical beast used as a heraldic

Figure 3.9. The estates of Bo Jonsson (Grip).

device by Bo Jonsson's family. For this method of identifying families see "Inheritance in practice" in chapter 8, and figure 9.3.) Bo Jonsson had held twelve royal castles (solid squares in fig. 3.9), together with their tributary regions; three castles of his own (large dots in the figure); and land scattered throughout the country (in the parishes indicated by open circles in the figure). The executors of his will, two bishops and eight secular magnates, recognized Margaret as regent and handed over most of the property to her. In 1389 her forces decisively defeated Albrekt and took him prisoner. Although it was some years before his faction gave up their opposition to her, the way was prepared for the unification of the three Scandinavian kingdoms. In 1389 Margaret's nephew Erik of Pomerania was elected king of Norway, but Margaret retained her leading role as regent until her death,

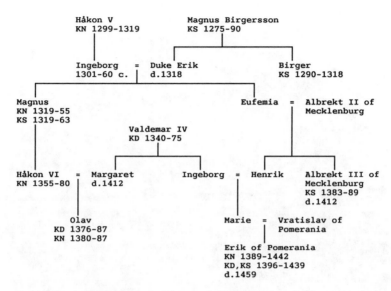

Figure 3.10. Erik of Pomerania's claim to be king of the Union (KD = King of Denmark; KN = King of Norway; KS = King of Sweden).

both there and in the other kingdoms in which Erik was made king in 1396. The Union was sealed, literally, at Kalmar in 1397. One document drawn up on that occasion was the so-called coronation letter, on parchment with the seals of sixty-seven bishops and magnates, testifying that they had witnessed the coronation of Erik as king of all three kingdoms, promising him all due loyalty and love in return for his, and recognizing that Erik and Margaret had the authority to lay down the terms on which castles and fiefs should be held. Another much-discussed document known as the Union letter was probably drawn up on the same day. It is on paper and names only seventeen witnesses, mostly Danes and Swedes, but includes the seals of only ten of them. It appears to be a draft of a declaration confirming the election of Erik as king, emphasizing that he had to consult his councillors in all kingdoms in dealing with foreign powers. That a formal version on parchment was not produced has been explained as the result of Margaret's opposition to its implied limitation of royal prerogative.

Erik's seal incorporates the arms of all three kingdoms in the Union (fig. 3.11). The Norwegian lion of Saint Olav with his ax is central, flanked by the Danish leopards and the three crowns of Sweden. The bottom quarters depict the lion used by Birger Jarl's family and the Pomeranian griffin, a fabulous beast with an eagle's head and wings and a lion's body. The three

Figure 3.11. The seal of Erik of Pomerania as Union king. Photograph from Riksarkivet, Stockholm.

crowns, which on the seal may have represented the three kingdoms of the Union, had been used earlier in Sweden, apparently first by Magnus Eriksson after 1332 when he claimed to be king of Skåne as well as of Norway and Sweden (Lagerqvist 1985).

The victory of Margaret and the establishment of the Union is the key to the final stages of the period. It was in effect a revival of the Danish empire with which this chapter began, with some measure of direct control in Norway but often no more than an overlordship in Sweden. The Union was welcomed by many, who thought that it would end the costly and destructive wars between the kingdoms and would reduce the costs of kingship, for one court would be less expensive than three. The Danes were especially keen for the Union, as it offered them larger opportunities.

Margaret ruled a far more extensive territory than had her father, but with no less skill or industry. Their reigns are good illustrations of the importance of individual ability and personality as factors in successful kingship. Like Valdemar, Margaret was able to exploit the dislike many Scandinavians had for foreigners, especially Germans, although she did cause some offense by giving fiefs in Norway and Sweden to Danes and Germans who had long been settled in Denmark but then failing to reward Norwegians or Swedes with Danish fiefs. With the help of the papacy she was able to reward her supporters with bishoprics. One of her most remarkable achievements was to reduce the amount of land that was not taxed because it was held by the church or, in Denmark and Sweden, by aristocrats. She did this by depriving aristocrats and even some churches of land that they had acquired since the deposition of Magnus Eriksson in 1363. The lower ranks of the aristocracy were affected by this change more than were families of high status. Indeed, the richer nobles were willing to cooperate in this campaign of reduction, for it was in their interest to maintain the gulf separating them from the lower aristocracy and, as far as possible, to prevent the dilution of their own ranks by the recruitment of men of lower status.

Margaret's skill as a ruler was made more obvious by the progressive failure of Erik after her death in 1412. The contrast should not be exaggerated; she encountered increasing opposition in the last years of her life, but Erik destroyed any hope of establishing a strong Union monarchy on the foundations laid by Valdemar and Margaret. His attempt to become the leading power in the Baltic aroused the hostility of the Hanseatic towns, in particular Lübeck, and this ambition, combined with his persistent but unsuccessful attempt to wrest control of south Jutland from the Holstein aristocracy, resulted in a series of costly conflicts. Erik increased his revenue by levying an English gold noble as toll on every ship sailing north through Øresund. This was a significant increase on the toll that had earlier been demanded from merchant ships returning to ports in western Europe from the Skåne Fair (Hørby 1966). Other attempts to increase his revenues by additional taxation and debasing the coinage provoked opposition, especially in Sweden where the aristocracy resented his willingness to grant lucrative fiefs to Danes, Germans, and other foreigners. Sweden was also seriously affected by the interruption of normal trade caused by disputes with the Hanseatic towns, one of whose weapons was to blockade Scandinavian ports, stopping the export of Swedish iron and copper. Significantly, it was in the mining district of Dalarna that open rebellion broke out in 1434. This rebellion was led by Engelbrekt Engelbrektsson, a member of the lower aristocracy, who was supported by large numbers of miners and merchants, quickly joined by many ordinary farmers. Their main targets were the castles, symbols of power and the main collecting centers for taxation, and many were taken and destroyed. The rapid success of the revolt alarmed the magnates, and by the end of 1436 they succeeded in taking over the leadership of opposition to the king; Engelbrekt was murdered and his leading lieutenants were executed. Erik failed to recover power in Sweden, and in 1438 a young Swedish noble, Karl Knutsson (Bonde), was chosen as Captain of the Realm (*rikshövitsman*). There were similar disturbances at the same time in Norway, but the Norwegian aristocracy rallied to the support of King Erik, who continued to be recognized there longer than in the other kingdoms.

The Breakup of the Union

The Swedish rebellion ended any hope that Erik's ambitious policies could succeed, and in 1439 he was deposed and spent the last twenty years of his life in exile. The Danes chose Christopher of Bavaria, Erik's nephew, to replace him. In 1441 Christopher was recognized in Sweden, and a year later in Norway. The Union had been restored, but in his reign effective power was in the hands of the councils of each kingdom. While the Danish and Norwegian aristocrats were in general in favor of the Union, powerful elements in Sweden were against it, and after Christopher's death in 1448 the competition between hostile Swedish factions for control of the Swedish council resulted in many changes of regime. Although Sweden continued to be, in theory, part of the Union until 1523, in practice it was virtually independent for much of the time.

After Christopher the Swedes elected Karl Knutsson as king and hoped that he would also be recognized in Norway. The Norwegians, after some hesitation, instead accepted the king who had been elected by the Danes, Christian of Oldenburg, a very distant kinsman of previous kings; his mother was a descendant of Erik Glipping. Karl abandoned his claim to Norway, but representatives of the Swedish and Danish councils agreed in 1450 at Halmstad that when both kings were dead the Union would be restored by the joint election of a single monarch. The election did not happen, but the union of Denmark and Norway proved to be permanent, with Christian's descendants as kings. Christian died in 1480 and was succeeded by his son Hans, who in turn was succeeded in 1513 by his son

Christian II. Ten years later Christian II was driven out by his father's brother, Frederik I. In 1531 Christian attempted but failed to recover his throne and was imprisoned.

Christian I promised to consult the Norwegian council on important matters but did not keep his word. In 1468–69, for example, he mortgaged Orkney and Shetland to the king of Scotland without referring to the council. He rarely interfered with episcopal elections, however, and he did keep his promise to grant Norwegian fiefs to Norwegians, the main exception being the crucially important castle of Bohus, which was normally in the charge of a trusted Dane. There were some local revolts against unpopular royal agents, but the most serious challenge to royal authority in Norway in Christian's and his son's reigns was the revolt of Knut Alvsson, a leading Norwegian nobleman, in 1501–2. He was of Swedish descent and took part in the rebellion that ended Hans's short period as acknowledged king in Sweden (1497–1501). The Norwegian rebellion was thus an extension of the Swedish one, but it was not so well supported, and Knut was forced to seek terms in the summer of 1502. Despite being promised safe conduct he was murdered, and most of his supporters soon gave up the struggle.

One result of this revolt was that King Hans began to take a closer interest in Norway and in 1506 made his son, the future Christian II, regent in Norway, with full powers. Both as regent and as king, Christian asserted Danish authority to the full. Norwegians were taxed more heavily than ever before; he disregarded the council and took over many of its functions. He also granted the most important fiefs to his Danish supporters, many of whom were not members of the aristocracy. He interfered in episcopal appointments and began to limit church privileges, which had recently been greatly enhanced. With the decline of the native secular aristocracy, the bishops began to be more prominent and in the fifteenth century formed a significant group in the council, which in the second half of the century was presided over by the archbishops. The bishops were in effect the representatives of Norwegian identity, which was consequently seriously weakened by the Reformation.

In 1536 the archbishop, Olav Engelbrektsson, who had built the first private Norwegian castle on Steinviksholm in Trondheim Fjord, declared his opposition to the Danish king Christian III, who favored the reformers, but he gained little support and in 1537 sailed to exile in the Netherlands. The year before, King Christian had declared that Norway was not a kingdom but a Danish province, like Jutland or Skåne. It was not until 1814 that the Norwegian kingdom was restored.

The main concern of the first three Oldenburg kings was to regain their authority in Sweden. They had little success. Each of them was only recognized there for a short while: Christian I from 1457 to 1464, Hans from 1497 to 1501, and Christian II in 1520–21. Karl Knutsson was king for three periods, 1448–57, 1464–65, and 1467–70, but was virtually powerless. After Karl's death in 1470 without a legitimate son, Sweden was more clearly than ever before an aristocratic republic with a council of bishops and magnates presided over by a regent. The attempt by Christian I to recover power failed; his forces were defeated at Brunkeberg overlooking Stockholm in 1471 by a coalition led by Sten Sture the elder, who was regent from 1470 until his death in 1503, except when Hans was king. Sten was succeeded by Svante Nilsson, a member of another family. Both these men worked in close cooperation with Archbishop Jakob Ulfsson, who had an exceptionally long period of office (1469–1514). Svante died in 1512, and after a short while was succeeded by his son, confusingly known as Sten Sture the younger; he was no relative of the earlier Sten Sture but was glad to be associated in this way with his remarkable predecessor. When Jakob Ulfsson was succeeded as archbishop by Gustav Trolle, the cooperation broke down completely. The regent contrived a quarrel with the archbishop, who was deposed and imprisoned. This strengthened the hand of Christian II, and in 1520 his third attempt to gain recognition in Sweden by force succeeded. Early in the year Sten Sture the younger was mortally wounded in a battle fought near Falköping in Västergötland against a Danish army that then advanced into Mälardalen. Christian's fleet besieged Stockholm, which surrendered in September, and Christian was then recognized as king. He was crowned in Stockholm on 4 November by Gustav Trolle. The following customary feasting was interrupted by proceedings against those who had supported Sten Sture the younger in his persecution of the archbishop. Those who were found guilty, together with others, were executed in what is known as the Stockholm Bloodbath. Over eighty people were killed, including two bishops, several members of the council, and many leading Stockholm burgesses. Christian then returned to Denmark, executing others on the way. This ruthless attempt to destroy all opposition had the reverse effect. Many were willing to join forces against Christian "the Tyrant," and early in 1521 Gustav Eriksson (Vasa), whose father was one of those executed in the previous year, emerged as their leader. In August he was chosen as regent and two years later was elected king, marking what proved to be the end of the Union. One of Gustav's advantages was that many potential opponents had been removed from the scene in 1520.

The loss of Sweden combined with revolts in Denmark undermined Christian's authority. In 1523 he went into exile, leaving his uncle Frederik as king. During Frederik's reign reformers were free to spread their message. Frederik's son Christian, however, was an ardent supporter of the Lutheran reformers, and when Frederik died in 1533 Christian's election as his successor was opposed by Catholics. A short period of civil war followed. This conflict has been called the "Count's feud" because it was led by Christopher, count of Oldenburg, who first supported the restoration of Christian II but was himself later chosen king by a faction. Not until 1536 was Christian III finally in effective control of the whole of Denmark. He then arrested his episcopal opponents and laid the foundations for the reformed church in the kingdom. With the departure of the archbishop of Nidaros he was also free to make similar changes in Norway, which was by then treated as a Danish province. In Sweden Gustav Vasa had advanced against the old ecclesiastical establishment more quickly, and at Vadstena in 1527 he took over responsibility for the church from the papacy. In both kingdoms the Reformation offered the opportunity to confiscate church wealth, which could be used to reward supporters, and also to lay claim to a share of regular church income from tithes.

The Union was ended, and both Danish and Swedish kings were supporters of the Protestant Reformation, but that did not bring peace to Scandinavia. For over a hundred years Danish and Swedish kings struggled for mastery of the region, a conflict that had wider ramifications in Europe. The end result was Danish defeat. In 1658 the Danes accepted the loss of Skåne, Blekinge, and Halland (Jämtland had been surrendered in 1645), fixing the frontier that has remained until the present day.

4

Things and Kings

Until the thirteenth century the basic institutions of government were the same in all three kingdoms: district and provincial assemblies commonly called *things* (Old Norse [ON] *thing*), and the royal retinue, or *hird* (ON *hirð*). The enlargement of royal authority and its extension into remote regions largely depended on the success of royal agents in gaining influence in the traditional assemblies. Many of these agents were members of the king's *hird*, which also included magnates who had great influence in assemblies in their own regions. In these ways the two elements (popular assemblies and royal retinues) were gradually linked, a process that was well advanced by the end of the thirteenth century, when new institutions of central government (councils and, in Denmark and Sweden, national assemblies) had begun to take shape. These acquired many of the functions that had earlier been the preserve of provincial assemblies, and by the fourteenth century it was as councillors that the higher aristocracy and clergy tried to guide royal government. Local government continued to be administered in communal assemblies in which local elites played a leading role, as they always had done (Imsen).

Early Assemblies

Little is known about assemblies at the beginning of the medieval period (*KHL*, s.v. "Ting"). By the thirteenth century, when contemporary texts begin to provide detailed information, generations of churchmen and royal officials had changed the assemblies in many significant ways, but some common and apparently ancient features can be discerned. Something can also be learned from the arrangements made in the ninth and tenth centuries by the Scandinavians who settled in the British Isles and Atlantic islands, especially Iceland. It appears that in ninth-century Scandinavia the public affairs of each local community or district were regulated in assemblies known as *allthings* because all the freemen of the area had the right to attend. The more important assemblies and those held at regular times were generally called *things*, but another common word, used especially for meetings called at irregular times, was *stefna* (cognate with a word meaning "voice"; a *stefna* was summoned). Both words were used by Scandinavians who settled in the British Isles in the ninth century.

These assemblies had many functions. In them individuals made the public declarations needed, for example, when an heir was recognized, a slave freed, or land changed hands. They dealt with accusations of theft and disputes about the ownership of land, or over boundaries. They were occasions for political discussion, for social contacts, for buying and selling, for sporting contests, and, most important of all, for religious ceremonies. It is significant that many of the places in which the major assemblies met were, to judge by their names, cult centers. Thus the place-name Viborg, the most important place of assembly in Jutland, meant "the sanctuary in the hill(s)," and Odense, "Odin's sanctuary." Both these places became sees of bishops, as did other pre-Christian cult centers. The association of assembly places with both pagan and Christian religion is sometimes confirmed in other ways. Thus Fröson, where the assembly of Jämtland met, not only has a pagan name, "the island of [the god] Frey"; it also has a runic inscription commemorating the Christianization of Jämtland, and traces of pagan rituals have been found under Fröso church (Hildebrandt; Jansson, 118–19). The rituals conducted in such places must normally have been the concern of people living in the region, but some festivals—for example, Distingen, the winter festival at Uppsala—attracted people from distant parts of Scandinavia (see "Markets and Fairs" in chapter 9).

By the thirteenth century churches and markets had taken over many of the diverse activities of the earlier *things*; assemblies were then largely concerned with legal matters. In practice many of those entitled to attend *allthings* did not; in some only a quarter was needed to constitute a quorum. Meetings were normally held in the open air. A small area was fenced off, with special places reserved for those who were directly involved, such as accusers or accused, and for the leading men, who were generally responsible for conducting the meeting. Others observed the proceedings and normally, but not always, approved decisions. One method of showing consent was by brandishing weapons, *vapnatak* (ON), a name and presumably procedure that was introduced into England in the ninth century by Danish settlers, who called the local assemblies they organized (or took over) *wapentakes*.

In relatively densely populated regions, local assemblies were held weekly for much of the year. Where population was sparse and scattered, the districts were much larger and the meetings less frequent. There were also differences in the frequency of provincial assemblies. In late medieval Denmark they were held every fourteen days. In Sweden they were mostly quarterly, but in Norway they were annual, although extra meetings could be summoned for special purposes. Where assemblies were infrequent, disputes were often referred to arbitrators or commissioners chosen by the disputing parties or appointed by an assembly. Resort to a formal assembly was avoided as far as possible, and normally only when no agreement could be reached, or when the decision of the arbitrators was not accepted.

Proceedings were highly ritualistic. Accusations and responses had to be made in traditional formulas. Decisions were sometimes made by appeals to the supernatural—for example, by casting lots, a procedure that gave power to those responsible for interpreting the signs. Decisions could also be reached by a duel between parties to a dispute or between their representatives. Another method was by compurgation, a procedure in which an individual was supported by oaths sworn by other people. As the value of their oaths depended on their status, it was an advantage to have the support of men of high rank.

In the early Middle Ages assemblies had no executive power; their effectiveness depended on social pressures, reinforced by the religious element in the proceedings. The ultimate sanction was outlawry, exclusion from the society represented by the assembly. The imposition of lesser penalties and the implementation of decisions about, for example, landownership lay in the hands of the individuals concerned. For the protection of their rights individuals therefore depended on their own resources and what help they could obtain from others. One source of support must often have been the family, but many disputes were within families, and then the support of friends was needed, if possible the more powerful men in the community. The support of a lord or chieftain who could call on his sworn supporters was particularly valuable. By acknowledging such a lord, a man could gain protection for himself and his family without losing his free status, and lords gained in prestige and influence. The most prestigious and normally most powerful lords were kings, and they were the best guarantors of individual rights, an important factor in the extension of royal authority and the formation of the medieval kingdoms. The role of kings as upholders of justice was greatly emphasized by churchmen, who also encouraged kings to act as lawmakers, in the first place in the interest of the clergy and their churches.

Lawmaking

By the tenth century special assemblies were beginning to make or change laws for provinces, some of which were very large (*KHL*, s.v. "Lagting"). In thirteenth-century Norway there were only four of these special assemblies. The Norwegian provincial assemblies, known as law-*things* (ON *lög-thing*), were, in contrast to the traditional *allthings*, representative, and were attended by a limited number of men chosen in different parts of the province. For that purpose the district or communal *things* were grouped in what were in west Norway called *fylki*, which were subdivided, generally into quarters (*fjörðungr*). Thus Gulating, which in the eleventh century legislated for west Norway from Agder to Sunnmøre, had six *fylki* that were believed originally to have sent about 400 representative landowners to the annual *thing* held near the entrance of Sognefjord. The number of representatives was reduced in the twelfth century to 246 and a century later still further to 146. By the eleventh century, and probably in the tenth, the representatives were nominated by royal agents, most of whom also attended the annual law-*thing*, together with numerous clergy chosen by the bishop.

The creation of these Norwegian law-*things* was closely connected to the growth of royal authority. The earliest, Gulating, was established in the tenth century in the part of Norway in which the foundations of the Norwegian kingdom were laid by Harald Finehair (fig. 3.3). Harald's son, Håkon the Good, was described as a lawmaker in an early eleventh century poem, which suggests that the tradition, reported by Snorri and others, that he "set" the law of Gulating may be sound. He had been educated in the court of King Athelstan in England, where there was a long tradition of royal lawmaking. It is indeed likely that the process of Christianizing the law of Gulating began in Håkon's reign, although it was apparently Harald, possibly influenced by the example of the Danes, who made it the central assembly for his newly established kingdom. Håkon was also credited with "setting" the law of Frostating. An even earlier origin was claimed for the east Norwegian law-*thing*, Eidsivating, which was said by Snorri and others to have been established by Harald Finehair's father, Halfdan the Black, but in the twelfth century there were said to be four provinces in that region (*Historia Norwegiae*, 81). They are unlikely to have been reorganized into a single law-province before that part of Norway was firmly under royal control, and that may not have been until the early thirteenth century.

In other parts of Scandinavia there were similar lawmaking assemblies known as *landsting*, where *land* has the sense of "province," not "kingdom." In the twelfth and thirteenth centuries some met in places (including Viborg and Odense) that were apparently sites of assemblies in pre-Christian times, but the pagan assemblies were probably for smaller districts than the medieval provinces, most of which, like Eidsivating, were formed by combining several self-governing districts. The medieval Swedish province of Småland, for example, a plural name meaning "small lands," was a region with several separate districts or provinces that apparently remained largely independent until the mid-twelfth century. North of Mälaren there were three provinces (or folklands) until the end of the thirteenth century, when they were united to form the province of Uppland, another plural name first recorded in 1296. South of Mälaren there were also three districts that were brought together, probably in the eleventh century, to form what was called Södermanland (land of the south men), with a newly organized assembly called Samting (the gathered *thing*), at Strängnäs. Similar provinces in Finland were formed even later, after the Swedish conquest in the thirteenth century.

The creation of the medieval law-provinces was an important stage in the formation of the kingdoms. Kings influenced the laws made in such assemblies from the outset, but they ruled by consent and had to respect existing rights. They needed the support of powerful members of the community in order to alter local customs and traditional procedures. Consequently, in each kingdom there were significant differences in the laws of different provinces when written versions were produced between the twelfth and fourteenth centuries.

Iceland was exceptional: its lawmaking *thing* was not established by a king. According to Ari the settlers originally set up numerous *things*, but shortly before 930 their leaders decided to have a central assembly for all free Icelanders, the Althing. The Icelanders were in close touch with their homeland, and at the same time that they founded the Althing they decided to base their law on that of Gulating. It does, therefore, seem likely that the Icelanders' decision to establish the Althing was an echo of developments in their Norwegian homeland.

Administrative Districts

The growth of royal authority also affected the local assemblies that continued to regulate the affairs of their own districts. They were expected to implement the laws and procedures determined in the provincial law-making assemblies, and these provided for the intervention of royal agents in local assemblies in various ways; by the thirteenth century they had become an important element in royal administration. This development apparently happened first in Denmark. Some time before the eleventh century administrative districts known as *syssel* were established in Jutland, but not in other parts of Denmark. This pattern suggests that they were organized when kings had direct control in Jutland but not in other parts of the medieval kingdom. The *syssel* were replaced by a new type of administrative district, called *herred* (plural *herreder*) in modern Danish, that were responsible for the collection of renders due to the king and for the imposition of military obligations (or the collection of tax levied instead). By the end of the eleventh century *herreder* had been organized in most parts of the kingdom, possibly including Skåne.

The Old Norse word *herað* was originally used to describe a settled district, which could be quite small and generally had well-defined natural boundaries. Most, if not all, presumably had their own *things*. Some were simply converted into administrative *herreder*, but others were too large and were divided into two or more *herreder*. By the thirteenth century some had been further subdivided to form half or even quarter *herreder*. Danish influence was probably responsible for the adoption of the same word for local assembly districts in southeast Norway (including Bohuslän), as well as in Götaland and the adjacent Swedish provinces. This terminology did not last long in Norway; after Norwegian kings gained firm control of the whole country, the system of *fylki*, familiar in west Norway, was introduced. Administrative districts in Svealand were not called *herað* (Modern Swedish *härad*) until the fourteenth century. Before that the inland districts were called *hundreds* (Old Swedish *hundare*, earlier *hund*). The districts may well have been very old, but it is most unlikely that they were called *hundreds* before the ninth century, when that word began to be used widely in Europe for administrative districts; the name may have been a novelty when it is first evidenced on an eleventh-century runic inscription (Murray 1988; *Sveriges Runinskrifter*, hereafter *SR*, Uppland no. 212). By the early twelfth century those north of Mälaren, in what was later Uppland, were grouped in three so-called folklands: Tiundaland, "the land of ten hund," Attundaland, and Fjärdrundaland, with eight and four *hundreds* respectively. The coastal region was divided into *skeppslag*, "ship-laws," reflecting the obligation of those districts to provide ships for military expeditions.

Kingship

The early development of kingship in Scandinavia is exceedingly obscure. According to Saxo there were many *reges* and *reguli* in early Scandinavia, as well as *praefecti* and *duces*, although there is no reliable evidence for the existence of such small kingdoms. The Byzantine historian Procopius was too remote for much weight to be given his statement that in the sixth century there were thirteen *ethnoi* in Scandinavia (*Thoule*), each with its own *basileos* (Procopius, 414–15). There may well have been thirteen distinct groups, but we do not know how they were ruled. The additional information about Scandinavia included in the Old English version of Orosius mentions only one ruler in Scandinavia, a king in Bornholm, possibly because such a small kingdom was itself remarkable. The only other ninth-century kings mentioned in contemporary sources were of the Danes and the Svear.

Of course, there may have been many other kings who are not mentioned in contemporary texts, but Rimbert and other Frankish sources do give a clear impression that the Danish and Svea kingships were extensive, and, according to the late-tenth-century poem *Vellekla*, Norway was then ruled by sixteen jarls, who all acknowledged one ruler (who was himself a jarl). Many of the armies attacking the British Isles and Frankia in the ninth century were led by kings or jarls; the *Anglo-Saxon Chronicle* names seven Scandinavian kings in ninth-century annals, four in one year (871), but that is not necessarily a reliable guide to the situation in Scandinavia. Leaders in exile may have claimed or been given by their followers a status that would not have been recognized at home; in 1014 Knut was elected king by the Danish army after his father's death, but it was several years before he became king of the Danes. Several of the leaders of Viking armies in Frankia were or claimed to be members of the Danish royal family, and it is possible that the kings named in the *Anglo-Saxon Chronicle* claimed that rank because they too were members of that or another prestigious royal kin.

As suggested in chapter 3, the best clue to the character of Scandinavian society in the ninth century is provided by the settlement of Iceland, where in the eleventh century power was divided between several dozen chieftains, called *goðar*, who were lords of men, not territory. Two hundred years later a much smaller number of territorial lordships, *ríki*, had been formed there, and it is likely that there had been a similar development in Scandinavia. There were, of course, fundamental differences between Iceland and Scandinavia. Iceland was not threatened by invasion, nor was it a source of luxuries that attracted foreign merchants. There was no king; the focus of unity in Iceland was in the Althing, which all *goðar* attended with

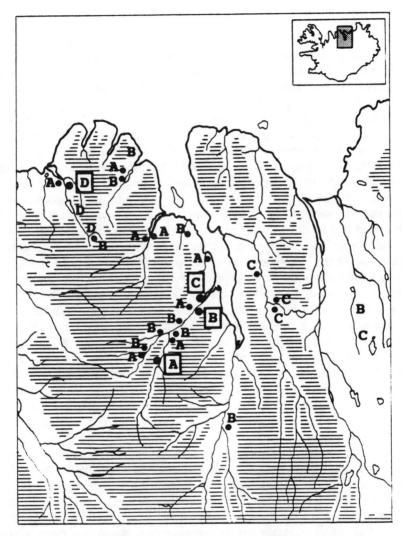

Figure 4.1. Four *goðar* and their *thingmen* in the Eyjafjörður district, circa 1190. This map, based on the *Saga of Guðmund dyri*, illustrates the nonterritorial power of Icelandic *goðar*. A boxed letter marks where a *goði* lived; the same letter unboxed indicates the farms of his *thingmen*. **A** represents Guðmund and his men. The small *goðorð* **D** was later given to Guðmund (Byock, 114–17).

their followers. Not until the years 1262–64 were Norwegian kings formally recognized by the Althing. It is significant, however, that in the eleventh century some Icelandic *goðar* already acknowledged the Norwegian king as their personal lord. Similar submissions by otherwise independent Scandinavian chieftains must have been a very important factor in the extension of royal authority in all three kingdoms.

The main source of information about Norway in the ninth century is the account of the voyages of Ottar. The description of his voyage to Hedeby does not mention any king or other type of ruler in Norway or Denmark. The explanation may be that the English reporter wanted to emphasize that Ottar recognized King Alfred as his lord. By submitting to Alfred, Ottar gained the king's protection; he would have needed similar protection in parts of Scandinavia away from his own district. It is explicitly stated that he did not dare to enter the territory of the Bjarmar, living by the White Sea, because he had no peace with them, the implication being that he did have such a peace elsewhere (Fell). It may be that Norwegian chieftains and rulers accepted Danish overlordship in order to have safe passage through Danish waters for themselves or their agents and access to Danish markets. It seems likely that Ottar was an example of a fairly common pattern, a local chieftain operating within the framework of an overlordship exercised by a distant king. It is possible that Danish kings were already overlords of much of the Norwegian coast as well as Viken by the ninth century. If so, Harald Finehair's kingship may have been an entirely new creation, modeled on that of the former overlords. A similar process can be observed in Frankia in the late seventh century. When the Merovingian Empire collapsed, various districts, including Frisia, briefly gained their independence and emerged as kingdoms.[1]

Rimbert, in his *Vita Anskarii* (Life of Anskar), provides much valuable but tantalizing information about kings of the Svear in the ninth century. One of the four he names, Erik, was a former king whom some people had begun to worship as a god, the implication being that that was a special honor; the kings of the Svear were not divine ex officio (*VA* 26). He says nothing about the way they were chosen, where they came from, or the extent of their authority, apart from reporting that one took part in an expedition to assert Svea overlordship over Kurland (*VA* 30). He implies that they did not have the same authority as their Danish contemporaries. His account of the decision to allow Anskar to revive the mission in Birka is especially revealing. The king had to secure the consent first of the chieftains and then of the people, in two assemblies (*VA* 27). Rimbert mentions no such consultations, or even assemblies, in Denmark.

The *Vita Anskarii* combined with later texts and archaeological evidence suggests that there were many chieftains (*principes*) among the Svear, whose power largely depended on their ability to obtain a share of the produce brought to the region from the north and from across the Baltic (P. Sawyer 1991b). The topography of the region meant that no one individual could control or monopolize this traffic in the way that Danish kings controlled the entrance to the Baltic, but the Svear had a common interest in maintaining peaceful conditions so that foreign merchants were not dissuaded from visiting the market at Birka. One of the main functions of the Svea king was to provide a focus of stability. The fact that in the eleventh and twelfth centuries the Svear expelled several of their kings suggests that, although some may have won recognition by force, the position of most depended more on consent than coercion. It may, indeed, have been easier for the lords of the Svear to accept an outsider as king rather than one of themselves. In the eleventh and twelfth centuries several kings of the Svear were from Götaland, but any king they chose was expected to serve their purposes, not his own. In the eleventh century they were prepared to tolerate Christian kings, and many Svear were themselves converted, but they fiercely resisted attempts to interfere with the traditional religious rituals, on which they believed the prosperity of the region had long depended.

Kings and *Things*

Whatever the basis of their claims—success in battle, election, inheritance, or the murder of a rival—in all three kingdoms kings had to be recognized or accepted by popular assemblies (*KHL*, s.v. "Tronfølge"). In Denmark the assembly at Viborg traditionally had precedence, but kings were expected to obtain confirmation from assemblies in other parts of the kingdom, those held at Lund and Roskilde being particularly important. In twelfth-century Norway the election could be made in any one of the local assemblies, and sometimes different assemblies chose different men. The twelfth-century conflicts in Denmark and Norway were, however, civil wars to gain power in relatively united kingdoms. Although rival claimants were sometimes linked with particular regions, there was no serious threat of provincial separatism leading to the fragmentation of the kingdoms.

In Sweden, which was not united so early or so securely, the Svear claimed precedence. In the fourteenth century Swedish kings were elected by representatives from all the provinces of the kingdom in a ceremony at Mora Stone in Uppland. This was probably an elaboration of the traditional procedure by which kings of the Svear had been chosen. After the permanent unification of Svear and Götar in the twelfth century, new kings had to make a progress through the provinces, which by the end of the thirteenth century included Finland, to be recognized in their assemblies. This trek was known as Eriksgata, "Erik's way" (*gata* meaning "street"). The significance of this name is disputed. It has been claimed that it was used long before the twelfth century to describe a progress of recognition in Uppland, the word *Erik* meaning "ruler." Whether or not that claim is right, by the end of the twelfth century the name was certainly being associated with Saint Erik.

The church contributed to political stability by insisting that illegitimate sons could not become kings. This doctrine was only slowly accepted—in Norway not until 1240, and even then illegitimate sons were not excluded; it eventually reduced the number of possible claimants but did not prevent violent succession disputes. The church also favored hereditary succession, but this was only made law in Norway. In Denmark and Sweden the magnates were powerful enough to retain the right to elect their kings on most occasions. Churchmen also attempted to strengthen the position of kings against the claims of potential rivals by the ceremony of coronation (*KHL*, s.v. "kröning"). There must always have been inauguration rituals, but little is known about them before the twelfth century, when ecclesiastical coronation, on the model developed in tenth-century Germany, was introduced. The first Scandinavian coronation was of Magnus Erlingsson in 1163 or 1164. His rival and successor, Sverri, attempted to secure his position by coronation in 1194, but he and his supporters argued that he was king by God's grace, which was bestowed directly, not mediated by the church. The first Danish coronation ceremony, in 1170, was on the initiative of the king, Valdemar I, whose attitude seems to have been much more like Sverri's than like that of Magnus Erlingsson's circle. Valdemar had his eldest son designated as his successor and crowned in a ceremony in which the sanctity of the king's father, Knut Lavard, was proclaimed and his relics translated into a new shrine at Ringsted. In Sweden, where the first recorded coronation was in 1210, the claims of rival dynasties made such ecclesiastical confirmation all the more valuable.

Occasionally churchmen, especially archbishops, attempted to influence the outcome of succession disputes by refusing to perform the coronation ceremony. The archbishop of Nidaros would not crown Sverri, but the ceremony was performed by another bishop. Similarly, in the dispute between the descendants of Valdemar II's sons Abel and Christopher, the archbishop of Lund supported Abel's line and refused to crown Christopher's son Erik either as the designated heir during Christopher's lifetime

in 1258 or after his death a year later. Erik was nevertheless crowned, by
the bishop of Viborg in his cathedral.

The King's Resources

By the end of the eleventh century Scandinavian rulers could no longer
hope to base their power on wealth gathered in Russia, the Byzantine
Empire, or England. They were forced to rely on their own resources, together with what they could gather as plunder or tribute from each other
or from the peoples living around the Baltic. Military adventures could be
rewarding, but their outcome was uncertain; a more stable basis of royal
power, especially in the early Middle Ages, was the yield of royal estates.
In early sixteenth-century Denmark these accounted for about 10 percent
of the value of all Danish estates, but by then other resources such as the
profits of justice, tolls, urban rents, and, above all, taxes provided the
greater part of royal income and compensated for the loss of estates through
donations, especially to the church. Kings had various ways of increasing
the amount of land they held: by marriage settlements; as penalties made
to regain the king's favor after an offense, such as failure to perform military service; or by the confiscation of the property of rebels. Kings could
also claim land for which there was no known heir. The greatest increase
was by conquest, especially during the eleventh and twelfth centuries when
the Scandinavian kingdoms were consolidated by the permanent incorporation of territories that had earlier been independent or held by tributary
rulers.

Even in the early Middle Ages kings were not solely dependent on
the land they owned. They could claim hospitality for themselves, their
retinues, and perhaps even their agents (*KHL*, s.v. "Gästning" and "Våld-
gästning"). This right was enjoyed by many lords, including Icelandic
goðar, and was so abused that in the late thirteenth century attempts were
made in all three kingdoms to regulate it. The general obligation to contribute food and materials needed by the royal household as it traveled from
place to place was, in effect, one of the earliest taxes, and by the thirteenth
century had become a regular demand regardless of the king's itinerary,
although extra demands might be made if the king did visit an area.

Another obligation that seems to have been universal in early medieval
Europe, including Scandinavia, was the duty to defend one's own territory.
Until the twelfth century offensive expeditions against enemies abroad
were undertaken by royal armies that included the king's own retainers,
some of whom had their own retinues, together with warriors supplied by

allies and tributary rulers, but when defense was needed, all able-bodied men could be called on to fight or help in some other way; food and other materials had to be supplied and transported. Materials, transport, and labor could also be requisitioned to construct defenses. Support of this kind continued to be demanded throughout the Middle Ages, but there were significant changes in the method of fighting (*KHL*, s.v. "Krigskunst").

In the twelfth century cavalry began to play a decisive role in the struggles for power in Scandinavia. Relatively small numbers of mounted warriors could overwhelm much larger forces of foot soldiers recruited by the traditional system of levies. This was dramatically demonstrated in 1134 in the battle of Fotevik, when some sixty mounted knights shattered a large conventional force. The lesson was soon learned, and in both Denmark and Sweden, where the landscape was suitable for cavalry, kings and magnates recruited professional warriors, mainly Germans, to fight on their behalf, and these soldiers had to be paid. One of the main sources of revenue in all three kingdoms was the tax levied instead of military service, which by the end of the twelfth century most people were normally no longer required to perform. Even in Norway, where the landscape made cavalry warfare difficult if not impossible, so that royal armies were still based on local levies of amateurs in the fourteenth century, tax was demanded when the levies were not mustered (*KHL*, s.v. "Leidang").

The King's Men

Magnates and the wealthier landowners who had their own retainers were not exempt from military service; rather, they were expected to serve in person with their followers. In Denmark and Sweden all the land owned by these men was exempt from the payment of the levy tax. The Norwegian aristocracy did not enjoy such extensive privileges, for they were only exempt on the land they themselves occupied; the land of their tenants was taxed. The magnates and their armed retainers had a crucially important role in Scandinavian politics throughout the Middle Ages, especially in Denmark and Sweden. Indeed, the extension of the direct rule of a king in the eleventh and twelfth centuries depended in large measure on the support of formerly independent chieftains and magnates who acknowledged his authority and were prepared to act as his agents. Many royal agents were of low status—stewards of royal estates, for example, were not necessarily freemen—but the consolidation of royal authority in newly won territory, whether acquired by conquest or voluntary submission, was best *lendrmenn*

hird

done by men of high rank respected in their own communities, with their own retainers (Helle 1972).

In eleventh-century Norway such men were called *lendrmenn* (singular *lendrmaðr*), a word generally taken to mean "men given [land by the king]." Kings may have rewarded them, or their ancestors, with land confiscated from those who did not submit or who rebelled, but most of the land held by *lendrmenn* was apparently inherited. The title seems rather to reflect the grant of responsibility for the protection of royal interests in a particular district, generally to a local magnate. The responsibilities of *lendrmenn*, as described in twelfth-century laws, included leading the military levy from their district, supporting stewards of royal estates, arresting wrongdoers, and choosing representatives to attend the annual law-*thing*. Most also attended the provincial assemblies, although a few remained on duty in their districts. The laws contain several rules designed to prevent *lendrmenn* from abusing their authority by partisan interference in the legal process. According to Gulating law, for example, a *lendrmaðr* could not act as a judge or arbitrator; he was not even allowed to come so close that his voice could be heard by the men dealing with a case. It may be doubted that this rule was strictly obeyed, but its breach could be the basis for an appeal.

There was, of course, a danger that such men might put their own interests before the king's, even to the point of rebellion. This risk was reduced by making them members of the royal *hird*, thus ensuring regular contact with the king and other *lendrmenn*, and strengthening the bond between them. A royal *hird* was in origin the band of warriors, often called a *lið*, that kings and many others had for their protection, to enforce their will and fight on their behalf. The civil wars of the twelfth century were largely fought by retinues of this kind, and three hundred years earlier similar groups were responsible for Viking raids. The number of retainers in such a *lið* varied. Some were no larger than the crew of a ship, but the more powerful leaders had several ships. When the ninth-century Swedish king Anund was exiled, he was accompanied by eleven ships of his own, and he recruited twenty-two Danish ships to help him regain power; we do not know whether the reinforcements were supplied by the Danish king or by one or more Danish lords (*VA* 19). In the ninth-century Viking raids, several fleets of thirty ships were reported, but these must often have included the retinues of several lords. The contemporary annals of Saint Bertin described the Viking army that threatened Paris in 861 as consisting of several *sodalitates*, that is, sworn groups, that wintered in different places along the river Seine. Groups of this kind were not formed exclusively for overseas expeditions (although such raids made it easier to maintain the loyalty of followers), and they must often have had a decisive role in assembly decisions and in local affairs long before the twelfth-century wars.

The *Hird*

Hird was an English word meaning "family" that was adopted in Scandinavia by the eleventh century, especially for the retinues of rulers, kings, and jarls; the word *lið* then tended to be used in a more limited, military sense. As the kingdoms developed, the character as well as the name of the royal retinues changed. They began to include bishops, and although many members continued to be warriors with their own retinues, their role as administrators was increasingly important. Although some remained as companions of the king as he traveled from estate to estate, others had to stay more or less permanently in their districts. The military role of royal *hirds* increased during the civil wars, but once peace was achieved, the administrative functions of *hirdmen* became more important. Kings drew men from the *hird* for special missions or to act as royal agents, and the *hirdmen* gradually took a more active role in local and provincial assemblies.

In Norway the districts were reorganized or renamed as *syssel*, and in the thirteenth century the *hirdmen* who took charge of them, called *sysselmen*, were generally given charge of districts with which they themselves were not closely linked. As royal agents *hirdmen* were entitled to a wage graduated according to rank, and to a share of the penalties they collected. Their tasks included the supervision of stewards of royal estates, ensuring that the king's dues and taxes were collected, and they were responsible for seeing that local districts fulfilled the duties that the royal government imposed on them, such as maintaining roads and bridges. It was their task to see that new laws were published and obeyed, that the property of outlaws was confiscated, and that the king's share of any penalties was collected. They were also responsible for mobilizing the military levy, or for collecting the tax levied when the levy was not called out. They were given, or were allowed to appoint, assistants called *lensmenn*, who were chosen from among the richer and better landowners of each district, thus ensuring that local elites continued to have a leading role in local government (Imsen). The king could communicate with his agents by sending messengers, but on some occasions the whole *hird* was assembled; in Norway this happened regularly at Christmas, but a full meeting could be summoned at other times.

The organization and rituals of royal *hirds* naturally tended to become more elaborate as the men acquired additional responsibilities, and they developed into central institutions in the government of the expanding king-doms. Two constitutions are known: the Danish Vederlov, "penalty-law," was drawn up for the Danish royal *hird* in the late twelfth century; a century later a more elaborate constitution, Hirdskrå, was approved for the Nor-wegian one. No such detailed information is available for the Swedish *hird*, but there is no doubt that arrangements were similar in all three kingdoms. A royal *hird* was aristocratic and included men drawn from leading families. The members were the king's sworn men. New members were admitted by the king, but according to Hirdskrå members of the *hird* could refuse to admit a candidate. The *hirds* were hierarchical. Toward the end of the thir-teenth century the different ranks in the Norwegian *hird* were given names that were familiar in western Europe; the highest rank, *lendrmenn*, became barons, and below them were knights (*riddere*) and squires (*svenner*). There were also pages, young men who were in effect apprentices, recruited from the better families in the kingdom. Some members had formal responsi-bilities in the king's hall, such as serving or holding lights, and there were officers who performed specific functions such as marshal, butler, or staller, but these duties were most often ceremonial; the real work was done by servants.

Councils and Parliaments

Meetings of a *hird* provided a good opportunity to discuss important mat-ters with many (in late-thirteenth-century Norway, all) of the magnates, but kings also needed to consult a smaller group. They must always have had a close circle of advisers, but in the thirteenth century these acquired a more formal status as kings' councils (*KHL*, s.v. "Rigsråd"). These were chosen by kings and normally included bishops, chaplains who were re-sponsible for the royal writing offices, legal advisers, and magnates the king wished to consult as well as those he could not ignore. During the thirteenth and early fourteenth centuries there were, in all three kingdoms, periods when the king was a minor. These were opportunities for the coun-cils to gain authority and independence and for councillors to experience full responsibility for government. The long minority of Magnus Eriksson as king of both Norway and Sweden was especially significant in the de-velopment of councils. It was then that the king's council in each kingdom began to be the council of the realm, with its own seal. In Denmark the minorities of Erik Glipping (1259–64) and of Erik Menved (1286–89) and the interregnum (1332–40) led to a similar increase in the importance and independence of the council. In the absence of King Valdemar abroad it was the council that negotiated and agreed the Peace of Stralsund in 1370. The power of councils was restricted under Margaret and Erik of Pomerania, but in the last years of Erik's reign there was a resurgence of conciliar power that continued into the sixteenth century. In that period the councils in all three kingdoms assumed many of the functions—including lawmaking, enforcing justice, imposing new taxes, and even electing kings—that had earlier been matters for larger assemblies that included a wider representation of clergy and of the lower as well as the high aristocracy.

The *hird* sometimes acted as a representative assembly. That practice was more reasonable in Norway, where most magnates were in the *hird*, but in Denmark and Sweden the aristocracy was more numerous and powerful, and special meetings called Herredag in Sweden, and Danehof in Denmark were summoned. In such meetings new laws were approved, extra taxation was agreed, and some justice done. These parliaments developed in Scandinavia at much the same time as in other parts of Europe; at such a meeting in Denmark in 1241 and forty years later at Alsnö, a royal residence in Sweden, the privileged status of the aristocracy in these kingdoms was confirmed. In Denmark Erik Glipping even promised to hold such a parliament annually, but he was murdered, and his successors did not go so far. Larger assemblies of clergy and aristocrats were, however, summoned from time to time in all three kingdoms to deal with especially important or difficult matters, although in Norway they were never on the same scale after 1281 as they had been earlier in the century, when as many as eighty prelates and royal retainers took part (*KHL*, s.v. "Riksmøter"). Church councils were by then dealing with church affairs, and in secular concerns the parliaments were in time eclipsed by the councils, especially in Denmark where the last Danehof was held in 1413.

One of the most important tasks of these parliaments had been to agree to the extra taxation needed to meet the costs of royal government, which increased greatly during the twelfth and thirteenth centuries. This increase was partly a consequence of the greater size of the kingdoms; the agents necessary to make royal authority effective had to be rewarded. As the status of kings increased, so did the cost of maintaining their prestige with ceremonies and imposing buildings, such as the great hall built by Håkon Håkonsson in Bergen (fig. 3.6). Diplomatic contacts with foreign rulers, frequently to negotiate the marriage of kings or their children, required expenditure on gifts and hospitality. Royal marriages were expensive affairs. The marriage of a son could bring in a substantial dowry, but that might not be enough to cover the cost of the ceremony and the associated feasting. On the other hand, the marriages of daughters of kings were a serious drain on royal treasuries.

Another more serious drain was the high cost of new military techniques. In addition to the novelty of cavalry warfare, the twelfth century also saw major developments in castle building (*KHL*, s.v. "Borg"). As castles began to be more elaborate and larger, they were more expensive to build, for even if materials and labor were requisitioned, skilled craftsmen were needed to supervise the construction. Castles were also expensive to maintain and garrison. At first these were built by kings and were a significant factor in the extension of royal authority, with many of the royal revenues of the surrounding districts allocated to their support, but during the thirteenth century many castles with their districts and revenues were granted out as fiefs in return for loans (*KHL*, s.v. "Län"). This exchange reduced royal income, and the transfer of control of such strongholds was a threat to royal power, which was further challenged by the construction of private castles by magnates and even by churchmen, the archbishop of Lund's great castle of Hammershus on Bornholm being the most dramatic example. Norway was exceptional in this respect too; there were few castles, and all were royal until the end of the Middle Ages.

These increased costs were met in part by increases in the revenue from traditional sources; royal estates, tolls, and town rents all yielded more as the economy expanded in the twelfth and thirteenth centuries and as collectors became more efficient (*KHL*, s.v. "Kronans finanser"). The involvement of the king in the administration of justice was also a source of profit. The main additional income was the tax that most people paid instead of the military service that they were no longer required to perform.

In Denmark and Sweden the magnates and wealthier landowners were exempt not only from the tax due in place of military service but also from other regular taxes on all their land, including that occupied by tenants. This freedom was formally acknowledged in Denmark in 1241 and some forty years later in Sweden; in this way the aristocracy of these kingdoms was defined but not created (*KHL*, s.v. "Frälse"). They were liable to extra taxes that were later imposed from time to time, but they claimed the right to approve such extra impositions and were sometimes successful in preventing what they considered excessive demands (*KHL*, s.v. "Skatter").

The councils in all three kingdoms were normally composed of bishops and members of the privileged aristocracy. The councillors, even in Norway, claimed the right to approve new members proposed by kings; during minorities and vacancies they had great freedom as the representatives of the kingdoms, controlling royal castles and fiefs and choosing the next king. They could require a new king to make certain promises before he was formally elected, or crowned, but these promises were commonly broken. After 1448 the Danish councillors, although very powerful, had their freedom of action against the king limited by their common desire to see royal authority restored in Sweden.

In Sweden one of the main ambitions of the rival factions among the higher aristocracy was to gain control of the council and with it the opportunity to acquire lucrative fiefs and key strongholds. In their conflicts appeals were made for support from the provincial assemblies. This was in accordance with Magnus Eriksson's Landlaw, in which it was laid down that decisions about extra taxation were to be made by the bishop, lawman, six aristocrats, and six others from each province.

During the fifteenth century representatives of provincial assemblies were summoned to special meetings of the Swedish council to approve and publicize decisions rather than to help make them (*KHL*, s.v. "Riksdag"; Schück). A notable example (there are earlier ones) is the meeting in Stockholm in 1499, when Hans, then acknowledged as king in Sweden, had his son Christian elected as the future king in defiance of the Landlaw that prescribed election. The decision of 1499 was made by the lawmen of the nine provinces together with "twelve good men of each province as indicated by the law of Sweden." The record of the event names them along with others who were summoned and present but did not take part in the decision. These observers included nobles, miners, burgesses, and councillors of Stockholm and "all the other townsmen here in the realm." Meetings of that kind prepared the way for the development of the Swedish Riksdag with its separate estates of nobles, other landowners, townsmen, and miners that first appeared in a clearly recognizable form as the "Reformation Riksdag" held in 1527 at Västerås.

In the fifteenth and early sixteenth centuries the major Swedish fairs or religious festivals were also important political occasions. At the fair of Saint Erik on 18 May 1470, Sten Sture proclaimed that he had taken over the government of the kingdom, and in 1501 at the festival of Saint Peter at Vadstena he renounced his oath of loyalty to King Hans. In the following years many of the major church festivals were occasions when the regents attempted, with some success, to gain general support from a wider public. They also appealed, in writing or in person, to the regular provincial assemblies. As a prominent Swedish prelate, Hemming Gadh, later bishop of Linköping, advised Svante Nilsson, Sten Sture's successor, "popular provincial *things* are powerful" (Schück, 33). Few medieval Scandinavian kings needed to be reminded of that truth, for their authority rested in large measure on the power of assemblies, large and small, and their ability to make use of this power.

After Erik of Pomerania royal power was severely limited in Scandinavia, but as Gustav Vasa demonstrated in Sweden, and Christian III in Denmark, the institutions of kingship that had been developed in the medieval centuries provided the basis for very effective royal authority. Their success was not so much due to their remarkable determination and ability to use the resources their predecessors had created but rather owed more to the Reformation, which provided them with vast resources with which to reward friends and supporters, and a network of authority, from archbishops to country priests, that could now be used to support kings, not to check them.

5

Christianization and Church Organization

The Christianization of Scandinavia began in the ninth century.[1] Some Scandinavians had contact with Christians and their churches much earlier, even before the collapse of the Roman Empire in the west, and in the early eighth century Willibrord, an English missionary, made an unsuccessful attempt to convert the Danish king Ongendus. It was, however, in the 820s that missionaries first had the opportunity to preach the gospel to the Danes and the Svear. Knowledge of Christianity was also spread at that time by Scandinavians who, as Vikings, merchants, or envoys, or as hostages in the courts of Christian kings, must have been impressed by the enormous wealth and elaborate rituals of the great churches in the Frankish Empire and the British Isles. Some had even been baptized or prime signed, the first stage in the baptism ritual, but those who returned to Scandinavia would have found little to sustain them in the new faith. Converts who stayed in Frankia or the British Isles were more likely to remain Christian, and most of the settlers or their immediate descendants were soon converted; in the tenth century many clergy and monks in England were of Anglo–Danish descent, including three archbishops. Such men would naturally have been sympathetic supporters of missions to Scandinavia.

The successes of pagan Vikings must have cast doubt on the claim that the Christians worshiped the only true God, but at least some Scandinavians were prepared to accept that he was a god, if not the only one. By the middle of the ninth century Christianity was tolerated in both Denmark and Svealand; priests were allowed to preach and baptize, and churches had been built in Birka, Hedeby, and Ribe. The missionary archbishop Anskar claimed to be on friendly terms with Danish kings, one of whom, Horik II, sent gifts to Pope Nicholas I in 864 but refused to accept baptism. As the German chronicler Widukind remarked when describing the conversion of Harald Bluetooth a century later, "the Danes had long been Christians but they nevertheless worshiped idols with pagan rituals." That description probably applied to many other Scandinavians in the tenth century.

This period of religious toleration prepared the way for the next stage of Christianization, the formal acceptance of the exclusive claims of the Christian God. That acceptance meant the abandonment of old cults or their reduction to mere superstitions. It also made it possible for the missionaries and their patrons to begin to establish a regular church organization. Such a dramatic break with the past required the support of powerful forces, especially of kings who were before their conversion closely linked with the traditional cults. A king could not make such a decision arbitrarily; the consent, if not wholehearted approval, of the magnates and their men was needed, and that consent must have been formally expressed in assemblies that were themselves associated with pre-Christian rituals. In the mid-ninth century a king of the Svear had to consult the leading men (*optimates*) and the people before allowing Anskar to revive the mission in Birka (*VA* 27). Two centuries later more than one king of the Svear was driven into exile for preferring the new religion and threatening the old. In Iceland, where there was no king, the decision to adopt Christianity as the public religion was made in the Althing, but for a while pagan practices were tolerated.

Public Acceptance of Christianity

In most parts of Scandinavia this public acceptance of Christianity occurred in the last four decades of the tenth century. The main exception was in Svealand, where the most famous of all Scandinavian cult centers, at Uppsala, remained unconverted until about 1080 despite the presence in the Mälar region of many Christians. The old religion also persisted for a while in some remote regions; a raid on Småland by the Norwegian king Sigurd in 1123 was represented as a crusade, but that claim may have been made to legitimize what was in fact a plundering expedition (Gunnes 1989, no. 65).

The first Scandinavian king to be baptized, in 826 at Mainz, was the Dane Harald Klak, but he was driven into exile a year later and never returned. It was not until about 965 that another Danish king, Harald Bluetooth, was baptized. The event was described by Widukind a few years later (Sawyer and Wood, 69). According to him there was a dispute between a priest called Poppo and some Danes at a feast attended by the king.

"The Danes affirmed that Christ was indeed a God but that there were other Gods greater than him, as they proved by revealing greater signs and wonders to men." Poppo contradicted them and declared his willingness to prove that "there is only one true God . . . and that idols are in truth demons, not Gods."

> As a result, the next day the king had a large piece of iron heated and ordered Poppo to carry the glowing iron for the sake of the catholic faith. Poppo took the iron and carried it as far as the king determined. He then showed his undamaged hand and demonstrated to all the truth of the catholic faith. Consequently the king converted, resolved that Christ alone should be worshiped as God, ordered all people subject to him to reject idols, and thereafter gave due honor to priests and God's servants.

That conversion meant the cessation of pagan rituals in which the king took part. Some Danes continued to sacrifice to their old gods in traditional ways, but not for long; by the end of the century they had abandoned pagan forms of burial.

The Danish overlordship, reestablished by Harald Bluetooth, did not necessarily accelerate the public acceptance of Christianity by the local rulers who acknowledged his superiority. Håkon, jarl of Lade, remained a pagan despite recognizing Harald as his overlord. Tröndelag was, though, a long way from the heart of the Danish empire; southern Norway, especially Viken, and Götaland were more likely to be affected by the religious change in Denmark. There are, however, indications that the rulers of west Norway publicly acknowledged Christianity even earlier than did Harald Bluetooth. Håkon the Good and his nephews, who overthrew and replaced him, were all believed to have been baptized in England. Håkon was brought up in the court of the English king Athelstan and was remembered as the first king actively to encourage Christianity in Norway. The "Sigefridus Norwegensis episcopus" who was commemorated in the English abbey of Glastonbury as one of the members of that community who became bishops in the reign of Edgar (959–75) may well have been the bishop who, according to Snorri, Håkon invited from England. Snorri also said that Håkon encountered determined resistance in Tröndelag, which was then ruled by Jarl Sigurd, who was prepared to acknowledge Håkon's overlordship but not his religion. The king was consequently forced to conceal his Christian sympathies, at least in Tröndelag.

The religious mixture in tenth-century Norway was therefore much like that described by Widukind in Denmark, with the significant difference that in large parts of Norway pagan burial customs were abandoned earlier than in Denmark. In the coastal regions of south and west Norway the proportion of burials furnished with grave goods was already declining in the first half of the tenth century. The survival of the older forms of burial inland strongly suggests that the change reflects the success of the missionaries who were encouraged, or at least allowed, to preach. In the same coastal districts of Norway stone crosses from six to twelve feet high and rune-stones with crosses carved on them were erected in the tenth and early eleventh centuries (*KHL*, s.v. "Steinkors"). Many of them were put up in pagan cemeteries by, or in memory of, converts before Christian cemeteries were established.

The early progress of Christianity in Norway has been obscured by the emphasis later put on the role of Olav Tryggvason. According to Ari, Olav was responsible for the conversion of both Norway and Iceland, and later writers followed Ari's lead. Snorri, for example, was prepared to accept that some Norwegians in Viken had been baptized earlier, but he claimed that they had "reverted to heathen sacrifices as before and as the people in the north did." There is no doubt that Olav was an active supporter of Christianity, although he was only converted on the eve of his return to Norway. It is not known where he was baptized. He was certainly confirmed in England in 995 with the English king as his sponsor. A more reliable indication of his enthusiasm for Christianity than the traditions reported in the sagas is the fact that the court poets, who had earlier made great use of mythological kennings, began to show an aversion for such echoes of paganism in, or immediately after, his reign. It does, though, seem likely that any missionary activity that he undertook in western and southern Norway was to consolidate a process that had begun decades earlier. Olav's main contribution to the conversion of Norway was his conquest of Tröndelag, whose rulers had remained obstinately pagan. It may have been this achievement that is referred to in the runic inscription on the island of Kuli, about 70 miles (110 km) west of Trondheim, commemorating a man who died after "Christendom had been in Norway twelve winters."

Ari gave a fairly detailed account of the conversion of Iceland, based on what he had been told by Teit, son of Isleif, the first native Icelandic bishop. According to him, Christianity was formally accepted after a heated dispute at the Althing in the year 1000 (999 by our reckoning). The change was urged by Christian chieftains who had been baptized by Thangbrand, the missionary sent by King Olav, but the decision was left to the pagan Law-speaker who, after what appears to have been a ritual of divination, proclaimed that all men should have one law and one faith, arguing that "if we break the law in pieces then we break the peace in pieces too." It was agreed that all men should be baptized. A period of transition was allowed in which Icelanders could offer sacrifices in private, eat horsemeat and expose infants, but "a few years later this heathendom was abolished like the rest." Ari exaggerated the part played by his own family and friends, and he oversimplified; knowledge of Christianity reached Iceland through many channels, from the British Isles as well as from an incompletely Christianized Norway. Ari mentions a number of missionaries from various quarters but does not credit them with any specific achievements. As in other parts of Scandinavia they were probably invited by different chieftains.

In Sweden Olof Skötkonung was later generally recognized as the first Christian king, but the traditional date for his conversion, 1008, must be too late; he was already issuing Christian coins by 995 from Sigtuna, which had been founded about twenty years earlier and may have been a Christian settlement from the start. Christian rune-stones and pagan burials show that in Svealand Christians and pagans lived alongside each other throughout the eleventh century. Pagan cults continued to be celebrated at Uppsala, which was only 18 miles (30 km) from Sigtuna, until about 1080. The new religion was more firmly rooted earlier in Västergötland, but according to Adam of Bremen missionaries were still combating pagan cults there as late as the 1060s.

Transition Period

It is clear that in many parts of Scandinavia there was a long period, in some places as much as two hundred years, in which the old and new religions overlapped. Pagan beliefs and rituals must have been affected by contact with Christianity. It is likely, for example, that the concept of Valhalla, first evidenced in the mid-tenth century, was shaped under Christian influence. Poetry and pictures provide good evidence for some Scandinavian myths and the attributes of a few of their gods, but most of that evidence is not early enough to have escaped the risk of some Christian contamination. The main source of information about pre-Christian religion in Scandinavia (other than what can be deduced about burial customs) is provided by Christian authors, some of whom, including Adam of Bremen and Saxo Grammaticus, were hostile and prepared to believe that pagans indulged in obscene, inhuman rituals (see "Attitudes to Paganism" in chapter 10). The most authoritative source of information is the *Prose Edda* of Snorri Sturluson, who had a more positive attitude to the old religion (Faulkes). Although he was obviously influenced by classical as well as Christian authors, his account of pagan myths and his interpretation of the poetry is the starting point for most discussions of the subject. Some Icelandic sagas include details about pagan practices that have been given more credence than they deserve. The most extravagant, *Eyrbyggja Saga*, has been taken by some as proof that the pagans had temples served by a hierarchy of priests and supported by temple taxes, although these details are obviously based on the church organization familiar when the saga was written. Adam of Bremen's account of the temple at Uppsala, although based on hearsay and untrustworthy in detail, is nevertheless rather better evidence that there were pagan temples in Scandinavia, at least on the eve of the conversion. Pagan rituals were originally conducted in the open air or in the houses of rulers and chieftains, but pagans may have been influenced by the example of Christian churches to build a temple in Scandinavia's most important cult center, if nowhere else (O. Olsen).

Mutual influence of the old and new religions makes it difficult to assess what contribution the old made to the new, but there are some fairly clear signs of continuity. Many places where pagan cults had been celebrated continued to be religious centers after conversion. Several, including Uppsala, Viborg, and Odense, became bishops' sees, and pagan place-names of some parishes such as Ullevi and Frösvi suggest that there was similar continuity in some less important local religious centers. Such parish names are most common in Svealand, but they also occur in Götaland, with some significant concentrations—for example, near the episcopal town of Linköping. Excavation under the churches of Mære on Trondheim Fjord and at Frösö in Jämtland has uncovered evidence of pagan rituals, and many holy wells in all parts of Scandinavia were holy long before they were converted. Some pre-Christian rituals survived conversion in a Christian guise, including the custom of taking holy objects in procession to ensure good harvests, but much was suppressed or treated with contempt as mere superstition.

Before A.D. 1100

Conversion meant accepting not only Christian beliefs but also the rules and rituals of the church. These were not uniform; many different traditions had developed in the Christian world, but there was general agreement in western Europe on the creed and the main structure of the church. The key figures in church organization were the bishops, a title deriving from a Greek word meaning "overseer." Only they could perform all liturgical functions. Some rites—for example, baptism—could be delegated to priests; confirmation, by which people were admitted to full membership in the church after they had been baptized, could not. Bishops were also needed to consecrate churches and churchyards and to ordain priests. Their most important function was, perhaps, to consecrate new bishops, thus ensuring, at least in theory, the continuity of tradition reaching back to the early years of the church, the so-called Apostolic succession. Bishops normally had authority over a well-defined area originally called a parish (*parochia*). By the eleventh century that word was used for smaller districts in the charge of priests; a bishop's district was then known as a diocese. A bishop supervised his diocese from his cathedral church, so called because he had his throne there (in Greek, *kathedra*). A cathedral, and by extension a diocese, may also be called a bishop's see, a medieval form of the modern word "seat." The bishop of Rome, as the successor of the apostle Peter (who, it was believed, had been described by Christ as the rock on which the church would be built), had very great, if until the eleventh century ill-defined, authority in the church. One way in which his special status was marked was the designation pope, ultimately from the Greek word *pappas*, "father." Until the eighth century any bishop could be so described, but the term then began to be reserved for the bishop of Rome. Long before the eleventh century it was accepted that only the pope could create new archbishoprics and that all archbishops required papal authorization, which was granted symbolically by the presentation of a pallium, a distinctive band of white woolen cloth worn by the pope, and which he gave to his special representatives. The profession of obedience and faith that an archbishop had to make to the pope before receiving his pallium was a means of maintaining orthodoxy and papal authority.

By the eighth century it was customary to seek papal approval for missions to new regions, and when Ebo embarked on his mission to the Danes in 823 he had the permission of Pope Paschal I to preach the gospel "in northern parts" (*Diplomatarium Danicum* 1, nos. 22–23, hereafter *DD*). Three years later Paschal's successor named Anskar as Ebo's assistant. After Anskar's successful mission to Birka in 829–30 he was given the bishopric of Hamburg as a base, and a year or two later Pope Gregory IV made it an archbishopric, sent a pallium, and authorized Anskar, together with Ebo, to undertake missions to the "Svear [*Sueones*], Danes, Slavs, and other peoples" of the region (*DD* 1, no. 25). After Hamburg was sacked by

Scandinavian raiders in 845, Anskar was given the see of Bremen, thus creating the joint archbishopric of Hamburg-Bremen. The vague wording of Gregory IV's letter could be interpreted as including the whole of Scandinavia, but it was not until 1053 that Pope Leo IX explicitly extended the archbishopric's authority to include Norway, Iceland, and Greenland (*DD* 2, no. 1).

The archbishops were proud to claim such extensive responsibilities, but in fact they did little to spread the gospel in the north. Anskar and his immediate successors, Rimbert and Unni (who died in 936 at Birka), were indeed active as missionaries but achieved few, if any, permanent results. Later archbishops were more interested in their prestige than in evangelism and were not able to claim the credit for converting a single Scandinavian ruler in the tenth and eleventh centuries. According to Adam of Bremen, Archbishop Adaldag (937–88) consecrated a number of bishops to work in Scandinavia, but with three exceptions none was assigned to a particular see. The exceptions were the bishops he consecrated in 948 for the sees of Schleswig, Ribe, and Århus. His reason for doing so was that, having no suffragan bishops, his status as an archbishop was questionable. They were more valuable to him in Bremen than in Denmark, for he needed two suffragans in order to consecrate a new bishop (Refskou). Nothing more is known about two of them; like two of the bishops consecrated for the Swedish see of Skara in the eleventh century, they may never have left Germany. According to Adam, the third, Liafdag, worked as a missionary in Norway and Sweden as well as Denmark, which does not suggest that his association with Ribe, if any, was close (Adam of Bremen 2.26). Schleswig, Ribe, and Århus may well have been bases for missionary activity before the Danish king was converted, but they cannot have been regular sees until that happened.

Missionary bishops needed protection and support and it is likely that in tenth-century Denmark, as in eleventh-century Norway, they were attached to the royal retinues, accompanying the king as he traveled around his estates, one of which was at Jelling, and visited centers of royal power such as Schleswig, Ribe, and Århus. After Harald's conversion, churches (some of which became cathedrals) were built in these places and in similar centers in other parts of the kingdom, including Odense and Roskilde. Harald Bluetooth had extensive authority as overlord in Scandinavia, and it may have been under his protection that missionaries like Liafdag were able to preach in Norway and Sweden. This extensive evangelism continued under Sven Forkbeard, in whose reign churches may have been built in Lund and Oslo, but it was Sven's son Knut who, apparently in the light of his experience as king of the English, began to organize regular dioceses in Denmark. Knut hoped to keep the Danish church independent of Hamburg-Bremen and in 1022 had a bishop of Roskilde consecrated by the archbishop of Canterbury, but he was soon forced to accept the German archbishop as the legitimate authority. Danish diocesan organization was soon completed, and by 1060 all eight medieval dioceses had been established with well-defined boundaries.

According to Adam of Bremen, when he was writing his book in the 1070s, in Norway and Sweden "none of the bishoprics has so far been given definite limits, but each one of the bishops, accepted by king or people, cooperates in building up the church, going about the region, drawing as many as he can to Christianity, and governs them without envy" (4.34). The bishops were still itinerant members of royal retinues, but by the end of the century regular dioceses had begun to be established, at least in Norway. Icelanders accepted the authority of the archbishops of Hamburg-Bremen, extended in 1053, more quickly than the Norwegians. In 1056 Ísleif, the son of one of the leaders of the Christian party in 999, was consecrated at Bremen as the first Icelandic bishop and used his own farm at Skálholt as his base. His son and successor, Gizur, made Skálholt the episcopal see, and in 1106 a second see was founded for northern Iceland at Hólar. Soon after that a see was also created for Greenland at Gardar.

Dioceses and Churches

A list of Scandinavian *civitates*, meaning "bishoprics," was compiled soon after 1100, probably in connection with the creation of the new archiepiscopal province of Lund, and survives in a clumsy copy made a few years later (Kumlien). It names three in Norway: Oslo, Bergen, and Nidaros. When Nidaros was made an archbishopric in 1152–53, sees had also been established at Stavanger and Hamar. The same list names six or seven places as *civitates* in Sweden, but the situation in that part of Scandinavia was obscure, and the compiler seems to have had little reliable information. One of the places named, Skara, was certainly a see by then; at least two others probably were—Linköping (which the list treats as two names, Lionga and Kaupinga) and Sigtuna. Some places seem to have been named as potential sees, one of which—Tuna—never became one. That the list concludes by naming fifteen regions of Sweden and around

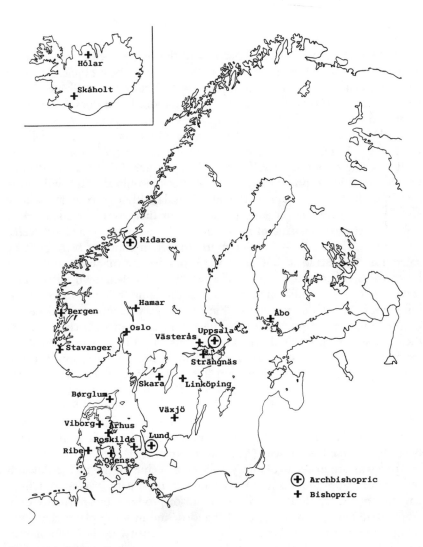

Figure 5.1. Bishoprics.

the Baltic as "islands of the Svea kingdom," including large parts of the later dioceses, suggests that the extent of the Swedish bishoprics had not been settled. It was not until about 1170 that the diocesan organization of Sweden was complete, with three sees in Svealand: Uppsala (which replaced Sigtuna and was made an archbishopric in 1164), Västerås and

Strängnäs, and Växjö in Småland. The Finnish see of Åbo was founded early in the next century.

At the same time that the dioceses and the first cathedrals were being established, a large number of smaller churches were being built. Adam of Bremen's claim that there were in his day 300 churches in Skåne should perhaps not be treated as an accurate enumeration, but it does give a good impression of the scale of this activity. Excavations have revealed many eleventh-century timber churches that were rebuilt in stone in the following century. In Lund diocese, with 540 medieval churches, some 300 were built in stone during the twelfth century or earlier. Lund was, of course, an exceptionally important and rich diocese; the only diocese with more medieval churches is Skara, with 630. Uppsala, although covering a huge area, had only 280, but a large proportion of them were founded before 1200, and the same is true of most parts of Scandinavia (Högberg; *KHL*, s.v. "Biskop," cols. 618–19). The more important churches were built by rulers for their bishops, but most were founded by magnates and richer landowners either at the request of a bishop or on their own initiative to serve as their own family churches, and at the same time as a mark of status. Proprietary churches of this kind were very common in eleventh-century Europe. Responsibility for the maintenance of such churches and their priests initially rested with the patrons, but others who needed the services of the priest had to pay fees. Adam of Bremen complained that in this time "baptism and confirmation, the dedications of altars and the ordination to holy orders are all dearly paid for among the Norwegians and the Danes. . . . As the barbarians still either do not know about tithes, or refuse to pay them, they are fleeced for offices that ought to be rendered for nothing. Even for the visitation of the sick and the burial of the dead—everything there has a price" (Adam of Bremen 4.31).

Tithe was originally a voluntary offering to a church, but by the eleventh century it had become a compulsory render in most parts of western Christendom. In theory it amounted to a tenth of produce, but normally only crops, farm animals, or fish were demanded, and in many places there was an agreement to render a smaller but regular quantity. In the Scandinavian world tithe was first imposed in Iceland, and by the end of the twelfth century it was probably being collected in all Scandinavian dioceses (*KHL*, s.v. "tiend"). It was initially demanded by patrons in support of their churches and clergy, but they commonly kept part of it for themselves. This lay ownership of tithes was regarded as a serious abuse by the church reformers in the eleventh century, and its prohibition was one of their first objectives. In many parts of Scandinavia, however, laymen were still taking part of the tithe in the thirteenth century, a custom condemned by William of Sabina in Sweden in 1248, but which persisted in Iceland until the Reformation. Tithe created the need for parish boundaries, a connection that is reflected in the word used in Scandinavia to describe a parish, *sokn*. It is commonly asserted that this word, related to the word "seek," refers to the choice of a church by its parishioners and defines the district whose inhabitants all "sought" the same church. It is more likely that the word refers to the district within which tithe was collected (cf. German *suchen*, "gather"). The Danes who settled in England in the ninth century used the word to describe estates whose inhabitants rendered produce and services to a lord. Parish boundaries are consequently not necessarily ancient, and some were certainly changed in the course of the Middle Ages. The assumption made by some legal historians and archaeologists that medieval parishes preserved the structure of pre-Christian units is therefore fallacious (P. Sawyer 1988b).

The attitude of many people toward their local church and their sense of communal responsibility must have been affected by the imposition of tithe as a general obligation. A sense of community was, of course, not new, but it was encouraged and reshaped around the churches in which people were baptized and buried. When all or even most people paid tithe to support their local church, it became in a very real sense the church of the community. When that happened there was a natural tendency to assume that it had always been so, and to believe that churches were from the beginning communal enterprises. This firmly held belief has tended to distract attention from the many indications that most churches were founded and built by rulers and landowners. By the end of the thirteenth century responsibility for the upkeep of most churches had passed to the parishioners, although the descendants of the original patrons sometimes retained privileges. Bishops were eager to obtain a share of the tithe paid to the churches or their owners but encountered serious opposition when they tried to do so. Absalon was bishop for thirteen years before he won the right to a third of the tithe in his diocese, but by the end of the thirteenth century all Scandinavian bishops were entitled to claim some part, commonly a third or quarter, of the parochial tithes in their dioceses, a significant additional source of income.

Until the middle of the twelfth century most bishops in Scandinavia were English or German. In organizing the new churches they were naturally influenced by the ecclesiastical traditions with which they were familiar. In Norway, for example, a hierarchy of churches was established that was very similar to that in Anglo-Saxon England. The words needed for innovations such as feast days, churches, church furnishings, and clerical dress were borrowed from both English and German or were adaptations of Latin terms. Thus Good Friday, which in Low German was *de gude* [or *stille*] *vridach*, was called Long Friday in Scandinavia as it was in England, but the German or Latin *pascha* was used for Easter, not the Old English *eastre* (Hellberg 1986).

Church Reform

The eleventh and twelfth centuries, when Scandinavian dioceses were being formed and hundreds of churches built, were a period of fundamental change in the Western church as a whole. This was brought about by reformers who had two main aims. First, they wanted to free the church from lay control, in particular by ending the private ownership of churches and of tithes; they also wanted the church to appoint its own priests and bishops, and to free clergy from secular jurisdiction. Their second key aim, for its own sake as well as a means of implementing other reforms, was to assert the superior authority of the papacy. The pope, as God's vicar, claimed to be subject to no earthly power. This authority was to be used to effect reforms not only within the church but also in society generally. The reformers succeeded in enhancing the authority of the papacy (by the end of the twelfth century the pope was generally recognized as the supreme authority within the church), but they were unable to free the church from all secular influence. The reformers did succeed in making the church a distinct and privileged institution, with the pope as its supreme head on earth, in most respects free to regulate its own affairs. The clergy were separated from the laity not only by their dress and the rule of celibacy (a rule not well observed by the lower clergy), but more significantly by their freedom from secular jurisdiction.

The desire for reform in the church was also manifested by new religious orders that emerged between 1075 and 1125 to challenge the traditional Benedictine communities. The Augustinian and Cistercian orders were especially popular. The Augustinians were canons, not monks, who sought to return to the primitive simplicity of the early church and to serve the world in a great variety of ways: relieving the poor, ransoming prisoners, caring for the sick, and running schools as well as preaching. They had great appeal to all sorts of people; many bishops and several twelfth-century popes belonged to the order, and by the thirteenth century there were thousands of Augustinian houses, most of them very small. The Cistercians were monks who wanted to withdraw from the world as completely as possible and live according to an austere and rigorous rule. The movement began in 1098 when a group of dissident monks left the abbey

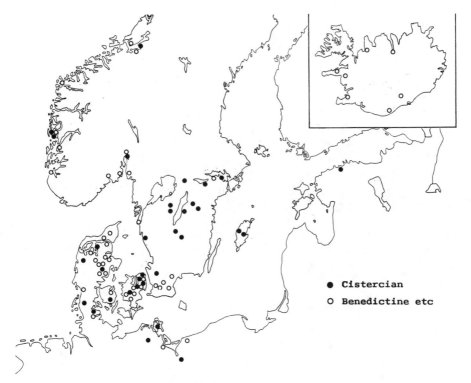

Figure 5.2. Monasteries founded before 1230.

of Molesme in Burgundy to found their own community nearby at Citeaux. Twenty years later six daughter houses had been founded, but the rate of expansion then increased dramatically, and by 1152 there were over three hundred houses, many on the frontiers of Christendom, including seven in Scandinavia (Götlind). They were united in an elaborate organization with annual councils that initially all abbots were expected to attend, a rule that had to be eased for those from Scandinavia and other distant regions.

New Provinces

News of the changes being made in the church reached Scandinavia quite quickly despite its relative remoteness from the centers of reform in Italy and Burgundy. Several bishops who worked in Scandinavia visited Rome

Figure 5.3. Dominican and Franciscan houses founded before 1300.

before 1100, and in that year the Danish king did so, too. These personal contacts were reinforced by the letters sent to Scandinavian kings and bishops by Pope Gregory VII and his successors. Some rulers and bishops were early enthusiasts for reform, especially in Norway, but in Scandinavia as elsewhere there was naturally much resistance from conservative clergy as well as from rulers who, although they might be willing to accept the guidance of the church on spiritual matters, were reluctant to surrender the control and influence that they had been taught was theirs by right. Kings and lay patrons of churches were in particular unwilling to lose the right to choose clergy for *their* churches, or to give up their claim to share church revenues. The German emperors were among the most vigorous opponents of the reforms demanded by Gregory VII and his colleagues. The attempt of Henry IV to retain his control not only over the German church but also over the papacy itself resulted in a conflict that had important consequences for Scandinavia. In the quarrel between Henry and Gregory, Liemar, archbishop of Hamburg-Bremen, supported the emperor and was therefore deposed by the pope. This had little effect on his position in Germany, but the situation encouraged the papal curia to consider reducing Hamburg-Bremen's authority by creating an independent Scandinavian province. This was done in 1103 (or possibly 1104) with Lund as the archbishopric. Hamburg-Bremen vigorously resisted this development for the rest of the century, with the support of the emperors, but without substantial success. It is true that in 1133 the German archbishop succeeded in obtaining a series of bulls from Pope Innocent II, who was then entirely dependent on the Emperor Lothar, deposing Archbishop Asser of Lund and restoring Bremen's authority, but these bulls never went further than Bremen, and Asser continued to function as archbishop without hindrance until his death in 1137 (*DD* 2, nos. 57–61).

By then disputes over the Danish succession had led to civil war in which several contenders submitted to the German emperor in order to gain his recognition and support. The papal curia responded to this new threat by creating two new archbishoprics. In May 1152 Frederik Barbarossa invested one of the Danish rivals as king in return for his homage and fealty, but in March of that year a papal legate, Nicholas Breakspear, had already set out for Norway where, early in 1153, he consecrated Jon Birgersson, bishop of Stavanger, as archbishop of Nidaros and invested him with the pallium. The new province included the five sees in Norway together with six others established in the predominantly Norwegian colonies in the British Isles and the Atlantic islands: Orkney and Shetland, the Faroes, the Isle of Man, and the Hebrides (from a Norwegian perspective these were the Southern Isles [*Suðreyar*], and the see was therefore known as Sodor and Man), as well as Iceland and Greenland. The archbishop's authority over this province was confirmed by the pope in 1154 (Gunnes 1989, no. 92). Later in 1153 Nicholas went on to Östergötland but was unable to create a Swedish archbishopric, probably because of disagreement about its location. It seems likely that King Sverker wanted it to be in Linköping but could not overcome the opposition of the Svear. It was only after Sverker's death that Nicholas, now Pope Adrian IV, granted Archbishop Eskil of Lund authority to create a Swedish province subject to the primacy of Lund (I. Andersson). He did so in 1164 and consecrated Stephen as archbishop of Uppsala with authority over the sees of Skara and Linköping in Götaland, and of Strängnäs and Västerås on the shores of Mälaren. By the early thirteenth century Uppsala's province also included the sees of Växjö in Småland and Åbo in Finland.

Figure 5.4. Nidaros Cathedral. The chapter house, on the right, was built by Arch-bishop Øystein. He also began to build the octagon at the east end of the church to house the shrine of Saint Olav, but this was not completed until early in the thir-teenth century. This cathedral shows many signs of English influence, and there are close similarities with Lincoln Cathedral. Photograph from Nidaros Domkirkes Restaureringsarbeider.

Bishops and Kings: Before A.D. 1200

The archbishops, who owed their enhanced authority to the papacy, naturally tended to accept papal claims to primacy more readily than did many others, and it was their responsibility to implement the church law defined by popes and by church councils. This obligation often brought them into conflict with kings. For Eskil, archbishop of Lund, there was the additional complication that for a while King Valdemar I recognized the imperial antipope Victor, while Eskil remained faithful to the legitimate pope Alexander III, a conflict of loyalties that eventually drove Eskil into exile. Only after Valdemar and Alexander were reconciled in 1166 did Eskil return home and endorse the king's authority by canonizing his father and crowning his son at Ringsted in 1170.

Six or seven years earlier Magnus Erlingsson had been crowned king in Norway, probably by Øystein, archbishop of Nidaros, and he promised loyalty to Alexander III and his successors. In his reign the church was granted many of the privileges that the reformers demanded, but Magnus's rival and successor, Sverri, considered the concessions excessive. He demanded, among other things, a say in episcopal elections and the restoration of his right to appoint priests to royal chapels and many other churches. In the face of Sverri's hostility Archbishop Erik, Øystein's successor, went into exile in 1190, and both king and archbishop appealed to the pope. Sverri refused to accept the judgment, which was in favor of Erik, and before the end of the century all the Norwegian bishops had joined their archbishop in exile in Denmark. In 1198 Pope Innocent III put Sverri and his supporters under interdict, prohibiting the celebration of mass and many other services in his territory. Sverri did not submit, but he recognized that in the long run compromise was unavoidable, and on his deathbed in 1202 he advised his son Håkon to come to terms with the church, which he did.

The church emerged from these conflicts with enhanced authority and greater freedom to regulate its own affairs, but, although later Danish and Norwegian kings were eager to have the spiritual and practical support of the church, they were unwilling to concede all the privileges that the most ardent reformers wanted. In Sweden, where royal authority was weaker, bishops were able to take advantage of the dynastic dispute that began with the death of Sverker to gain concessions, and by 1200 they had obtained freedom from royal exactions, including military obligations not only for themselves but also for all church land, a more extensive and general privilege than the church enjoyed in either Denmark or Norway.

Figure 5.5. Ribe Cathedral. No visible traces remain of the first church built on this site. The present building was built at much the same time as Nidaros Cathedral (fig. 5.4) but displays German, not English, influence. The main building material is tufa, a porous volcanic stone, from the Rhineland. The original design was Romanesque but in the thirteenth century Gothic style became fashionable, and Gothic vaulting was added and the windows were enlarged. Many of the structural details and sculptures are very similar to those current in Germany at the time. Photograph by Niels Elswing. © Ribe Domkirkes Menighedsråd.

Ecclesiastical Organization

The organization the church needed in order to function effectively was developed more quickly in Denmark than in the other kingdoms, but by 1250 great progress had been made almost everywhere; the only exceptions

Figure 5.6. Suntak Church, Västergötland, Sweden. The first churches were built of wood, and many remained timber structures until modern times, but in Denmark and Sweden patrons began early in the twelfth century to rebuild their churches in stone, which was considered more prestigious. Suntak is a good example of such a rural stone church, probably built in the middle of the twelfth century. Like many others in Götaland it has a nave, chancel, and apse. Its overall length is only fifty-four feet. In Denmark many Romanesque churches were enlarged or extensively rebuilt in the late Middle Ages; this did not often happen in Sweden until the eighteenth century. The main change at Suntak, for example, has been the enlargement of the original windows, which were about five inches wide. Photograph by Ragnar Sigsjö.

were the peripheral regions in the north of Scandinavia and in Finland, which were not yet converted, and Iceland. By then most medieval Scandinavian churches had been built, although many were rebuilt in the later Middle Ages. The first wave of monastic foundation was over, and the mendicant orders of the Franciscans and Dominicans were well established with houses in most of the more important towns. Church, or canon, law was generally respected by the clergy in the thirteenth century, although the rule of celibacy was not observed by the lower clergy in Scandinavia any better than in other parts of Europe. By the end of the twelfth century one of the most fundamental principles of canon law was the ultimate au-

Figure 5.7. Urnes Church, Sognefjord, Norway. This remarkable timber church was probably built at much the same time as Suntak Church (fig. 5.6). Only about a quarter of Norway's medieval churches were built of stone. Photograph from Riksantikvaren, Oslo.

thority of the pope; as a result many appeals were made to Rome by Scandinavian rulers, churchmen, and even laymen who could afford the expense. Scandinavians were also made aware of new legislation by papal legates. One of the most important was William of Sabina, who held reform councils in both Norway and Sweden in 1247–48. Religious orders also contributed to the integration of Scandinavia in the wider church, and from the end of the twelfth century many of the leading Scandinavian clergy were educated in the universities of Paris or Bologna. In these and other schools young Scandinavians met students from throughout Europe, some of whom later rose to positions of great power in the church. Pilgrimages and exiles also provided opportunities to learn about new ideas and to meet church leaders.

During the thirteenth century bishops gained greater control over the clergy and churches in their dioceses. They did this partly by formal visitations, but these were not always welcomed by the laity, who were expected to provide hospitality. A more effective way of keeping in touch with and influencing the clergy was by summoning them to meetings or synods. These were held twice a year in Danish sees and once a year in other parts of Scandinavia, generally in connection with a major church festival celebrated in the summer. In several Swedish sees synods were held immediately after the Feast of Peter and Paul on 29 June. Synods were good opportunities to inform the clergy about new, and to remind them about old, church legislation; to discuss matters of concern; to lay down rules for local churches; and to deal with disputes involving clergy (*KHL*, s.v. "Synode").

At an early stage in the development of many dioceses some clergy, commonly called provosts, were given a supervisory role over the churches in districts that were based on the districts used for secular government, although in Jutland the *syssel* were used for this purpose, even though they had been superseded by *herreder* (*KHL*, s.v. "Provst"). In the thirteenth century these local provosts in Denmark were replaced by rural deans. During that century diocesan organization became more elaborate in all parts of Scandinavia, a development made necessary by the large amount of property owned by the church, but even more by the church's greatly increased responsibilities. By then the church had jurisdiction not only over the clergy but also over laymen in cases involving offenses against church law, which included disputes over agreements that were made under oath, such as marriages and contracts. A hierarchy of diocesan clergy was created in which superior clergy, including archdeacons, deans, and provosts, gained larger responsibilities. Archdeacons, for example, inspected church buildings and the accounts of churchwardens. In districts remote from the cathedral the local superior—for example, the provost of Jämtland—had a great deal of independence, while in all parts of dioceses these men, who were originally intended to assist their bishops, came into conflict with them, most commonly over rights of jurisdiction.

Cathedral Chapters

The most fundamental institutional development was the creation of cathedral chapters (*KHL*, s.v. "Domkapitel"). Bishops always had a retinue of clergy of various grades to help them and to accompany them on journeys around the diocese. In Västergötland in the thirteenth century, for example, when the bishop consecrated a church he could expect hospitality for three days and two nights for himself and twelve companions, all of whom were entitled to mead; later only the bishop and his chaplain were entitled to that relatively luxurious drink. Clergy were also needed to maintain regular worship in the cathedral church. Ideally cathedral clergy lived a regulated communal life. There were some well-established models. In England some cathedrals were served by monastic communities, and that arrangement was exported to Denmark; Odense Cathedral had a monastic chapter, a daughter house of Evesham Abbey in England. A more common pattern in Europe was to have canons living under rules laid down in a reform council at Aachen in 816. The earliest Danish chapters, including Lund and Roskilde, were of that type but in the twelfth century some adopted the Augustinian rule. It was difficult to maintain communal life in cathedrals, however; canons preferred to live separately, drawing their income from a part of the endowment, called a prebend, that was set apart for each of them. Most Scandinavian chapters were sooner or later organized in that way. Chapters were established in Norway after the visit of Nicholas Breakspear. The chapter in Nidaros was closely associated at an early stage with the nearby Augustinian abbey of Helgeseter, and a similar arrangement may have existed in Bergen. In Sweden there was an unsuccessful attempt in the 1220s to establish an Augustinian chapter in Skara, and the Swedish chapters, most of them founded after William of Sabina's legation in 1247–48, were of the secular type. By 1288 all Swedish cathedrals, including Åbo, had chapters. The number of canons varied. In 1085 Lund had nine; four were added after the see was made an archbishopric, and on the eve of the Reformation there were thirty-four. Ordinary bishoprics normally had between eight and twelve.

Chapters were led by a senior member, often called a provost or dean, and by the fourteenth century most had two or three other senior prelates or dignitaries, one of whom was, in most cases, an archdeacon. Until the thirteenth century, when popes began to interfere, provosts, deans, and other prelates were elected by the canons, who also, together with the bishop, chose new members. Some canonries, however, were in the gift of kings or lay patrons; in 1381, for example, Bo Jonsson (Grip) founded and endowed an archdeaconry in Strängnäs with hereditary patronage.

Chapters were responsible not only for the worship in the cathedral but also for the school in which new clergy were educated. After finishing their studies and being ordained, clerics were expected to complete their training by serving in the cathedral for a year or more, joining the lower clergy who, in the absence of many of the canons, did much of the work. Some young men studied abroad. Most were members of wealthy families, but bishops and cathedral chapters were prepared to support promising candidates, and in some dioceses a part of the tithe was devoted to this purpose. In the twelfth century some leading Scandinavian clergy had already been educated in European schools. Archbishop Eskil of Lund studied at Hildesheim, and both Øystein, archbishop of Nidaros, and Thorlák, bishop of Skálholt (who died in 1193), probably studied in the famous school of Saint Victor in Paris (Bagge 1984). The main center for legal studies was the University of Bologna. Anders Sunesson, archbishop of Lund from 1201 to 1222, studied there, as well as in Paris and Oxford, and in the period 1285–1300, for which there are good records, nineteen Danes, eleven Swedes, and six Norwegians studied in Bologna. Most were clergy, but two of the Norwegians were prominent laymen, who became councillors. In the thirteenth century most Scandinavians who studied abroad went to the University of Paris, where, shortly before or after the year 1300, two Swedish colleges and a Danish one were founded. Attempts were made to require new cathedral canons to study in a university for at least two years, and although this ideal was not achieved, many did have such an education. It is likely that in the first half of the fourteenth century up to half of all Norwegian canons spent some time in a university, although only seventeen of them graduated. All Norwegian bishops in office between 1309 and 1369 had had some university education.

Bishops and Kings in the Late Middle Ages

One of the most important functions of a cathedral chapter was to elect their bishop. Theoretically the cathedral chapters had a free choice, but in practice they were subject to pressure from both king and magnates, who were often kinsmen of chapter members. The importance of magnate influence is very clear in Denmark. The see of Roskilde was occupied for over a century by members of the Hvide family, the dominant family in Sjælland, and in 1252 their candidate, Jakob Erlandsson, was elected despite royal opposition. The wishes of kings were, however, often respected. Kings were naturally eager to have bishops with whom they could cooperate, for bishops not only had great moral authority as spiritual leaders, they had exceptional influence over the diocesan clergy. Many were employed in important diplomatic missions to the papal curia or to other kings, and at home they were a ruler's natural advisers. Their support was valuable, but their opposition could weaken royal authority, as Sverri discovered.

Kings nevertheless occasionally came into conflict with bishops and, more often, with archbishops. Between 1250 and 1320 Danish kings had heated disputes with a bishop of Roskilde and three successive archbishops, two of whom were imprisoned. In these quarrels the kings were often supported by a majority of the bishops. These disputes also illustrate the growth of papal authority and its use in support of kings. The kings and their opponents all appealed to the papal curia. The popes did not follow a consistent policy, but in the end they generally gave only lukewarm support to the archbishops. They had their own difficulties and needed the support of well-disposed kings, which affected the judgments they reached. Archbishop Jens Grand was in the end deprived of Lund and translated to the see of Riga (Skyum-Nielsen 1963; Hørby 1979).

Popes badly needed money to maintain the curia and the huge bureaucracy that papal supremacy generated and to pay for troops or allies needed against their enemies in Italy and elsewhere. One way of raising funds was to tax the clergy, often on the pretext of financing a renewed crusade. Bishops and clergy resented such exactions, but they were bound to obey. In order to gather the money papal agents needed the goodwill and cooperation of kings, which was obtained by allowing them to keep half or more of the proceeds (*KHL*, s.v. "Korstogsafgifter"). In 1329, for example, papal collectors gathered the equivalent of 4,340 pounds sterling in Sweden but gave half of it to the regent (Magnus was still a minor). In the thirteenth century the papacy began to claim the right to appoint the holders of some benefices, especially the richer ones (*KHL*, s.v. "provisioner"). Many valuable Scandinavian churches and prebends were given in this way to members of the curia who never set foot in Scandinavia but drew the income from their churches and appointed deputies to do the work. Popes claimed the same right in appointing bishops, but kings were naturally unwilling to have absentee curialists as bishops, and popes compromised. In return for a freer hand with other posts, they often gave bishoprics to the men nominated by rulers. Valdemar IV and his daughter Margaret were able, in this way, to fill sees with the men they wanted and so reward the administrators on whom they depended. This also enabled them to reduce the number of bishops who were members of the most powerful families, and thus to balance the influence of secular magnates.

If the papacy did not intervene, the right of presenting, or nominating, priests to many churches remained in the hands of kings or lay patrons as heirs of the original founders (*KHL*, s.v. "Patronatsrätt"). In Norway, however, the church had been given a great degree of freedom to choose priests. Håkon V compensated for this lack of direct influence by developing the chapels on royal estates and obtaining papal approval of the right to choose the chaplains (*KHL*, s.v. "Kapellgeistlighet"). There were fourteen chapels in his reign; four of them were organized as colleges. The largest was in Bergen with twelve chaplains, and Saint Mary's in Oslo had six. In 1308 the chapels were organized as a separate institution under the provost of the Bergen chapel, who was given special powers by the pope that were the subject of dispute with the bishop of Bergen. The chaplains formed a corps of clerks of great value to King Håkon, but as his successors lived most of the time in other parts of Scandinavia, they lost much of their potential importance. Many did, however, become bishops, and the provost of Oslo was normally chancellor; both he and the provost of Bergen were leading members of the Norwegian council.

Danish kings had more extensive patronage than did Norwegian kings, amounting to as much as 10 percent of all benefices, and did not need a special chapel organization. Valdemar IV did obtain papal confirmation of his right to choose chaplains in royal castles, a privilege that was a useful means of rewarding royal clerks, many of whom were later promoted to bishoprics. Magnus Eriksson apparently attempted to develop the Swedish royal chapels on the Norwegian model, but little came of his efforts. Like other kings before and after him, he had chaplains in his service, but they did not form a separate, privileged group as in Norway.

The Late Medieval Crisis

The plagues of the fourteenth century probably killed a disproportionate number of clergy, and the desertion of settlements led to the abandonment of many churches, especially in Jutland. The catastrophic decline of Norwegian rents combined with the declining enthusiasm for the older forms of monasticism led to the closure of many monasteries (Gunnes 1987). The richest in Norway, Munkeliv in Bergen, was virtually derelict in 1420, and the monastery of Selja was closed by 1474. Several other houses suffered a similar fate before the end of the century, and in 1520 Christian II began granting those that survived to his servants as fiefs on condition that the surviving members were cared for. Norwegian cathedrals and parish churches fared rather better, and gifts made after 1350 greatly increased the amount of land they owned; by 1500 the churches owned almost 50 percent of the total. The archbishops of Nidaros prospered. They were well placed to benefit from the increased value of the trade in dried fish from the northern part of the diocese, both as tithes and from their own estates in that region.

In Denmark and Sweden many monasteries survived the crisis rather better, partly because some of them were able to profit from the demand for cattle products and fish. A number of new Franciscan houses were founded in the fifteenth century in areas that were then becoming prosperous, thanks to the demand for fish. Their houses on Kökar in Åland and Torkö in Blekinge were the fifteenth-century equivalents of Marstrand in Bohuslän a century and half earlier. There were a remarkable number of new foundations. Ten Carmelite houses were established between 1410 and 1500, and other new orders were popular. The Order of the Holy Spirit founded six hospitals in Denmark between 1451 and 1485. The one order that originated in Scandinavia, founded by Saint Birgitta, was favored by the Union kings, and two houses were founded in Denmark: Maribo and Mariager, in 1418 and 1446 respectively. An attempt was made in 1420 to revive Munkeliv in Bergen as a Bridgetine house but it had little success. There was only one house of this order in Sweden, at Vadstena, but in the early sixteenth century it was the richest abbey in Sweden.

There were other signs of religious vitality in the fifteenth century. Many Danish churches were enlarged and their interiors adorned with elaborate paintings. In Sweden there was less rebuilding, but the walls of many of the Romanesque churches that had been built in the twelfth and early thirteenth centuries were covered with paintings (fig. 1.2). In many parts of Scandinavia churches were provided with sculptures of saints, and elaborate altar screens were bought from north German craftsmen. New cults flourished. That of Saint Anne, the mother of Mary, was especially popular, and to judge by the names given to children of ordinary farmers, Saints Severinus and Erasmus were extraordinarily popular in Denmark. Devotional literature was written and published in Denmark and Sweden, but not in Norway, which seems to have been rather more conservative.

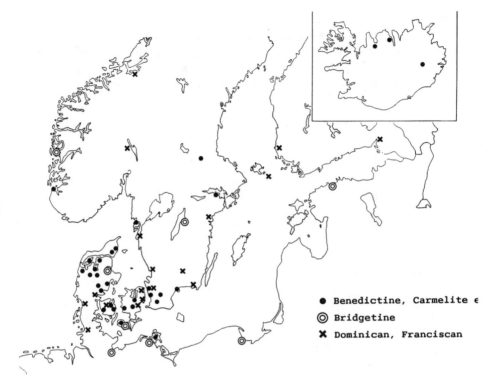

Figure 5.8. Monasteries founded 1230–1500.

Despite the efforts of generations of reformers the church in the late Middle Ages was deeply secularized by its wealth and by its involvement in politics and royal administration. Bishops were lawyers and administrators rather than theologians and devoted much energy to protecting their own interests and challenging others'. Disputes between bishops and their chapters or between bishops and monasteries were commonplace. Church leaders were, therefore, ill equipped to meet the challenge posed by the reformers whose ideas and demands were fermenting in many parts of Europe. The decisions of Gustav Vasa and Frederik I to renounce obedience to the pope were made for political rather than religious reasons, but in both Denmark and Sweden most of the bishops and clergy initially accepted the decision with little protest, and in Norway there was negligible support for the rebellion of Archbishop Olav Engelbrektsson.

By assuming the supreme headship of the church in their kingdoms, the rulers of Scandinavia gained many advantages. They were able to choose bishops and other clergy without outside interference, and their income was greatly increased when they took over a large part of the tithe, which their agents began to collect more efficiently. They also acquired a huge amount of land, including much of the best, by confiscating the property of religious houses, thus transforming the pattern of landownership.

6
Landowners and Tenants

Only a small proportion of the medieval owners of Scandinavian farms and other properties can be identified. The composition of a few estates is known, thanks to the surviving charters, surveys, wills, and accounts, mostly of the fourteenth century or later, but it is rarely possible to trace the owner of a particular farm for more than a couple of generations because lay property was repeatedly redistributed in marriages or when inheritances were divided. Church estates were more stable, but the full extent of only a few of them is known. It is, however, possible to discover how most land was classified on the eve of the Reformation, together with some indication of its relative value, measured in terms of tax assessments or rent. There were four main categories of land, determined by the status of the owner: the crown, a church or churchman, a member of the privileged aristocracy, or a free man or woman. There was also a huge area of common land shared between various landowners, including kings.

In the early sixteenth century the royal share of the total value of land was largest in Denmark, about 10 percent. In Norway it was about 7 percent, and in Sweden 6 percent.[1] Far more, including much of the best land, was held by the churches: in Norway 48 percent, in Denmark 35–40 percent, and in Sweden only about 20 percent. In both Denmark and Sweden the secular aristocracy had about as much as the church, but in Norway much less, only 12 percent. The rest was held by free landowners. Their individual holdings were small, but, as they were numerous, their combined share was large in Sweden (50 percent) and in Norway (33 percent). In Denmark they only had about 10 percent. In Iceland there were about four thousand farms. The crown had very few, accounting for less than 2 percent of the total value, and the church share appears to have been as large as in Norway, but that is misleading, for much of the church land was, in fact, controlled by laymen. The other farms were held by free landowners, among whom there was a small group of about thirty who owned about half of them.

These totals conceal great variations within the kingdoms. The proportion of unprivileged free landowners was highest in peripheral regions. They held almost all the land in northern Scandinavia and Finland and were relatively numerous in the mountain and forest regions of inland Norway. Such landowners were relatively few in the best farming districts of inland Norway—Tröndelag and Oppland—or in Sweden in the central parts of Götaland and the Mälar Valley, but they held most farms in the surrounding forests, where the population was sparser. Bornholm and Blekinge had the highest proportion in the Danish kingdom. Royal estates tended to be strategically placed in most regions, providing convenient bases for the king and his agents. At the end of the Middle Ages there were extensive aristocratic estates in most parts of Denmark, the main exception being Sjælland, where churches were the main landowners, but in Sweden they were concentrated in the relatively fertile, open regions of Götaland and the Mälar Valley. Farms belonging to local churches and their priests were naturally scattered. In Norway these accounted for about a third of the total value of all church land. The land of major churches tended to be concentrated in their vicinity; half of the farms owned by the bishop of Linköping were within about 3 miles (5 km) of his cathedral. There are many instances of monasteries exchanging distant farms they had acquired for others nearby, but many communities retained relatively remote properties from which they could obtain specialized produce. Sorö Abbey, in the middle of Sjælland, for instance, obtained the iron it needed from its estates in Halland, and several Swedish abbeys were careful to retain their right to salmon fisheries in Klarälven, the main river flowing into Vänern.

Most farms owned by kings, churches, and aristocrats were worked by tenants. Some free but unprivileged landowners, especially in Norway, found it was in their interest to let their own farms to tenants and themselves become tenants of more rewarding land owned by the church, but in Denmark and Sweden most of them farmed their own land. There were relatively few free, nonaristocratic landowners in Denmark because many had surrendered their farms to aristocrats in the fourteenth century. They did this not for the sake of protection, as many chose lords based in other parts of Denmark; the motive was economic. Danish aristocrats by then were exempt from paying normal taxes on all their property, including that held by tenants, a privilege also enjoyed by the church (*KHL,* s.v.

"Frälse"). Consequently the whole burden of regular royal taxation fell on the ordinary free landowners, who, by giving their land to aristocrats and becoming tenants, could expect to pay less rent to their new lords than they would otherwise have had to pay as tax to the king.

The proportion of land held by ordinary Danish free landowners was therefore smaller in the fifteenth century than in the thirteenth, but it is not possible to determine the scale of the change. The situation earlier than that, and in other parts of Scandinavia, is even more obscure. Attempts have been made to estimate the proportion of such landowners in twelfth-century Denmark, but the results are in wild disagreement, ranging from 80 percent to 25 percent.

Social Hierarchy

In many accounts of Scandinavian society it has been assumed that there were many more free landowners in the early Middle Ages than later, and that they had a leading role in society that was, by the fourteenth century, taken over by royal agents and the aristocracy. Some of these free people had more land than others, but, it has been supposed, they were all equal, with the same legal and social status. By the end of the Middle Ages circumstances were very different. Relatively few Scandinavian farmers owned the land they worked; most were tenants of a king, a church, or an aristocrat. The change has been explained by the submission of freemen and freewomen to major landowners. In medieval Scandinavia itself, however, some people seem to have believed that many tenants were descendants of former slaves.

Certainly there were slaves in early medieval Scandinavia (Karras). Many free landowners may have had one or more as household servants or farm laborers, and the large demesne farms of greater landowners could have had several. As in other parts of Europe this group was hereditary and could be enlarged either by the voluntary submission of freemen and free-women seeking protection and support in times of disaster or by the purchase of captives brought back by successful raiding expeditions. Scandinavian raiders certainly captured many slaves in the ninth and tenth centuries and may have brought some home, but most were sold in European or eastern markets; slaves were realizable assets rather than potential laborers. It has been claimed that slaves were so numerous and significant in early medieval Scandinavia that it had a "slave-economy," but that is no more than a theoretical assumption; there is no reliable evidence on which to base an estimate of the number of slaves in Scandinavia at any time. The church encouraged the liberation of slaves, but they were being freed long before Scandinavia was converted; freedmen of the Danes are mentioned in ninth-century England. Freedmen had a lower status than the fully free, and many must have continued as servants and laborers for their former masters or were given the chance to clear land in the forest for them, and so become their tenants.

In the early provincial laws, which provided for both slaves and freedmen, the leading role is generally assigned to freemen, many of whom are simply described as *bönder* (singular *bonde*). In the earliest Swedish laws, from Västergötland, four groups or classes under the king are recognized: slaves, freedmen, tenants, and *bönder*. The *bönder* included men of high status; bishops and lawmen of Västergötland had to be the sons of *bönder*. In fact the bishops and lawmen in thirteenth-century Västergötland who are identifiable came from the ranks of the magnates, and the lawman who has been credited with drafting the older law of Västergötland, Eskil, was brother not only of Bishop Karl of Linköping but also of Birger Jarl, who ruled Sweden after 1250.

In Denmark, too, the *bönder* included some exceptionally wealthy men in the twelfth century. A charter of 1145 for Lund Cathedral classifies the witnesses and lists the *bönder* (*bondones*) immediately after the royal family, including several of the most powerful Danish laymen, most of whom were called king's counselors in another charter apparently drawn up on the same day (*DD* 2, nos. 88, 91). It is also significant that the name Bonde was used by several families of first importance, including Karl Knutsson, who was Swedish king three times in the fifteenth century. It may be doubted whether such men would have had much in common with an ordinary freeman who owned a single farm. Attempts have been made in modern discussions to accommodate this range of wealth and power among the *bönder* by inventing such titles as *bonde-hövdingar* (*bonde*-chieftains) or *stor* [large]-*bönder*, for which there is no contemporary justification. The exceptional status of Swedish *bönder* is underlined by the extraordinary clause in the law of Östergötland: "If there is a dispute [over land] between *bonde* and king, the *bonde* always has the verdict" (*Östgötalagen*, 140 [Jordabalken II]). Such a law raises the question whether many *bönder* really owned no more than a single farm.

The Gulating law, which is earlier than the Swedish laws, shows that the word *bonde* did not have such an exalted meaning in Norway. It has a more elaborate scale of status, most clearly stated in clause 185 prescribing the penalty owed to someone who had been wounded:

When a freedman wounds someone, then he shall make amends with a 12 öre ring, and his son with two rings, and a *bonde* with 3 rings, *oðalboren maðr* with 6 rings, *lendrmaðr* or stallar [i.e. royal agents] with 12 rings, or jarl with 24, or the king 48. (Robberstad, 190)

The *oðalboren maðr*, "odal-born man," who is alternatively called a *hauld*, owned inherited land; the *bonde* did not. The land farmed by *bönder* may have been bought, but it is more likely that it was owned by someone else. In other words, in twelfth-century Norway *bönder* could be, and many apparently were, tenants.

The translation of the word *bonde*, therefore, poses a problem. It has variously been rendered "peasant" or "yeoman," but these have misleading, anachronistic connotations. The root meaning is "a dweller," which suggests that a good translation would be "a free farmer with his own household." That certainly fits the Norwegian usage but is less satisfactory for Denmark and Sweden, where *bonde* seems to be the equivalent of the Norwegian *hauld*.

The earliest evidence for the meaning of the word is provided by runic inscriptions of the late tenth and eleventh centuries. Some of the men they commemorate are described as *bönder*, and a few inscriptions show that the word implied responsibility for a household. In one a mother, together with her daughter, erected a stone in memory of two of her sons, only one of whom is called *bonde* (*SR* Södermanland, no. 208). There are also inscriptions in which men describe their dead kinsmen as their *bönder* (e.g., *SR* Södermanland, nos. 72, 346).

The sense "head of the family" is further evidenced by more than 175 inscriptions in which a widow refers to her dead husband as *bunta sin*, "her *bonde*"—as his wife she had been under his authority. It was, of course, unnecessary for a son commemorating his father to call him "his *bonde*," and it is significant that this only happened when the father was additionally described as "good *bonde*" (e.g., *SR* Södermanland, no. 19, Västergötland, nos. 92, 128, Östergötland, no. 119). That was not an empty formula but rather implied a special status. It is unlikely that "good" in these inscriptions refers to goodness of heart or special competence or skill; if that was its significance, such people were rare—only 10 percent of the people commemorated were "good." Almost all were men (there are only four "good" women), and many of them were also called *thegn* or *dreng*. In eastern Sweden, where such titles are exceptional, the epithet is also used for some fathers and sons as well as for a few *bönder*.

The interpretation of the epithet "good" as an indication of status is further supported by the fact that in Denmark and Sweden (there is only one "good" man in Norway) the "good" people seem to have been relatively rich. That is suggested by the lavish style of their monuments, and by the fact that some of these monuments name the place the dead person lived, implying ownership, a detail that is rarely given. Another indication of status is the additional information given in some of these inscriptions that a bridge, a relatively costly enterprise, has been built for the sake of the "good" departed.

The runic inscriptions thus support other evidence that in the early and central Middle Ages the *bönder* included men of wealth and rank; indeed, that seems to have been the normal sense of the word outside Norway, and even there may have had the same meaning earlier. The association of the word *bonde* with freemen of lower rank was in part a result of the formal recognition, in the thirteenth century, of the richest *bönder* as a privileged and distinct aristocracy. Another factor in the decline of the status of the word was the tendency for *bönder* to become tenants, as they already were in twelfth-century Norway. A similar change affected the equivalent English word *ceorl*, which by the sixteenth century, in the form *churl*, had come to mean a rude rustic. The later meaning of *bonde* has naturally colored much modern comment on early Scandinavian society, which has sometimes been made to appear a peasant democracy.

Church Land

The huge amount of land later held by churches was obviously acquired after the mid-tenth century. The earliest churches must have belonged to the people who had them built, their patrons; traditional laws certainly did not allow land to be alienated to strangers. By the eleventh century rulers and other landowners were providing their churches with land, but for some time they and their heirs retained rights over such gifts. The claim that Olav Haraldsson gave land rendering a mark a year to every *fylki-church* may not be reliable, but he may well have ensured that the priests serving his churches had some land for their support. The earliest documented grant to a church was by Sven Estridsen to Lund Cathedral (L. Weibull, 69). His son made a much larger grant, the subject of the earliest Scandinavian charter in 1085, and according to the *Roskilde Chronicle* his mother made an even larger grant to Roskilde Cathedral (*DD* 2, no. 21; C. Christensen). Bishops were also early donors, in particular to their own cathedrals. According to Adam of Bremen, Odinkar, the first bishop of Ribe, was "a noble of royal Danish stock, and so rich in land that they say the bishopric of Ribe was founded from his patrimony" (Adam of Bremen 2.36). In Iceland the farm of Skálholt, which became the first see, belonged to the first native bishops, Ísleif and his son Gizur. The endowment of the first Swedish see, Skara, was still modest in the year 1200, but it had recently been doubled by its bishop, Bengt "the Good," who gave it nine farms and fifty tenants (Lindquist, 46–47).

Kings, members of royal families, and bishops also founded and endowed most of the monasteries that were established in the eleventh and twelfth centuries. The original endowments of monasteries, cathedrals, and other churches were enlarged in various ways: by gifts, many of them to ensure that masses would be said for the soul of the donor and his or her kin; in payment of penalties for breach of church law; by purchase; and by the foreclosing of mortgages. As churches accumulated wealth, they were able to lend money or supplies that were needed, with land as security; if a borrower could not repay, the land passed permanently into church ownership (*KHL*, s.v. "Kyrkans finanser").

This process of accumulation continued to the eve of the Reformation. The large compact holdings then owned by churches generally represent major donations, although some estates had been consolidated by purchase and exchange. Most large gifts were made at an early stage; in the thirteenth century the demand that church land should be exempt from taxation led to some resistance in Denmark and Sweden to further large grants. The principle was firmly stated in the Lateran Council of 1215, and in Denmark only land acquired by the church before that date was exempted. In Sweden a similar, but later, limit was imposed, originally 1281 (*KHL*, s.v. "Det andliga frälset"). Swedish churches had very little land at the beginning of the thirteenth century. A large part of the endowment of Gudhem Abbey was a bequest by a queen in 1252 (Lundahl, 73–74), and almost all the 770 farms owned by the cathedral and chapter of Skara in 1540 were acquired after 1190. By 1280 in Sweden, as in other parts of Scandinavia earlier in the century, there was in effect a prohibition on the permanent alienation of royal land to the church, although kings could still donate land they had obtained, for example, by confiscation. The dispersed properties, single farms or parts, held by churches at the end of the Middle Ages were probably acquired piecemeal, a process that continued throughout the period. There were also losses. Some gifts were challenged by heirs of the donors, and in the fourteenth and fifteenth centuries some churches were forced to surrender land that had been acquired illegally.

Early royal grants to churches certainly included some land that had belonged to kings for generations, but the very large donations made by Danish and Norwegian kings in the eleventh and twelfth centuries were made possible by the confiscations that followed the formation of their kingdoms. Thanks to Harald Bluetooth's success in winning all "Denmark," his successors could afford to be lavishly generous to the cathedrals of Roskilde and Lund. Similarly, Nidaros Cathedral benefited greatly from the conquests made by eleventh-century Norwegian kings. The early poverty of the Swedish church was a result of the delay in the formation of an effectively united kingdom; Olof Skötkonung had limited resources with which to endow his bishop.

The grant of land to a church was not initially thought of as a loss. In the eleventh century a king who founded a cathedral expected that he and his successors would choose the bishops, who would continue to serve royal interests. Patrons of local churches had similar expectations. Both royal and lay patrons vigorously resisted the attempts of church reformers to deprive them of these assets (see "Church Reform" in chapter 5). Monastic foundations, despite their theoretical isolation from the world, were also expected to provide secular as well as spiritual benefits for their patrons and benefactors, in particular by providing hospitality. The demands could be burdensome. The Swedish nunnery of Gudhem, a royal foundation, even tried to move in the fourteenth century because it was too exposed to the demands of travelers (Lundahl, 74).

Kings' Land

The land with which kings were able to endow bishoprics, monasteries, and other churches was accumulated over a long period and in different ways. Many of the royal estates that can be identified in the twelfth and thirteenth centuries had belonged to previous rulers; some can be identified with the help of poetry, place-names, and archaeology, but there is no means of determining how large they were. It is likely that a ruler or chieftain was normally the largest landowner in his territory or area of influence. If, as argued here, some magnates had very large estates long before the twelfth century, it follows that the estates of some rulers in early medieval Scandinavia may have been very large indeed. It is, however, likely that some twelfth-century magnates inherited their property from earlier local rulers or chieftains who submitted when the medieval kingdoms were consolidated. Land held by those who did not submit, or who rebelled, was confiscated.

Throughout the Middle Ages kings increased their resources by confiscation. In 1502, for example, soon after the murder of the Danish nobleman Poul Laxmand, the confiscation of his huge estate of nine hundred farms was justified on the grounds of his having had treacherous dealings with the Swedes (Wittendorf, 35, 73). Kings could not retain all such confiscated property; much had to be given away to reward supporters.

Kings also had rights in common land. In the thirteenth century Swedish kings claimed the right to dispose of a third of such land in Götaland and gave much of it to monasteries and magnates. Later kings claimed the whole territory of Norrland. According to the law of 1241, in Jutland the landowners had the wood and the king the ground, apparently meaning that landowners could graze animals and collect wood, but the king could claim that any new cultivation was liable to royal taxation. The thirteenth-century laws of Sjælland and Skåne show that in those provinces royal rights to common land were limited to the vicinity of royal estates; other landowners had comparable rights (*KHL*, s.v. "Alminding").

A distinction was already being drawn in the twelfth century between crown land and land inherited by the king or acquired in some other way— by conquest, confiscation, purchase, gift, or as a penalty. It has been argued that from an early date kings were free to give away acquired but not inherited land, but that rule was first stated toward the end of the thirteenth century. In Denmark the royal coronation promises included an undertaking not to give land away, and in 1302 the Norwegian regency swore the same. In Sweden supposedly inalienable land was, in the thirteenth century, linked with the pre-Christian cult of Uppsala and called Uppsala Öd. The distinction was, however, unreal. Kings treated property as they liked and cited the prohibition against alienation in order to recover what had been given away by their predecessors (*KHL*, s.v. "Iura regni"; Knudsen). It was part of the reaction to the erosion of rights and property by the excessive generosity of earlier generations. The doctrine of inalienability was, in fact, most vigorously invoked by Valdemar IV and Margaret in their attempts to recover property.

The Land of the Aristocracy

The lay aristocracy was defined by privileges granted in the thirteenth century exempting it from many taxes in return for service, especially military service (*KHL*, s.v. "Det världsliga frälset"; Benedictow et al.). This group came to be distinguished by special titles and by heraldic devices. There was a huge range, from people with vast estates to gentry hardly distinguishable from ordinary freemen. The division between the higher nobility and the lower is nowhere well defined, but in Denmark those who had less than a hundred tenants were generally treated as belonging to the lower

Figure 6.1. Stone house at Tjele, near Viborg, north Jutland. This small house (only fifty-five feet long) was built in the early years of the sixteenth century and served as a storehouse with a dwelling, consisting of two rooms and a toilet, on the upper floor. It was not fortified but provided some security for the family that lived in it and for their documents and valuables; there was less risk of fire than in a timber house (R. Olsen, 90–92). Photograph by Hans Henrik Engqvist. © National Museum, Copenhagen.

aristocracy. Some who had little more than a single farm were only distinguished from their neighbors by their freedom from taxation.

The number of aristocrats at any one time cannot be determined exactly. In early sixteenth-century Denmark there were about 250 noble families entitled to a coat of arms, and many of them were represented by two or more adults. Only about a fifth of these families would have been considered as high aristocracy (Ulsig 1968, 399–403). The numbers in Sweden were probably much the same, but there were very few Norwegian high aristocrats; after 1523 only one such family survived, represented by two brothers. There were, however, a surprisingly large number of Norwegian families with coats of arms, about 500 in the early fourteenth century and still about 200 in the middle of the fifteenth century (Bagge and Mykland, 36). The higher aristocracy was eager not only to preserve its privileges but also to prevent anyone else from sharing them; in the thirteenth century the Norwegian *hird* already claimed the right to veto new members. Members of the higher aristocracy tended to marry women from families of similar status, and, although the laws of inheritance meant that much family property necessarily passed into other hands, it normally remained within the charmed circles of families who shared common interests. Rival constellations competed for power, especially in Sweden where attitudes to the Union monarchy were an issue, but the higher aristocracy of Scandinavia formed a separate segment of society whose members enjoyed enormous power and privileges and who were often able, as councillors, to obtain lucrative fiefs that in turn gave opportunities to acquire still more land, by fair means or foul.

Some of these aristocrats of the later Middle Ages were descended from men of relatively humble origin who were successful royal servants, but most were members of families that were prominent earlier as church benefactors and had bishops as their kinsmen. Some apparently traced their ancestry back to former local rulers, who by submission to conquering kings succeeded in retaining their wealth, status, and power. Others may have been descendants either of local magnates who survived the conquest, or of men who were installed by the conquerors to look after their interests. Whatever their ancestry, in the eleventh and twelfth centuries in many parts of Scandinavia, magnates owned or were lords of very large areas of land. A few of them can be glimpsed in twelfth-century records, notable examples being the Hvide family, who, it has been claimed, owned a thousand farms in Sjælland, and their rivals, the Thurgots of Jutland (Nørlund). Their wealth and therefore their power may have partly depended on successful campaigns but was more securely founded on the revenues from their estates. Some families also had the advantage of controlling the routes by which valuable produce reached markets where it could be sold. From the estates of such families, some bishops were able to make lavish benefactions to their own sees. Twelfth-century kings could no more ignore the heads of these families than could their successors three hundred years later. The privileges "granted" in the thirteenth century were the recognition of existing status, not the creation of a new group in society.

The other group of landowners in late medieval Scandinavia were the free but unprivileged. They were most numerous in peripheral regions. As explained earlier the proportion of these landowners in Denmark was greatly reduced in the fourteenth century, a consequence of weak royal power. In Norway, where aristocrats were few, relatively poor, and underprivileged, and royal authority remained strong at least until the mid-fourteenth century, the *bönder* continued to play a leading role in local government, and, most significantly, the traditional military levy continued to have military importance there longer than in other parts of Scandinavia.

The Norwegian *bönder* were not all equal in wealth and prestige, however. A social hierarchy existed even in superficially egalitarian districts, and some families continued to take the lead in the affairs of their localities for generations (Imsen).

Tenants

Even in Norway many *bönder* became tenants.[2] Subdivision could reduce the separate holdings to the level that they could not pay what was due to church and king and so remain independent. A farm could be split, but it could alternatively be kept intact and farmed by one heir, who would then either have to buy out the coheirs or pay them a rent. This system, combined with the effects of gifts in alms, marriage portions, and penalties for offenses, could produce complicated results (*KHL*, s.v. "Bygsel").

The proportion of land cultivated by tenants increased throughout the Middle Ages. The evidence of Vorbasse combined with the indications, discussed earlier, that there were many large magnate estates in early medieval Scandinavia suggests that many, perhaps a majority, of Scandinavian farmers were tenants in the twelfth century, and probably much earlier. The laws generally assume that tenancies would be for short periods (up to three years was common), and surviving tenancy agreements from the later Middle Ages were often for such short terms, but in practice they were for life and commonly proved to be hereditary. Short terms were in the interest of landowners, who could demand extra payment for renewal. Tenants were expected to maintain both buildings and land in good order, and they therefore had an obligation to maintain a certain amount of stock.

Tenants who worked land on the main farms of major landowners or who lived nearby often rendered services, but these were rarely burdensome. More distant tenants paid rent in kind to the owner, who could use it in his own household or sell it. In Norway rents were generally the equivalent of one year's sowing. The yield was about threefold, but farmers also had some income from stock and hunting, and it has been concluded that, very roughly, rent amounted to a fifth or sixth of income. Rents were paid in many different kinds of local produce. Dried fish or *wadmal*, a coarse cloth, was a normal payment in Iceland; many farms in Sweden and Norway paid in butter; and in Denmark payment in grain was common. Some rents were expressed in terms of money, most commonly in areas with good access to town markets, but in practice they were often paid in kind, an arrangement preferred by landowners to compensate for the debasement of the coinage in the later Middle Ages (Gissel et al., 145–54).

The recurrent plagues in the late fourteenth century greatly improved the economic conditions of the tenants who survived. In Norway it has been estimated that by the end of the century rents were on average only a quarter of what they had been earlier. The landowners who survived the crisis best were those who could obtain produce that was then fetching high prices—that is, stockfish, salt herring, cattle, or butter (see "The Black Death and Its Consequences" in chapter 7). Many others were less fortunate, and some families lost their property. In Norway the church was best able to take advantage of the new situation.

Thus the *bönder* who owned land in the sixteenth century were not the remnants of a once much larger group, eroded by the pressure of church and aristocracy. Most were descendants of families who had established new farms on common or waste land in the eleventh and twelfth centuries and were therefore treated as free landowners owing tax to the king—what in Sweden were by the end of the fourteenth century called *skattebönder*, tax-*bönder*. Some large areas of land suitable for colonization had been granted to churches or aristocrats, but they were often unable to retain their rights over the settlers in the remoter regions. By the sixteenth century Norrland in Sweden was almost entirely held by *skattebönder*, although this vast region had been granted earlier to the archbishop of Uppsala and a few magnates. Many of the Danish free landowners who became tenants in the late Middle Ages were probably surrendering land that had been colonized in this way in the eleventh and twelfth centuries.

The distribution of landownership revealed by the relatively abundant records of the sixteenth century was the result of many changes during the Middle Ages, but some ancient patterns can be discerned. Kings and magnates had given much land to the church, especially in the eleventh and twelfth centuries, but in 1500 their descendants still held large estates that included much land that had been passed on by inheritance for many generations; some royal estates can be traced back for centuries. Although partible inheritance caused estates to be frequently redistributed, large parts of them remained in the same families or had been acquired by members of families of similar rank in marriage settlements. Much of the land held by magnates in the thirteenth century was still in aristocratic hands three hundred years later. The main concentrations of aristocratic property in the sixteenth century were in the open and fertile regions of Scandinavia, from Denmark to Tröndelag, and probably always had been. The new element was the large group of free but unprivileged *bönder*, who were concentrated in the peripheral regions.

Appendix: Rígsthula

The conventional picture of early Scandinavian society, which has been questioned here, was given a mythological basis in *Rígsthula*, a poem that describes the god *Ríg* visiting three households, representing three generations—great-grandparents, grandparents, and parents (*KHL*, s.v. "Rígsthula"; Karras, 60–63, 208–10). He shares the bed of each couple in turn and fathers a son in all three. The first son, Thræll ("Slave"), lives with a woman called Thír ("Servant"), and their children, both boys and girls, have names describing their ugliness or the heavy and dirty work they do. The second son, Karl ("Freeman"), marries Snör ("Daughter-in-law"); he plows, and she weaves. They are good-looking and prosperous, as are their many children, who include Dreng, Thegn, Hold, Bóandi, Brúð, and Víf (the last representing "Bride" and "Wife"). Ríg's third son, Jarl, and his wife, Erna, have only sons, among them Aðal, Arfi, and Konung ("Noble," "Heir," and "King"), none of whom works; they live in luxury, eating and drinking, hunting, and fighting.

The poem survives only in an incomplete fourteenth-century copy. It has been variously dated between the late ninth and the thirteenth centuries. The place of composition is equally uncertain; Norway, Denmark, the British Isles, and Iceland have all been suggested.

Those who accept that it is an early poem have taken it as a description of early Germanic social structure in which the *bönder* had pride of place. The presence of a distinct aristocratic class would, however, have been more appropriate in the thirteenth century. The indications of an early date, such as the prominence given to the slaves, the absence of overt Christian influence, the vocabulary, and the apparent description of old-fashioned dress, could all be deliberate archaisms. Moreover, it is unlikely that slaves would be described as masterless at a time when slavery was a flourishing institution.

The poem is obviously not a realistic description of social structure. Its author was clearly in sympathy with the *bönder*, who are idealized. There is a marked contrast between the virtues of Karl and his family and the qualities associated with the other classes: the near bestiality of the thralls, and the worthless luxury of the aristocrats. *Rígsthula* can be seen as a response, by someone who sympathized with the unprivileged *bönder*, to the changes in the thirteenth century that threatened them: the growing numbers of the landless and the formal recognition of the privileges of an aristocracy closely allied with kings. The poem offers an explanation, even a justification, for the many who were landless and unfortunate; it is implied that they were descendants of slaves and had inherited their inferiority. The message that the social order was divinely ordained and that all men were brothers is perhaps an echo of Christian teaching, albeit in a pagan guise. In criticizing rather than praising military prowess and unearned ease while commending industry and diligence, *Rígsthula* can, perhaps, be seen as the earliest statement of the Protestant ethic.

7

Trade and Towns

Early Trade

Toward the end of the seventh century, civil war in Frankia hindered over-land traffic within the kingdom and encouraged a dramatic increase in traffic along its coasts and between Frankia and the British Isles.[1] As a result Scandinavia, which had never been completely cut off from western Europe since the collapse of the Roman Empire, began to be visited by Frisian merchants from Dorestad, which was first established as a trading place at that time, and perhaps from other trading places around the North Sea that flourished in the eighth century. The merchants' main purpose appears to have been to obtain furs and other luxury goods, such as amber, walrus ivory, and, perhaps, falcons, that were highly prized by the rulers and aristocrats of Christian Europe. Scandinavians themselves may have sailed to western harbors in the eighth century, as they certainly did in the ninth. By the year 800 commercial links between western and northern Europe were well established. Contemporary texts name several ninth-century trading centers in Scandinavia, including Hedeby and Ribe in south Jutland; Skíringssal, near Larvik in southeast Norway; and Birka in Mälaren. There are also references to similar places on the south coast of the Baltic: Apuleia in Latvia, Truso near the mouth of the Vistula, and an unlocated place called Reric in Slav territory.

According to Rimbert, merchants regularly traveled between Hedeby and Birka, and between these Baltic ports and Dorestad. He also mentioned the presence of Saxon merchants in Hedeby. The fact that the ships taking Anskar to Birka in 829 were attacked by pirates suggests that this traffic was on a scale sufficient to make piracy worthwhile (*VA* 10, cf. 27). The accounts of the voyages of the Norwegian chieftain Ottar imply that he took furs, skins, and walrus ivory from north Norway to Hedeby and

England. The same text also includes an account of a voyage from Hedeby to Truso made by a man called Wulfstan, who was probably English. Archaeological investigations at Hedeby and Birka have confirmed that these were trading places in the ninth and tenth centuries, importing goods from distant parts.[2] The finds at Hedeby include barrels from Alsace and the Black Forest that presumably once contained wine, millstones from the Eifel region, pottery and glass from the Rhineland, and whetstones from Norway or Sweden. Similar imports also reached Birka. These and other excavations have shown some of the goods that were imported, but Scandinavian trade was then, as later, mainly in organic materials that do not normally survive as well as stone and metal. Furs were probably the most important northern export in the early Middle Ages. Rich and powerful people in Europe were eager to display their wealth and status by wearing fine-quality furs, the best coming from the Scandinavian peninsula, Finland, and north Russia, where the winters were very cold. Jordanes, writing in sixth-century Byzantium, noted that the Svear were "famed for the dark beauty of their furs" and that they sent "sapphire-colored skins" to the Mediterranean world. Five hundred years later Adam of Bremen noted that black foxes, hares, white marten, and polar bears were to be found in Norway and that the Swedes took beaver and marten pelts for granted (P. Sawyer 1982, 65, 72).

Some trappers and hunters may have sold furs to middlemen or to foreign traders, but it is likely that most of the produce that reached the trading places was collected as tribute. Ottar said that he himself hunted walruses and whales, but that his wealth was mostly in the tribute from the Finnas (that is, the Sami):

> That tribute consists of the skins of beasts, the feathers of birds, whale-bone, and ship ropes made from whale-hide and seal skin. Each pays according to his rank. The highest in rank has to pay fifteen marten skins, five reindeer skins, one bear skin and ten measures of feathers, and a jacket of bearskin or otterskin and two ship-ropes. Each of these must be sixty ells about long, one made from whale-hide the other from seal. (Lund, 19–20)

This tariff implies that there was a well-established tributary relationship between rich and powerful men like Ottar and the Sami, who were skillful hunters but ill equipped to resist the demands of well-armed outsiders. Later in the Middle Ages they were forced to pay tribute not only to Norwegians but also to Swedes and Russians.

In the ninth century traders known in Old Norse as *Bjarmar* were also active in the far north and were encountered by Ottar when he reached the White Sea (*KHL*, s.v. "Bjarmar och Bjarmaland"). The name derives from a Finnish word, *perm*, that was used for traveling merchants who operated in the vast region between the arctic and the upper Volga. They may have hunted, but they probably relied for most of their supplies on tribute exacted from the native Sami, as Ottar did. Tribute was similarly collected in many parts of Scandinavia, as well as in Finland and other lands around the Baltic. The defended site recently discovered in Finland at Varikkoniemi, with a harbor and unusually large houses, has plausibly been interpreted as a base from which the Lake Region of Finland was exploited before Swedish invaders did the same from the fort called Tavastehus, which they built nearby in the late thirteenth century.

Scandinavians and others began to exploit the lands around Lake Ladoga in the eighth century, if not before, and by 750 a base for gathering tribute from that region had been established at Staraja Ladoga, a short distance south of the lake.[3] By the mid-ninth century there were several similar centers in north Russia at Beloozero, Izborsk, Jaroslav, Pskov, and Gorodisce, which was replaced in the tenth century by Novgorod, "the new gorod," nearby. The furs collected in these places were not all destined for western Europe. It was not long after the foundation of Staraja Ladoga that the tribute collectors discovered that in markets on the lower reaches of the rivers Don and Volga, rich Muslim merchants were prepared to pay large amounts of silver for slaves, furs, and other northern commodities. As a result many Islamic coins began to reach Russia, where the earliest known hoard, containing coins struck before 787, is from Staraja Ladoga. Soon after the year 800 such coins were also reaching trading places around the Baltic as far west as Ralswiek and Hedeby.

The opportunity of trading with Muslim merchants led some Scandinavians to establish bases farther south. From one of these, at Kiev, they came into contact with the Byzantine Empire, but in the ninth and tenth centuries the Russian trade was with Muslims rather than with Byzantines. Muslim geographers of the tenth century and later provide valuable information about the goods that were available in Russia. Many of them, including different types of fur, slaves, falcons, wax, and honey, could be gathered there, but amber probably came from the Baltic coastlands, and walrus tusks, which they called "fish-teeth," must have come from arctic waters. Similar goods were also being exported to western Europe. The new markets in the south did not mean that the western commerce stopped. Many trading places along the Baltic coast and in Scandinavia flourished during the ninth and tenth centuries. One of the most important was at Birka, which was very well placed as a center in which produce from around the gulfs of Bothnia and Finland and from Karelia could be collected for shipment to Hedeby and beyond.

As Anskar discovered on his first journey to Birka, merchant ships were vulnerable to attack by pirates, who could operate from many islands and isolated stretches of coast around the Baltic with little fear of interference. Ships were particularly vulnerable when they were forced to pass close to land, as they had to in order to enter or leave the Baltic. From the eighth century to the end of the tenth, merchants preferred to sail through Store or Lille Bælt, for Jutland and Fyn were the heart of the Danish kingdom, and ships sailing along those coasts could hope for better protection than in Öresund. Until the eleventh century a channel connected Limfjord with the North Sea, and ships could thus avoid the dangerous currents around the point of Skagen. As early as 726 the Danish king had a base on the island of Samsö from which his agents could control traffic through the Belts (P. Sawyer 1988a, 20–21; Roesdahl 1991, 93). It could, of course, have been a defense against naval attack, but it would also have deterred pirates and been a means of controlling, and levying toll on, merchant ships.

Early Trading Centers

Danish kings were undoubtedly eager to encourage and control trade in the eighth and ninth centuries. They established trading centers in south Jutland, soon after 700, at Ribe, a port for ships from western Europe, and a century later on the eastern side of Jutland at Hedeby. According to the contemporary Frankish royal annals the merchants settled in Hedeby had earlier been at Reric in Slav territory and had apparently recognized Godfred as their overlord and paid him tribute. The annals imply that he wanted this prosperous trading center to be within his own territory. He chose a good site, close to the main land route along the spine of Jutland that continued south into Saxony. As it was south of the defensive barrier constructed in 737–38, the first phase of what is known as Danevirke, Godfred constructed a new rampart to protect it from external attack. The site was otherwise open and undefended until a German invasion threatened in 968, when a massive semicircular rampart was built around it; the king's peace was apparently sufficient protection against internal disruption. The Hedeby rampart enclosed an area of about 75 acres (30 hectares), but it was not all permanently occupied. There was open space in which temporary workshops could be sited and visitors accommodated, perhaps in tents. The population was, nevertheless, substantial. The adjacent cemeteries suggest that it had well over a thousand permanent inhabitants for most of the three centuries that it existed. The population of Ribe cannot be estimated in that way, but by the eleventh century it was bounded by a bank and ditch enclosing about 34 acres (14 hectares).

Ribe and Hedeby were valuable assets. Merchants brought luxuries as well as more commonplace but useful things such as millstones, and the tolls they paid were a source of revenue, one of the earliest forms of taxation. Traces of a toll station have been found in the harbor of Hedeby, and the emphasis in the Frankish annals on the single gate in the defensive wall of Danevirke through which wagons and horsemen could pass suggests that tolls were levied there too. Like rulers elsewhere, Danish kings could, through their agents, claim the right of preemption and so have the chance to buy the best goods, presumably at bargain prices, and merchants doubtless offered gifts. Itinerant craftsmen must have paid fees, probably in kind, and rent could be expected from permanent inhabitants.

Danish kings provided the security that merchants and craftsmen needed, if necessary by building defenses against external attack. They also tried to reassure Christian merchants that it was safe to venture into this pagan world by allowing churches to be built in Ribe and Hedeby. Rimbert reported that there was great joy at Hedeby after a church was built there because

> people of this race [Saxons] as well as merchants from this district [Bremen]
> and from Dorestad made for the place readily and without any fear—
> something which was not possible previously—and at that time there was
> an abundant supply of goods of every kind. (*VA* 24)

That may, indeed, have been one of the main reasons missionaries were invited to Birka.

According to Rimbert, piracy was a growing menace in the Baltic in the ninth century, but Birka was to some extent sheltered from attack by strangers because it could only be reached by sailors familiar with the channels in Mälaren; the one recorded raid on it was, in fact, led by an exiled king of the Svear (*VA* 19). It had no fortifications until the mid-tenth century, which suggests that, like Hedeby, it was relatively secure from local violence, but that security depended more on the common interest of the chieftains who dominated the region than on the authority of the Svea kings (see chapter 2). Pirates do not seem to have been a serious problem along the Norwegian coast, but it seems likely that anyone shipping northern produce of the kind collected by Ottar would have to give something from their cargoes to the men who controlled the central and southern sections of the North Way, for whom such payments would have been a welcome source of extra wealth.

Some merchants sought protection by recruiting warriors or were themselves leaders of a warrior band. Muslim writers report that in tenth-century Russia there were traders with such bands of retainers, some numbering hundreds, who enabled their leaders to extort tribute from the natives and to protect what was collected. The fact that Staraja Ladoga was fortified with a stone wall as early as 860 suggests that at that time it was more liable to be attacked than Scandinavian trading places, some of which were protected not only by rulers but also by religious sanctions. Markets that were incidental to traditional assemblies were, before the conversion to Christianity, subject to the taboos associated with pre-Christian cults. Such restraints were, of course, only effective among those who shared in the cult. Outsiders who did not could cause disruption (as the Vikings did in Christian Europe); they could, however, be allowed to attend if they promised to keep the peace. It was because he did not have peace with the Bjarmar that Ottar did not go into their territory.

Markets and Fairs

All but one of the pre-Christian assemblies in Scandinavia were "converted" and linked with Christian festivals. The exception was the winter fair held at Uppsala, called Distingen, "the thing of the Díser [female goddesses]." Throughout the Middle Ages it was held when the first new moon after midwinter was full. Its date could therefore be worked out by all who attended it, including non-Christian trappers and traders from the far north who would know from experience when to set out. Many other major assemblies, especially in Norway and Sweden, were held in the winter, when travel was easier than at other times of the year. Furs are best in winter, and furs of the highest quality could be obtained in the markets or assemblies held at that time of year, but foreign merchants could only reach Scandinavian and Baltic trading places in the summer. As the markets they visited were coastal, the furs and other winter produce had to be stored for several months and brought from the places of winter assembly and from collecting centers in Finland and north Russia. These goods were potentially valuable and had to be protected against pirates at sea and raiders on land. Chieftains and magnates were able to enhance their power by providing the necessary protection, but it seems likely that most of the produce offered for sale in the coastal trading places was gathered by such men as tribute and taken by them to the markets, as Ottar did when he sailed to Hedeby.

With one exception, Visby (see "1100–1300" later in this chapter), the trading places visited by merchants from western Europe were not, like the native places of assembly, associated with traditional cults. Both types of market were, however, linked in a complex network of exchanges within Scandinavia that existed before the demand for northern produce grew in the early Middle Ages. Excavations of rural sites in many parts of Scandinavia have begun to cast light on these early medieval networks by showing how some things, such as whetstones, were distributed far from the centers of production in Norway or Sweden, and how imports from outside Scandinavia were similarly spread; fragments of millstones from the Eifel region are found in virtually all village excavations in Denmark (Resi; Roesdahl 1982, 87–90).

Traces of early seasonal markets or fairs with remains of the activity of craftsmen have been recognized archaeologically in many places around the Baltic. Most were temporary and were either abandoned or moved after a while to form the nucleus of a town nearby. Old Lejre, for example, seems to have been the precursor of Roskilde, and Ålborg, on Limfjord, was apparently preceded by an ephemeral trading center at Bejsebakken, now on the outskirts of the town. Excavations sometimes reveal that towns had surprisingly early origins. So, for example, Skien, in southern Telemark, was granted a charter in 1358, but there is some evidence for a seasonal market there before the year 1000 (Myrvoll). Some inland trading places had extensive contacts. The apparently isolated valley of Setesdal in south Norway received imports from all directions in the Viking period, and it seems likely that there were seasonal fairs then much like those reported in the nineteenth century, when men traveled to Setesdal from the coast to exchange salt, cloth, leather, and fish for hides and skins (Larsen). At Ystad, on the coast of Skåne, remains have been found that led the excavator to describe the site as a market for nearby communities in the seventh and eighth centuries, if not earlier. Other places appear to have attracted visitors from far afield. Paviken on Gotland flourished in the ninth and tenth centuries, importing goods from many parts of the Baltic, and a similar site has been found at Skuldevig, just inside the entrance of Roskilde Fjord in Denmark (P. Sawyer 1986b). Many of these places had good access to the sea and could be reached by boat more easily than overland. In the later Middle Ages farmers from the Danish islands sold their produce in Lübeck, Norwegian farmers did the same in Denmark, and Finns bought food in Estonia. The archaeological evidence from several sites suggests that their predecessors did much the same in the early Middle Ages.

Some less important fairs or assemblies also had religious associations. One well-documented Swedish example was held at the spring at Svinnegarn, near Enköping in Uppland (Ahnlund). Before the Reformation votive offerings were made at the spring and to the nearby church by people of both high and low status. In 1488 an unsuccessful attempt was made to suppress that fair, but it still attracted thousands of people, some traveling sixty miles or more, every Trinity Sunday until the nineteenth century. In 1813 the local landowner reported that a fair was held there every year with booths specially set up, and he complained about the accompanying drunkenness and noise. In Denmark over thirty similar fairs were held at springs, some of which survived until quite recently.

Local trading places can also be indicated by place-names. The most obvious are Kaupang and Köping, equivalent to the English name Chipping, meaning "a market." The names are, however, unlikely to be earlier than the eleventh century. The word was borrowed from England in the early Middle Ages, and even in England it is rare before the twelfth century (Harmer). One distinctive name common in Norway and Sweden is Bjarkøy or Björkö. Many of these names mean no more than "birch island," but some, including Bjarköy in Troms in north Norway, and places with Finnish forms of the name, Birkala, near Tammerfors and Pirkkiö in the Torneå, were certainly medieval trading places. Their names indirectly echo that of the famous Birka in Mälaren. The law in many towns and trading places in medieval Scandinavia was known as Bjärköarätt, the Law of Birka, reflecting the importance of that place; use of the name does not mean that those laws were identical with that current in Birka when it flourished (*KHL*, s.v. "Bjarkoaratt"). In Norway *lade*, meaning "a landing place," was used to form numerous names, such as Laberg, Lahelle, or Lastein, but most such names may be relatively recent, even postmedieval, and they were not necessarily trading places. The one certain early example, Lade near Trondheim, was the base from which the jarls of Lade controlled the rich area around Trondheim Fjord in the tenth century; the medieval town developed later some distance away.

Currency

The development of trading places and towns in medieval Scandinavia was partly stimulated by the demand for Scandinavian produce elsewhere in Europe, but it was also a result of increasing exchanges within Scandinavia. Trade was facilitated in the tenth century by the availability of large quantities of silver (Blackburn and Metcalf). A little silver may have been a trade balance, but most was acquired as plunder, tribute, or pay in west or east Europe and was widely distributed among the Scandinavian population. Some was in the form of coins, but there were also rings that served as currency, ornaments (many of them broken), and simple rods or ingots of the metal. This silver was at first hoarded as a store of wealth to be used to make large payments—for example, when arranging a marriage or paying a ransom. For such purposes large lumps of silver were convenient, but for most purchases in local markets smaller pieces were needed. As markets became more active, the silver was cut into smaller fragments, many of them much lighter than the foreign coins that began to reach Scandinavia in the ninth century. This change began in the tenth century in Denmark, and by about 1075 Danish coins were normally used there instead of unminted silver fragments or foreign coins (Hårdh; Bendixen 1992). A similar change occurred later in Gotland (Lundström). From the ninth century to the eleventh more silver was hoarded on that island than in the whole of the rest of Scandinavia, but the transition from large units of the metal to small fragments happened about a century later than in Denmark. This evidence from Gotland shows that an abundance of silver did not itself stimulate economic activity. The silver accumulated by the Gotlanders did not often change hands; it was hoarded (Malmer and Rispling).[4] Until the middle of the eleventh century the coins on the island did not circulate much, and it was not until about 1140 that the Gotlanders began to produce their own coins. This contrast between Denmark and Gotland suggests that effective royal authority was a more significant factor in stimulating economic activity than was an abundance of silver, even if it was widely distributed. Kings had nothing to do with the development of Gotland as a major center of Baltic trade, however; that was the work of merchants.

Early Towns

Danish kings were the first to issue a continuous coinage in Scandinavia, and they founded the earliest towns.[5] By the beginning of the eleventh century Århus, Lund, Roskilde, and Viborg were all well established. Ribe, the oldest, continued to flourish, and so did Hedeby, although by 1100 it had been replaced by Schleswig on the other side of the fjord, apparently because Hedeby's harbor was too shallow for the larger ships that were then being used. At least two Norwegian towns were founded in the last years of the tenth century: Oslo, in a district under Danish overlordship, and Trondheim, which may have been initially established by a jarl, not a king. Norwegian kings claimed authority over both places before long, and by the end of the eleventh century had founded several other towns. This urban expansion was not only encouraged by kings; their power made it possible. They could best provide the protection traders and craftsmen needed and grant the privileges that enabled embryo urban communities to flourish. In the eleventh century Danish and Norwegian kings established episcopal sees in some towns and endowed churches in others. A few were established for strategic rather than economic reasons. Konghelle on Göta Älv, which was founded soon after the Norwegians gained control of Bohuslän in the mid-eleventh century and marked the southern limit of the kingdom, is a good example. In some there was a royal residence, and most of the mints in which coins were struck in the names of kings were located in these urban or proto-urban centers. The people who settled in these places were, in effect, royal tenants and paid rent to royal agents, who also collected tolls and other dues and probably supervised the urban assemblies in which disputes were dealt with and legal transactions were completed.

In Sweden royal power developed more slowly, and so too did urbanization. By the year 1100 many of the medieval towns of Denmark and Norway were firmly established, but there were only two—Lödöse and Skara—in Götaland and one—Sigtuna—in Svealand. It was two hundred years before most of the medieval towns in the central regions of the Swedish kingdom were well established, but urban development in the peripheral regions was slower. Finland, for example, had six towns by 1500, but only one of them, Åbo (Turku, in Finnish) existed in 1300. By 1500 there were 100 towns in the Danish kingdom, almost a third of them in what are now Swedish provinces; 40 in the Swedish kingdom; and 15 in Norway, 3 of them in Bohuslän. Most were very small and functioned as craft and market centers for their districts. The larger towns attracted numerous foreign merchants, but even these towns were small by European standards.

1100–1300

Scandinavians continued to supply other parts of Europe with luxuries throughout the Middle Ages. In the twelfth century walrus tusks were the main source of ivory in northwestern Europe; most probably came from Greenland. Falcons and hawks from Scandinavia, Iceland, and Greenland were also greatly prized by the rulers and aristocrats of western Europe. Some birds were sold, but many were given as presents, for example, by Norwegian to English kings. The first reference to Norwegian merchants in England shows that the English king was eager to retain their goodwill (P. Sawyer 1986a, 186). In 1095 the earl of Northumberland attacked and robbed four ships traveling from Norway to England. The merchants appealed to the king, and when the earl disregarded an order to restore the stolen goods, full compensation was paid from the royal treasury. Norwegians appear to have been as welcome then, at least in the royal court, as Gotlanders were in the early thirteenth century, and for the same reasons. They both supplied luxuries that were in great demand, especially in the royal court. They may have brought a variety of goods as well, but the earliest references in English royal records are to purchases of falcons and furs.

In the eleventh and twelfth centuries the demand for furs in western Europe greatly increased as they became more fashionable (P. Sawyer 1986a, 191). One indication of the change was the development of an elaborate terminology to describe different types of fur; until the eleventh century the English had been content with the word *fell*, which they used for all types of animal skins, even (in poetry) dragon skins, but by 1200 there was a huge vocabulary for furs in England as well as France. The new fashion provoked protests. In 1127, for example, an English church council ruled that abbesses and nuns were not to wear garments more precious than those of lambs' wool or black cats' fur. In 1138 the prohibition was made more explicit: "We forbid that nuns wear fur of vair, gris, sable, marten, ermine or beaver, put on gold rings, or make up their hair." The best-quality furs fetched very high prices; the English king Richard I was willing to pay as much as £13 for a fur of ermine and four sable skins, the cost of eighty-six oxen at that time.

Norwegian as well as Russian furs are mentioned among the exotic goods that could be obtained in London at the end of the twelfth century. The importance placed on the fur trade by Scandinavian rulers is indicated by the efforts they made to claim the right to exact tribute from the rich fur-producing regions in the north and east, but by the end of the eleventh century most of the furs reaching western Europe came from north Russia, not Scandinavia. Danes and Swedes could still exact tribute from the people living around the Baltic, but they could no longer roam as freely in Russia as they had earlier. Russian princes then had more effective control over the region, and Novgorod took particular care to retain control of Karelia. Merchants who wanted to obtain the best furs in large quantities had to buy them in the increasingly important market of Novgorod.

This naturally enhanced the importance of Gotland. Earlier there had been many small trading places on its coast, and in the eleventh century one of them, Visby, began to grow rapidly to become one of the major towns of northern Europe. Unlike other towns in Scandinavia, it does not seem to have been established by a ruler. Its name shows that it was a pre-Christian cult center, and it appears to be the only one that became an international market; perhaps it was a religious center for seamen in the Baltic long before it became a major market. Visby was visited by merchants from many parts of Scandinavia and from western Europe as well as from

Figure 7.1. Model of Visby, Gotland. This model of Visby circa 1300 (in Gotlands Fornsal) is here seen from the harbor. By then many of the houses were built of stone. Those along the waterfront combined the functions of warehouse and merchant's dwelling, with shops at street level. The large building in the middle is the Rådhus, the meeting place of the town's government and courts. The harbor was sheltered by a sand reef, part of which is represented in the model, and the town was surrounded on its landward side by a stone wall with towers and frequent intervals. Photograph by Raymond Hejdström. © Gotlands Fornsal.

Baltic towns. Some settled there permanently, and by 1225 the German burgesses were a sufficiently important group to be granted special privileges by the bishop of Linköping, whose diocese included Gotland. The Gotlanders also engaged in this expanding trade. As there were no deep natural harbors in the island, their boats had to be light and easily beached, like many of the ships used by the Vikings. In such boats the Gotlanders could reach Novgorod, while most of their rivals had larger ships with deeper draughts and had to transfer their cargoes to smaller boats to navigate the River Volkhov.

German Merchants

The expanding market for northern produce in western Europe encouraged Germans to engage in the Baltic trade.[6] The lead was taken by merchants from towns in Westphalia, who early in the twelfth century began to visit the Slav trading place at Lübeck, their nearest Baltic port, and in 1143 a German colony was established there. After a disastrous fire it was refounded in 1158–59 by Henry the Lion, duke of Saxony, who encouraged Danish, Norwegian, Swedish, and Russian merchants to trade there. He also renewed the privileges that had been granted to the Gotlanders by the emperor Lothar III. At first the Germans bought goods from visiting merchants, but they soon began to travel across the Baltic themselves, and before the end of the century they were visiting Novgorod. It was, however, not until the thirteenth century that Germans began to dominate Baltic trade. Between 1200 and 1250 numerous German towns were established along the Baltic coast, from Wismar and Rostock to Riga and Tallinn (or Reval); the coast was nominally under Danish control, an expansion made possible by the Danish and German conquests along it. The Germans, the merchants of Lübeck in particular, were well placed to take advantage of the decline of Danish power that began in the reign of Valdemar II. A more important factor in Lübeck's development was the rapid growth of the Skåne fair in the early thirteenth century, which was made possible when Lübeck merchants began to obtain large quantities of salt from Lüneburg. Lübeck was not only the German gateway to the Baltic, it was also one end of an important route overland to Hamburg and the North Sea. By the twelfth century Limfjord, which had formerly provided a convenient entrance to the Baltic, had been closed at its west end by drifting sand. Ships traveling between the North Sea and the Baltic then had to sail around Skagen, the northern tip of Jutland, which was a hazardous enterprise, especially for small boats. This made the land routes more attractive, at least for merchants trading in furs, which were both light and valuable. The shortest route was across the base of Jutland from Schleswig to Hollingstedt, but although the road from Lübeck to Hamburg was longer (about 30 miles), it had many advantages and was used by Gotlanders when they began to visit England in the 1230s (P. Sawyer 1986a, 189–90).

Initially the main attraction for German merchants in the Baltic was the trade in furs, and throughout the Middle Ages furs were an important part of their commerce, but they soon began to trade in bulkier goods such as grain, for which there was a demand in Norway.[7] In the twelfth and thirteenth centuries Norwegians imported grain from England, but by 1250 Germans were also supplying them with grain produced by colonists who had settled along the Baltic coast between Lübeck and the Oder. By then merchants from Lübeck and other new German towns along the Baltic were visiting Scandinavian ports to buy a variety of raw materials for which there was a demand elsewhere in Europe. Iron may have been exported from Norway and Sweden in the Viking Age, but production increased in the thirteenth century, especially in the Swedish region known as Bergslagen, thanks to improved mining and smelting techniques. Copper began to be produced in the same district at much the same time. Other exports included timber (the English king Henry III bought paneling for Windsor Castle from Norway); skins of goats and other animals; and lamp oil obtained from fish, seals, and whales. Iceland could supply sulphur, wool, and the coarse cloth known as *wadmal*. Danish horses were highly prized. These and many other goods were shipped from Scandinavian ports in the thirteenth century by German and other merchants, but they accounted for a relatively small part of Scandinavian exports at that time, whether measured by volume or value; dried cod and salt herring were far more important.

The Fish Trade

There was at that time, and long after, a demand for preserved food that could be eaten in the late winter and spring. The need was most acute in the towns that were rapidly developing in many parts of Europe in the eleventh and twelfth centuries. There were four main methods of preserving food: smoking, fermentation, salting, and drying. The simplest and cheapest was drying, which is best done in a cold climate; in warm weather food tends to rot before it is dry. Conditions in northern Norway were ideal, with its arctic climate and strong winds, and cod were abundant especially in the coastal waters around Lofoten and farther north. By the fourteenth century dried cod, known as stockfish, accounted for 80 percent of the value of all Norwegian exports, and there are indications that large quantities were already being produced early in the twelfth century (*KHL*, s.v. "Fiskehandel").

The main production center was in Lofoten, and stockfish from the whole of north Norway was collected there to be shipped south in the spring, initially to Trondheim, which probably owed its rapid development in the eleventh century largely to this traffic. Many towns in western Europe, especially in England and Flanders, were already large in the eleventh century, and stockfish would have been as welcome then as it was in 1200. By then Bergen had displaced Trondheim as the main market for the export of stockfish. It was founded in the late eleventh century, apparently by King Olav Kyrre, and soon flourished; it was more convenient for foreign merchants than distant Trondheim and certainly attracted many of them.[8] It was also the best port for ships sailing to the Norwegian settlements in the Atlantic islands. A vivid description of the town at the end of the twelfth century is given in an account of the journey of a band of Danish and Norwegian crusaders who set out from Bergen in 1191:

This town is the most famous in the country, graced with a royal fortress and with the relics of many virgins; the Holy Sunniva's body rests there, upon an elevation in the cathedral church. In addition, there are both monasteries and nunneries. A very great number of people live in the town, which is rich, and abounding with wares. There is dried fish (known as *skrei*) beyond telling. Ships and men arrive from every land; there are Icelanders, Greenlanders, Englishmen, Germans, Danes, Swedes, Gotlanders, and other nations too numerous to mention. Every nation can be found there if one only takes the trouble to look. There are also quantities of wine, honey, wheat, fine cloths, silver and other commodities, and a busy trade in all of them. (Helle 1972, 12)

A similar impression is given by a speech attributed to King Sverri in his saga. The king thanked the English for bringing wheat and honey, flour and cloth, but complained that the Germans came "in great numbers and impoverish the land by carrying away butter and dried fish, and encourage drunkenness by importing wine" (P. Sawyer 1986a, 190). A fuller list of Norwegian exports is given in the Norse translation of the Saga of Tristram, which was made in 1226. The translator elaborated on the original by describing a cargo taken to France by a Norwegian ship. It included beaver, bear, sable, and squirrel skins, walrus tusks, hawks and falcons, wax, hides, goatskins, stockfish, tar, oil, sulphur, "and all sorts of northern wares" (Nedkvitne 1983, 22). The emphasis on luxuries is natural in a tale of chivalry, but it is likely that stockfish was already at that date Norway's most important and lucrative product.

Scandinavia was also then exporting large quantities of salt herring, which came not from Norway but from southern Scandinavia (*KHL*, s.v. "Sildefiske"). There were several important herring fisheries, some of them significant only for limited periods, thanks to the periodic migrations of the fish. For example, large quantities of herring were caught and dried along the coast of Bohuslän in the thirteenth century, but in the mid-fourteenth century that fishery ceased and was not revived until about 1500. The main and continuous fishery was in Öresund, where huge shoals arrived in the late summer. That was not a good time of year for drying the fish, so they had to be salted, as smoking and fermentation were not convenient methods of preservation when large quantities had to be processed. Öresund had the great advantage that the fish were caught close to the shore and could be salted quickly when they were still fresh. Until the end of the twelfth century production was on a small scale, limited by the shortage of salt (*KHL*, s.v. "Salthandel"). Salt could be obtained in England, France, and the Low Countries, but much of it was of poor quality, and the best, from the Bay of Biscay, was expensive. Shortly before 1200

Lübeck merchants began to obtain large quantities from the salt deposits at Lüneburg, about forty-five miles away, which made it possible to process very large quantities of fish. Merchants from many parts of Europe came to collect supplies and sell their wares, making the Skåne Fair, which opened annually on 15 August, one of the major fairs of medieval Europe (*KHL*, s.v. "Skånemarkedet," "Öreshundshandel"). Some merchants came overland, others from ports around the Baltic and in Scandinavia. From about 1250, seagoing ships from western ports regularly sailed around Jutland to visit the fair. Lübeck's control of the supply of salt gave it a great advantage and was an important factor in that town's later domination of Scandinavia's overseas trade. The Skåne Fair was also responsible for rapid urban development around Öresund; several towns, including Copenhagen, Dragör, and Köge grew rapidly after 1200, initially thanks to the fair.

Towns

The main town in Sweden was Stockholm, which was founded in the mid-thirteenth century and was the primary outlet for the produce of not only the Mälar region but also Bergslagen (Dahlbäck). It soon began to play much the same role on the east coast of Scandinavia that Bergen did in the west, and efforts were made to give Stockholm a monopoly of trade in the region, including the parts of Finland that began to be brought under Swedish control in the thirteenth century. Stockholm, with a population of at most 7,000 at the end of the Middle Ages, was much the same size as Bergen but far larger than any other Swedish town, only five of which ever had more than 1,000 inhabitants in the period. Even the largest Scandinavian towns were relatively insignificant in comparison with many of those along the south Baltic coast: Lübeck had 40,000 inhabitants in 1300, and a century later Rostock had 15,000 and Stralsund 10,000.

Scandinavians towns, although small, had an important economic role. They were centers in which craftsmen produced tools, equipment, and clothing; in the regular town markets imports were distributed and surplus produce gathered, and some were the sites of major seasonal fairs that attracted large numbers of people from wide regions. Even small towns were key parts of complex networks through which the larger cities and the households of rulers, magnates, and bishops, as well as religious communities, were supplied with their needs. The towns were also centers for the collection of produce that eventually reached customers in Germany, England, and many other parts of Europe. Towns were more than economic

centers. They were centers of authority—royal, ecclesiastical, or both—
and in the fifteenth century some Swedish towns had a crucially important
political role. They were also places through which new ideas and artistic
styles were disseminated.

Local trade was normally in the hands of natives, and much interregional
trade was also in their hands. Throughout the Middle Ages fishermen,
farmers, and major landowners shipped their surplus produce to sell or exchange. Finns crossed to the southern shore of the Gulf of Finland, and
Norwegians sailed to Jutland or the Danish islands (*KHL*, s.v. "Bondeseg-
lation"). This activity supplemented the economy of households, both
great and small. It was often undertaken by the producers themselves,
without middlemen, but neighbors sometimes pooled their resources and
allowed one or two to act on their behalf. Such arrangements naturally led
to some people being, in effect, part-time merchants who could undertake
extensive operations. There was, for example, a regular traffic by men
from south Finland who sailed to Österbotten and took what they bought
there to Stockholm, or to ports on the south side of the Baltic. Norwegian
farmers also traded on their own account, not only in Denmark but even
in Iceland and Greenland. Trading of this kind was undertaken by major
landowners or their agents as well as by small-scale farmers. Some had
their own ships. There are, for example, references in English customs records of the thirteenth and fourteenth centuries to ships owned by the archbishop of Nidaros and by Norwegian bishops and abbeys.

Scandinavians were also active in regular long-distance trade across and
outside the Baltic. They had to compete with foreign merchants who in
normal times were welcome and actively encouraged by Scandinavian rulers to visit and even to stay for long periods; some settled permanently.
Those who stayed for a year or more had the same rights and obligations
as natives, but most foreign traders came for shorter visits, as "summer
guests" (*KHL*, s.v. "Gæster," "Vinterliggare"). For much of the thirteenth
century they seem to have enjoyed a great degree of freedom, but in the
following century their rights were restricted. In Norway, for example,
foreigners were not allowed to travel north of Bergen, and in Sweden there
was, at least in theory, a similar restriction on foreigners trading north of
Stockholm or in Finland. Attempts were made to concentrate all trading in
towns, for natives as well as foreigners. Some foreign merchants were
granted special privileges, such as freedom from tolls, in the hope of ensuring a supply of necessary imports. In Norway privileges were commonly granted to German merchants in return for a guaranteed supply of
grain, and when in 1316 there was a disastrous shortage of food throughout
Europe the Norwegians only allowed merchants who brought grain and

grain products to buy stockfish. Another consideration was a plentiful supply of goods in order to keep prices lower than they would otherwise have been. Birger Jarl granted the merchants of Lübeck freedom from tolls in Stockholm in order to ensure that his newly founded town would flourish. Another reason for granting privileges to the merchants of particular towns was to obtain financial or military backing.

German Domination, 1300–1500

Foreigners, especially Germans, had great advantages over Scandinavian merchants, who were gradually excluded from most overseas trade.[9] German merchants had large financial resources and access to markets in Europe where they could sell Scandinavian exports and buy what Scandinavians needed to import. German towns sometimes came into conflict with each other, but their merchants often cooperated, thus gaining flexibility in planning trading ventures. In the second half of the thirteenth century German merchants began to dominate trade in the Baltic. After the 1280s Gotlanders were no longer able to travel from the Baltic to the North Sea, and the Germans in Visby monopolized the island's trade. In the early fourteenth century they also took over most of the trade across the North Sea; by 1330 Scandinavian merchants were virtually excluded from trade with England, although English merchants fared better.

The fourteenth-century customs accounts from English ports and Lübeck make it possible to study Scandinavia's overseas trade in some detail (C. Weibull; Nedkvitne 1977). They show that at the beginning of that century by far the most important Scandinavian export was fish, dried or salted. At least 4,000 tons of dried cod from north Norway was shipped abroad each year, and accounted for 82 percent of all Norwegian imports to England between 1303 and 1311. At the end of the century, after the Black Death, the quantity exported was much smaller, but it fetched higher prices. It was not until the sixteenth century that Norway exported as much dried cod as it did in the early fourteenth century. In the 1390s some 300,000 barrels of salt herring were being distributed each year from the Öresund fishery, and it is unlikely that less was being produced before the Black Death. The English customs accounts show that substantial quantities of oil were imported (7 percent between 1303 and 1311). This oil probably came mostly from cod livers, herring, seals, and whales and was used mainly for lighting and for treating leather. Next in value was timber (4 percent) and skins, mostly goat and sheep (3 percent). The remaining 1 percent consisted of small quantities of a wide range of goods including butter, falcons, whetstones, tar, furs, and *wadmal*. Apart from salt herring from Öresund, the Danes exported relatively little to England. Their main markets were in the Low Countries, Lübeck, and other German towns, and their exports consisted mainly of butter, cattle, hides, and horses. Danish exports to Lübeck and other Baltic towns included some things that they had themselves imported, notably cloth, which they could have acquired in direct trade with England or Flanders, or indirectly in the Skåne Fair. At the end of the Middle Ages the main Swedish exports were iron, copper, butter, and skins. Most were shipped from Stockholm, but other ports on the east coast had a share; for the western parts of the kingdom the most convenient port was Lödöse on Göta Älv. The most important Scandinavian imports were grain (mainly rye) and flour from the Baltic, ale from Germany, salt from Lüneburg, and cloth from England or Flanders.

The customs accounts also make it possible to discover the routes taken by many ships. Lübeck's traffic with Denmark and Sweden was by means of a large number of fairly small boats, many of them making more than one round trip a year, in effect operating a shuttle service. For the voyage to the main Norwegian port at Bergen larger and more seaworthy ships were needed; there were about thirty of them at the end of the fourteenth century, and much the same two hundred years later. A few sailed directly between the two ports, but Lübeck's direct trade with Bergen was on a small scale. The normal pattern was for ships to sail from Baltic ports with grain, flour, and beer to Bergen, and then with dried cod to England or Flanders, returning to the Baltic with cloth as the main cargo.

The Black Death and Its Consequences

The situation changed dramatically following the Black Death (Nedkvitne 1983, especially chapters 2, 6). The reduction in the population in Europe had the overall effect of lowering the price of grain, but as wages increased, many people had more money to spend on what had earlier been regarded as luxuries, such as animal produce. The prices of fish, cattle, and butter in European markets were significantly higher at the end of the fourteenth century than at the beginning. Scandinavians were well placed to take advantage of this situation. Scandinavia was already Europe's main source of preserved fish, and many areas were better for pastoral farming than cultivation. In Denmark and south Sweden there was an increase of cattle farming, especially on land that was no longer cultivated.

The merchants of Lübeck and other German towns, who by then controlled most of Scandinavia's overseas trade, also profited. To take full advantage of their opportunities they organized a formal association known as the Hanseatic League, which was first mentioned in 1358. In Bergen they established a center known as the Kontor, which was given, or took, privileges and virtually monopolized the trade in stockfish. Interest in the Skåne Fair also increased. The Danish king Valdemar IV recovered Skåne from Magnus Eriksson in 1360 and conquered Gotland the following year. This expansionist policy and attempts to restrict the privileges of German merchants in the Skåne Fair led to open conflict, which ended with the defeat of the Danes, who in 1370 had to renew the privileges enjoyed by the German towns and pay compensation. Divisions between the Hanseatic towns soon weakened their position, which was further damaged by their attempt to monopolize trade in the Skåne Fair by excluding foreigners. This encouraged the Dutch and English to seek alternative sources of both dried cod and salt herring. New types of ships were developed on which the salting could take place in the North Sea fishing grounds, and the high price of salt herring made it worthwhile to import good quality salt from the Bay of Biscay. The Germans did their best to exclude the English and Dutch from Bergen, but the English began to import dried cod from Iceland instead.

The Hanse towns were not even able to maintain their domination of trade in the Baltic. The Prussian towns were willing to supply Dutch merchants with rye despite the objections of Lübeck and its close allies. The supply of squirrel skins from Novgorod also declined, a result of overexploitation. What is more, such huge numbers had been exported that during the fifteenth century they were no longer a mark of prestige. The rich then wanted other furs, such as sable, that came from other parts of Russia. In 1494 the Hanse Kontor in Novgorod was closed by the prince of Moscow, who had recently conquered the republic. The Kontor in Bruges lasted longer, but the Hanse merchants faced growing competition from the Zuider Zee towns and their herring fisheries, and by 1500 Lübeck's trade was largely limited to direct traffic between Scandinavia and Germany.

In the late Middle Ages there were three economies in Scandinavia. The Danes, who lived in the most fertile part, had a surplus that they could sell in north German markets, which most Danes could easily reach overland or by a short sea crossing. They were also able to take advantage of the herring fisheries in Öresund and, in the fifteenth century, in Limfjord. These attracted foreign merchants who provided the Danes with a great variety of wares. Within Denmark there was an active economy in which coins were commonly used (Poulsen; Jensen). Many towns, even though most were small, provided a network of markets, held weekly or more frequently, within easy reach of all Danes.

Most Norwegians and Swedes, in contrast, had a subsistence economy, and after paying rent, tax, and tithe they had little left over with which to buy the necessities they could not produce themselves. In Norway the buying and selling that did happen was mostly in seasonal fairs; few Norwegians could reach an urban market in a day.

Norway and Sweden did produce some goods that fetched high prices in foreign markets. As a result those who lived along the coast of north Norway and in the mining districts of Sweden prospered; simple fishermen and miners as well as magnates and prelates benefited from this international commerce.

Remarkable evidence of this is provided by an account written by Pietro Querini, a Venetian nobleman, of a disastrous voyage in 1431 (Helland, 865–908). His ship, bound for Flanders with a cargo from Cyprus, was caught in a violent and prolonged storm that forced the crew and passengers to abandon ship for two boats. Only Pietro's boat survived, stranded on an uninhabited island at the tip of the Lofoten chain. After a while he and ten survivors were rescued by fishermen living on the nearby island of Röst, where the Italians stayed for over three months until they were able to sail south with the year's harvest of dried fish. Pietro's description of life on Röst gives an extraordinary, perhaps unique, glimpse of the life of ordinary Scandinavians in the fifteenth century, albeit seen through the eyes of a sophisticated Italian aristocrat with the help of the island's priest, a Dominican, who knew Latin and was Pietro's host and interpreter.

Pietro gives a great deal of fascinating information. There were 120 inhabitants on the island, which had an area of only 1.4 square miles. They lived by fishing cod and halibut, and took the wind-dried cod—stockfish—to Bergen, a thousand miles south, every May. There they exchanged it for cloth from London and elsewhere, firewood, salt, spices, rye to make bread, and ale to supplement a diet of fish, eggs of seabirds, butter, fresh milk (each family had four to six small cows), and some meat. Thanks to their key role in the international fish trade, they had a higher standard of living than most of their contemporaries in Europe, although they had no coins and used dried fish as currency.

Lübeck's virtual monopoly of this trade could cause problems, as Pietro discovered when, approaching Trondheim, he learned that the boats could not continue their voyage to Bergen because of war between the Germans and Erik of Pomerania. They made their way overland to seek the help of a fellow Venetian, Giovanni Franco, who held the castle and territory of

Stegeborg, on the Baltic coast of Östergötland, as a fief from King Erik. They were well received and eventually, after visiting Vadstena, made their way home via Lödöse, where Giovanni had a house. Lübeck's monopoly was indeed directly responsible for destroying the Kalmar Union. The war that prevented Pietro from reaching Bergen also prevented the miners of Sweden from exporting their iron and copper, which not only caused Engelbrekt's rebellion in 1434 but gave it sufficient force to undermine Erik of Pomerania's authority and end his reign.

8

Family and Inheritance

A widely held interpretation of early Scandinavian society has been that, like other Germanic societies, it was based on clans (*ätter*), in the sense of descent groups that were responsible for many of the functions that were later taken over by kings and the church, an encroachment that the clans are supposed to have vigorously resisted. This view of Scandinavian society is repeated in modern textbooks and has been widely disseminated by Perry Anderson in his very popular *Passages from Antiquity to Feudalism* (107–8, 176–77). There is, however, no evidence for such well defined descent groups in Scandinavia; belief in their existence largely depends on interpreting the provincial laws as reflecting such a clan society in the last stages of dissolution. Some provisions in these laws have been taken to be relics of a time when rights and obligations were matters not for individuals but for the clan, which is supposed at some time to have owned land collectively and been collectively responsible for protecting its members. In the absence of any superior authority, conflicts between members of different clans are supposed to have been resolved (or not) by blood feud; if an individual was dishonored, injured, or killed, the clan took revenge on the clan of the wrongdoer.

For such a society to function each clan would have to be a well-defined, distinct group, which in turn requires that descent was traced from either fathers or mothers. The Scandinavian clans are supposed to have been patrilineal; upon marriage, a woman left her own clan and joined that of her husband. As a consequence, women are supposed to have had no right to inherit land; otherwise clans could not have had permanent rights over their own land. The existence of such a society in Scandinavia cannot be proved at any time. The laws that have been taken to show its transformation do nothing of the sort. The rules in question deal with three topics:

inheritance rights, birth rights, and the right to take revenge and to receive compensation.[1]

The belief that Scandinavian kinship systems were originally patrilinear has been based on the medieval rules of inheritance, which have been interpreted as always favoring men. They do not. On the contrary they show that for purposes of inheritance kinship was traced through both sexes, and they all recognize that women have a right, if limited, to inherit. Men are not always given priority in the order of inheritance claims. It is true that daughters are given a weaker claim than their brothers, but they have priority over their uncles and grandfather. What is more, the laws provide for reverse inheritance, when a surviving parent inherits from a child. In that way a widow could acquire her husband's inherited land, which would after her death pass to *her* heirs, and thus to a different family (Winberg, 24–27; B. Sawyer 1991b).

The right of relatives to buy back land that they should have inherited but that had been alienated has been interpreted as a survival from the time land was owned collectively by a descent group. In fact, the medieval laws on this *bördsrätt* were not intended to keep land within a patrilinear clan. On the contrary, they assume a bilateral kinship system, and *bördsrätt* therefore facilitated the transfer of land from one family to another. If, for example, a father sold land to a male relative, his daughters, being closer in succession, had a right to buy it back (Winberg, 25).

The laws on the rights of relatives to take revenge after a killing and to receive compensation cannot be interpreted as evidence for the collective responsibility of a clan. They do not imply a right to take revenge collectively but allow the closest heir to refuse compensation and, instead, to have the wrongdoer outlawed. Laws prescribing how responsibility for the payment of compensation, or *wergeld*, should be distributed among the relatives of a killer (and similar rules governing its distribution among the victim's relatives) have been taken as evidence that revenge or compensation was originally a matter for the collective action of the clan. These detailed tariffs were, rather, a response to the growing power of kings and their intervention in lawmaking. When a king confiscated the property of a killer as a penalty, any compensation to the victim's family would have had to be paid by the killer's kin. The legal responsibility of a killer's family was a way of ensuring that when the king imposed a heavy personal penalty on a killer, the victim's family could still hope to be compensated (Bagge 1989a).

Thus the earliest Scandinavian laws do not show a patrilinear clan society in dissolution. If such a society ever existed in Scandinavia, which is extremely doubtful, it had disappeared long before these laws began to be compiled in the twelfth century. The runic inscriptions of the tenth and eleventh centuries confirm this conclusion, for they show that society then consisted of nuclear families. Most rune-stones were erected in memory of people by their closest relatives—by children for their parents, by siblings or spouses for each other. They show that the kinship system was then bilateral; men sponsor memorials to their relatives by marriage, including brothers-in-law and mothers-in-law (*SR*, Uppland, nos. 897, 914b). Many inscriptions name the wife, mother, or daughter of a dead man, and in some, a husband, when commemorating his wife, named her father and occasionally even her grandfather. The fundamentally bilateral character of kinship is further underlined by the words used in inscriptions for some relatives; an uncle, for example, is either mother-brother or father-brother.

The Early Middle Ages

The inscriptions that explicitly deal with property and inheritance clearly show that property rights were individual and that women were entitled to inherit from their father and from their children. Relatively few inscriptions are so explicit, but many others can cast light on the ownership of property and inheritance rights in the early Middle Ages. Because most inscriptions were sponsored by the heirs (or their guardians) of the person being commemorated, a systematic study of all inscriptions can yield information about customs of inheritance among those who sponsored runic monuments in tenth- and eleventh-century Scandinavia. They suggest that daughters did not inherit from their father if sons, brothers, or parents of their father were still alive, but that they inherited before his more remote kinsmen. In many areas mothers appear to have had a prominent place in the order of inheritance, immediately after sons and the father. Customs were apparently not the same in all regions. In Denmark, Norway, Småland, and Gotland, women in general seem to come very low in the order of inheritance, but in Uppland there are indications that they could inherit *together with men*, for example daughters together with sons, sisters with brothers (B. Sawyer 1988).

There is no way of discovering the antiquity of the inheritance customs implied by the rune-stones. They were erected at a time of fundamental change. The growth of royal authority and the establishment of the church possibly, even probably, influenced inheritance customs and property rights. The church vigorously supported the right of women to inherit and dispose of property. By promising eternal bliss and threatening eternal damnation churchmen encouraged everybody, women as well as men, to give to pious causes "for the sake of their souls." That the inheritance customs indicated by the runic inscriptions may have been to some extent a result of such teaching is no more than a possibility. It is certain, however, that the runic inscriptions reflect a society with bilateral kinship and nuclear families much like those in modern times.

The Family

The inscriptions show that in eleventh-century Scandinavia a woman did not sever all links with her own family when she married. In the new family she and her husband created, they both, together with their children, had property rights or expectations. There is no proof that wives owned a share of the household property at that time as they did later, but it does seem likely that they did. That many inscriptions were sponsored by widows, either on their own or together with other members of the family, suggests that as wives they had a leading role in their families, most probably as co-owners. With some regional exceptions it seems to have been the widow's task to sponsor her husband's memorial if his sons, brothers, or father did not survive him, or if his sons were too young. In such a situation the widow apparently took over leadership of the household, guardianship of minors, and control of the property, suggesting that she had well-defined rights as co-owner when her husband was alive. The many memorials sponsored jointly by a widow and sons confirm the nuclear character of families and possibly imply that in those families the inheritance had not yet been divided among the heirs.

Marriage

The inscriptions also show that families were formed by monogamous marriages. A man may have had relationships, and children, with several women, but when he died, only one wife was acknowledged. We do not know how couples were married, but there is no doubt that then, as later, marriage was based on a contract between their families. Reciprocally binding agreements were needed, especially between wealthy families, for reverse inheritance could result in the transfer of large estates from one family to another. Contracted marriages were not the only form of partnership. Concubinage, or informal relationships without legal consequences, was common later, and, although the inscriptions do not provide any evidence for the custom, some eleventh-century rulers—for example, Sven Estridsson—had concubines, and there is no doubt that it was a common practice. Concubinage should not be confused with brief relationships; a concubine was a permanent, or at least long-term, partner of a man, and their children could, if he acknowledged them, inherit from him. In the higher levels of society a man could hope to ensure that he would have one or more sons to survive him by having a concubine as well as a legal wife; in lower levels such informal relationships may have been the normal form of partnership between men and women. There is nothing to suggest that these relationships were considered improper at any social level before the church condemned them, only approving of relationships that met its requirements for a Christian marriage. Church law not only required monogamy and faithfulness, it prohibited divorce and forbade marriage between people related within seven (later four) degrees of kinship.

The Size of Families

Runic inscriptions provide some information about the size and composition of families in parts of eastern Sweden (Uppland, Södermanland, Öland, and Blekinge) where men and women jointly acted as sponsors. Inscriptions with more than three or four children are rare, but as a high rate of infant mortality can be assumed, many more children must have been born. Daughters are significantly fewer than sons. In Uppland inscriptions with both, the ratio of sons to daughters is 3:2. This circumstance cannot be explained by the exclusion of married daughters, for they are sometimes named. It was probably the result of a deliberate attempt to control the size of the population by limiting the number of girls who were allowed to survive (see "Demography" in chapter 2).

Christian missionaries objected to this infanticide, and in Iceland it was prohibited soon after conversion. Christianity was certainly responsible for many other changes that affected families. Too little is known about the pre-Christian situation to say much about the immediate impact of the new religion. The runic inscriptions, most of which are Christian, may give some clues to the early stages of transition, at least in the upper levels of society. They may give a misleading impression of circumstances in general; only a small number of Scandinavians were rich or Christian. Later evidence does show how many Scandinavians reacted to and resisted the policy of the church on families, inheritance, and property in the twelfth and thirteenth centuries. The struggle between secular and ecclesiastical interests has left many traces, and the thirteenth-century laws show that the church was then still meeting determined resistance.

Marriage and the Church

Marriage and Concubinage

The only form of cohabitation between men and women accepted by the church was Christian marriage. Permanent and monogamous concubinage based on the consent of both parties was classified as marriage if the partners were not too closely related. Such customary marriages were treated like more formally contracted marriages; they were all subject to church law, which prohibited divorce and condemned extramarital relationships as sinful. Only children born in wedlock could inherit, and the distinction drawn between legitimate and illegitimate children caused many difficulties that were particularly serious when the children in question were the sons of kings. Because several Danish and Norwegian kings were sons of concubines, the church had great difficulty in gaining acceptance of its demand that kings should be legitimate. The Norwegian succession law of 1163, which required the successor to be legitimate, was not followed. It was not until 1240 that the principle was accepted, and illegitimate sons were not completely excluded from the order of succession as laid down in 1260. An illegitimate son could be accepted as an heir if his father formally acknowledged him, but only on condition that his parents were not related more closely than church law permitted.

Incest

Until 1215 the limit of kinship set by the church within which marriage was not allowed was the seventh degree. As the first degree, according to the church, covered siblings, and the second degree covered cousins, the seventh extended to a very large group including distant kin. It was clearly unworkable in practice, and the limit was therefore reduced in 1215 to the fourth degree, meaning that marriage with third cousins was not allowed without special dispensation. The prohibition against marriage with relatives is found in most Scandinavian laws, but not in the Danish law of 1241, which has been taken to show that in Denmark marriage was already by then subject to ecclesiastical law, not to the traditional secular jurisdiction.

Although divorce was not allowed in church law, marriages between people who were too closely related were considered invalid and could therefore be annulled. According to Adam of Bremen this was the reason the Danish king Sven Estridsen parted from his wife, after pressure from

Archbishop Adalbert. Adam exaggerated Sven's respect for church law; he had at least fourteen sons by various mothers, and five of them were recognized in succession as kings by the Danes. The break was almost certainly made for political reasons. This law was, in effect, a convenient means of circumventing the church prohibition of divorce, and it could be used as a weapon in political disputes. So, for example, in 1288 the Swedish king Magnus had the children of his opponent Folke Algotsson declared illegitimate on the grounds that their parents were too closely related and had married without dispensation. That decision was, however, reversed after appeal to the pope (*KHL*, s.v. "Skyldskap").

Clerical Marriage

The attempt to impose Christian standards of marriage was hampered by the fact that many priests were married or had concubines. In early medieval Scandinavia married priests were common, and several Icelandic bishops were married, the last being Magnus of Skálholt, who died in 1237. By then married clergy were unusual, but many priests continued to have concubines. Until the Reformation zealous bishops and church councils repeatedly demanded, but with little effect, that priests should be celibate, and many lower clergy serving rural churches in all parts of Scandinavia had concubines who bore them children. The many requests for permission to ordain the sons of priests show that the practice was widespread. Priests themselves were supposed to be legitimate, but dispensation was frequently requested, often for the sons of priests. In 1346, for example, the archbishop of Nidaros asked for papal permission to ordain forty illegitimate men, thirty of whom were priests' sons. It was not only the lower clergy who had concubines and children; so too did canons of Nidaros. Bishops normally did not, but many of them separated from their concubines when they were promoted. At least two thirteenth-century archbishops of Nidaros had sons, and so too did the last pre-Reformation bishop of Iceland.[2]

The laity were not united in their attitude to clerical celibacy. Some approved, partly in the belief that the prayers of a celibate priest were more effective, but also because church endowments were safer in the hands of such men; there was a risk that priests with children might try to provide them with land belonging to the church. Others claimed to be against it, in part, it was said, to save their own wives and daughters from priests "who in the morning honored the Virgin Mary, but at night embraced Venus" (Skyum-Nielsen 1971, 51). These different standpoints were dramatically demonstrated in twelfth-century Denmark. In 1123 a revolt in the diocese of Roskilde, led by a magnate of Sjælland, Peter Bodilsen, was directed in particular against married priests. The opposite attitude was expressed by the Scanian landowners who revolted in 1180, mainly against the policy of king and archbishop, but according to Saxo Grammaticus one of their demands was that priests should be married (Saxo 15.13).

Christian Marriage

It is not surprising that church reformers found it difficult to demand that the laity keep to the Christian standard of marriage, avoiding incest and limiting themselves to one wife. Only the relatively rich could afford both a wife and a concubine, and such men were not as susceptible to clerical pressure as were less powerful people. One famous example is the unsuccessful attempt of Thorlak, bishop of Skálholt, to force Jón Loftsson, a leading Icelandic chieftain, to separate from the concubine he had in addition to his legitimate wife. The concubine was Thorlak's own sister, Ragnheid, who bore two of Jón's sons, one of whom, Pall, was Thorlak's successor as bishop of Skálholt (*KHL*, s.v. "Slegfred").

Tensions also developed over the definition of a valid marriage. Canon law required a clerical blessing, but a marriage ceremony in church was not necessary until after the Reformation. In 1215 it was decided that a church ceremony could only be held after the publication of banns, and after that date marriages celebrated without banns were considered clandestine, even if the couple had been blessed by a priest. A penalty could be imposed for this neglect, but such marriages were still valid. What constituted a marriage was the voluntary consent of both partners and the absence of impediments such as too close kinship between them, or one of them already being married. When the union was made, the marriage was a fact and could not be ended, although it could be annulled if it could be proved unconsummated.

The ecclesiastical concept of marriage as a voluntary and indissoluble union of two individuals contrasted with the prevailing secular view that it was above all an alliance between two families, based on an economic agreement that could be canceled. This secular attitude is found in the Scandinavian laws, in which the role of the family in negotiating marriage contracts is generally emphasized, in several of them at the cost of the woman's consent; Norwegian and Icelandic law even allowed divorce. Fidelity was required only from a wife; there is no mention of banns or church ceremonies. Instead, detailed regulations concern the reciprocal economic obligations of the two parties.

Thus, in Scandinavian laws, marriage is based on an economic agreement between the families of the married couple. The initiative is assumed to come from the man, who, either in person or through a negotiator, approached the woman's guardian, normally her father, otherwise her closest kinsman. If the guardian accepted the proposal, a formal betrothal was arranged, where, in the presence of witnesses, the size of the dowry (the contribution made by the woman's family) and of the dower (the contribution made by the man's family) was agreed. According to some laws, the consent of the woman was also necessary; in the Law of Jutland of 1241 it was required only if the guardian were someone other than her father, brother, or son. A valid marriage was constituted by the betrothal and the wedding, when the bride was formally given away, followed by the bedding, an act symbolizing the union, by which the woman gained her right to a share of the uninherited property of the couple, commonly a third.

All Danish and Swedish provincial laws except that of Gotland assume that married couples have movable wealth and land that was not inherited and was owned jointly, but at the husband's disposal. This common property was called *fællig* in Denmark, *félag* in Norway. It has been convincingly argued that *fællig/félag* was a novelty introduced to compensate for the indissolubility of marriage. The permanence of marriage was not accepted everywhere; west Scandinavian provincial laws allowed divorce and gave the woman the right to keep both dowry and dower if she was blameless. In Norway and Iceland the spouses owned their property separately, unless it had been agreed to create a *félag*. In the Gulating law the husband could demand a *félag*, provided that the couple had heirs in common who consented to its creation. By the end of the thirteenth century divorce was no longer allowed in Norway and Iceland, but even then the property of married couples had to be regulated by special agreements. In time *félag* became general, but in Norway and Sweden it included just husband and wife; only in Denmark did it include the children.

Although Scandinavian laws were strongly influenced by canon law, the church's rules were not fully accepted and on some matters seem to have been deliberately rejected. The Scandinavian laws should, therefore, be seen as the result of compromises between ecclesiastical and secular interests. The resistance to canon law is also reflected in other sources (Nors; B. Sawyer 1990).

Consent: A Contentious Issue

From a secular point of view it was out of the question that a decision to marry could be made by the couple themselves. In the higher ranks of society especially, marriage was a family concern with far-reaching consequences. By means of marriage contracts magnates and other landowners could build up networks of alliances, in which economic and political considerations were significant. It was in the interest of the families involved that the marriages by which such alliances were formed, or confirmed, should function, and it is therefore reasonable to suppose that some consideration was commonly given to the attitudes of the future couple; even though a woman's consent was not necessary, if her active opposition to a match was disregarded, there could well be problems later.

The emphasis of the church on the voluntary character of marriage with consent as the sole requirement posed a serious threat to the existing social order. The demand that the woman's wishes should be respected was particularly disturbing. If a daughter could decide whom to marry, her father and family lost the opportunity of using her marriage as a means of advancing their interests. What was worse, she might marry someone unsuitable, possibly from a hostile family. One means of bringing pressure to bear was that a woman who married against the wishes of her guardian could be disinherited. The church's insistence on consent also meant that a daughter could cause a problem by refusing to marry the man chosen for her. To avoid that possibility many marriage agreements were made while the daughter was too young to know her own mind. This was often done in the upper strata of society, especially in royal families. For example, Ingeborg, daughter of the Norwegian king Håkon V, was betrothed to Duke Erik when she was one year old, and the marriage took place when she was eleven. She disposed of her own daughter Eufemia in the same way by betrothing her at the age of four to the three-year-old Albrekt of Mecklenburg.

The lack of consent could be used to annul a marriage. A good example is described in *Sverris Saga*. During the 1180s Cecilia Sigurdsdotter left her husband, Folkvid, in Värmland and took refuge with her brother, King Sverri. When, with her brother's consent, she married a Norwegian magnate, Archbishop Øystein refused to allow it and ordered her to return to Folkvid. Cecilia claimed that she had been given to him against her own wish and had not known what to do about it until her brother came to Norway. The truth of Cecilia's claim was confirmed by witnesses, and Øystein was forced to annul that marriage and approve the second (Jochens 1986a, 142).

Several episodes in sagas turn on the right of a woman to make up her own mind, even against the interest of her family. According to the legendary saga of Saint Olav, the Swedish king Olof Skötkonung agreed to the marriage of his daughter Ingegerd to the Norwegian king Olav but changed his mind and arranged her marriage to a Russian prince instead.

Her sister Astrid, on Ingegerd's advice, then married the Norwegian king without her father's consent. In this way Olav revenged the insult he had suffered by the Swedish king's breach of promise.

Håkon's Saga, written at about the same time, but about events 250 years later, describes Håkon's efforts to arrange a marriage between his son Magnus and Ingeborg, daughter of the Danish king Erik Plovpenning (see the appendix to this chapter). Eventually Ingeborg's closest relative, Margaret Sambiria, gave her consent but later changed her mind and for safety confined Ingeborg in a nunnery. The Norwegians, who knew that the Swedes were planning a marriage alliance with the Danish royal family, sent Håkon, bishop of Oslo, as envoy to the nunnery. He admonished Ingeborg to decide for herself about her own marriage, to trust God and King Håkon. Ingeborg, having been promised rich bridal equipment, is said to have let herself be persuaded.

These episodes, among others, in thirteenth-century sagas suggest that women's consent to marriage was a live issue at that time, and they illustrate ways in which it could be used for political purposes. The demand for consent was perceived for what it was, a means of manipulation. It emancipated neither daughters nor sons from psychological or social pressure, and there is no reason to believe that the traditional pattern of marriages arranged by families was seriously disturbed. There are, on the other hand, clear indications that the attempt to interfere with customary practice by not only requiring consent but treating it as all that was necessary met with deep disapproval. Toward the end of the twelfth century the church began to press its demands seriously, and after that the issue of consent is given a significant place in both laws and literature.

Some authors, notably Saxo Grammaticus and Snorri Sturluson, even imply disapproval of church policy on this matter. In both *Gesta Danorum* and *Heimskringla* most girls are married without being consulted, and, especially when the proposer is a king or magnate, women are given an entirely passive role. The examples of women who were consulted only show that their wishes were of no account, or that the consequences of allowing them to have their own way were disastrous.

In the saga of Olav Tryggvason Snorri describes how Olav met stiff resistance at the Gulating until he agreed to make some gesture in return for the support of the people. When the *thingmen* suggested marriage between their leader, Erling Skjalgsson, and Olav's sister Astrid, the king consented on condition that his sister answer for herself. Astrid had no wish to marry someone so much beneath her and preferred to wait for a better proposal. Olav responded by plucking all the feathers from a hawk belonging to his sister and then sending the naked bird back to her. Astrid took the hint and agreed to accept his decision about the marriage (Snorri Sturluson, "Olav Tryggvason's Saga," chaps. 55–57).

In *Gesta Danorum* Saxo offers many examples showing how untrustworthy women's judgment is. He was probably commissioned, among other things, to give the ecclesiastical demand for consent a historical basis. That is suggested by his assertion that "it was ancient custom to allow women of marriageable age to choose their husbands" (10.9) and that this custom was made law by King Frode, who was supposed to have ruled the Danes when Christ was born. It is significant, however, that his text clearly implies disapproval of this custom. Of the 175 women who figure in his work, only 14 are said to have been consulted about their marriages; those who refused their consent were overruled or punished, while those who tried to make their own choices either failed or suffered disaster. The implication is underlined by the fact that only in the pagan—imperfect—period of Denmark's history are women said to have had any influence; in the Christian period they are generally described as passive and obedient tools of their men (Strand).

In the Icelandic family sagas the message is the same; some marriages to which women explicitly consented are total failures, while marriages arranged without consulting them last. Because, however, all marriages arranged *contrary* to a woman's will had catastrophic consequences, it can be concluded that, even if a woman's consent was not considered necessary, it was still unwise to disregard her strong protests (Frank 1973, 477). This, together with common sense, suggests that, in practice, some account of a woman's wishes was normally taken both before and after the introduction of the canon law on consent. Why, then, did the thirteenth-century authors make consent such an issue, and why did it meet with such stiff resistance?

The answer is, in part, that consent was not only necessary but was also *sufficient* for a valid marriage, and this could be a serious setback for the head of a family planning an alliance in his own interest. Even though a woman who married against her family's will could be disinherited, she was considered a wasted asset if the marriage could not be annulled in some way. Another reason for the reaction to the law on consent was that it meant that a woman who chose to become a nun could not be forced to marry, and it can safely be assumed that the church fully supported women whose families objected to them taking vows—or simply deciding to lead a chaste life. It is therefore significant that Saxo and Snorri wrote at a time when many nunneries were being founded in Scandinavia. Women who entered a nunnery took property with them, thus diminishing the amount that their fellow heirs could hope to inherit. This threat to family property may well have been a major factor in the contemporary objections to the independence of women and lifelong chastity (B. Sawyer 1990).

Women who did not wish to marry could in this way turn to the church for help. This way of escape was entirely new. So too was the right of appeal that Danish law gave women who wanted to marry against the wishes of their families. According to Danish law a girl was under the guardianship of her father until she married, but if her guardian was someone else, she could in certain cases turn to the king. According to the Law of Jutland brothers could not stop a sister over the age of eighteen from marrying, and she could "demand herself married away" at a *thing*. A medieval Danish folk song describes a woman going to a royal *thing* to seek help against her uncle who administers and mismanages her patrimonial inheritance. Because he has abused his position as guardian, the girl delivers herself with all her property to the king, who, at her request, marries her to one of his men, with the paternal inheritance as dowry. This illustrates how royal authority, as well as the church, could undermine the influence families had over their women (Blom 1990).

Marriage and Alliances

The demand of the church to have ultimate jurisdiction in marriage questions, its rules about impediments to marriage, and its prohibition of divorce were resisted throughout Europe, but opposition seems to have been even firmer in Scandinavia. This may have been partly because Christian values and ideals had not had so long to take root, but a more important factor appears to have been that in Scandinavia this interference in family affairs had especially serious consequences. In Denmark and Sweden especially magnates had exceptional power even in the reigns of capable rulers. To maintain their leading role they depended not only on their own resources but also on networks of alliance that were often created or reinforced by marriage. The custom of partible inheritance gave marriage alliances even greater significance than they had in other parts of Europe where primogeniture was common, especially among the aristocracy. It was therefore important for Scandinavian magnates and other landowners to retain their influence in arranging the marriages of their children.

The importance of marriage in the struggle for power in Scandinavian society is vividly illustrated by the career of Snorri Sturluson and his family, the Sturlungs, who gained control of a large part of Iceland in the early thirteenth century.[3] The family took its name from Sturla Thorðarson, who died in 1183. He only held one *goðorð*, with his main farm at Hvammur.

Figure 8.1. The rise of the Sturlungs.

He was defeated when he attempted to extend his power and died in 1183 leaving three sons, who by marriage alliances and negotiation rather than violence acquired bases on which they built up a concentration of power unprecedented in Iceland. The eldest, Thorð, took over Hvammur but in 1186 married Helga, daughter of Ari the Strong of Staðr in Snæfellsnes (a grandson of Ari the historian); Thorð then took over his father-in-law's farm and *goðorð*. The marriage was soon dissolved, but by marrying a rich widow Thorð was able to enlarge his power in Snæfellsnes. Sturla's second son, Sighvat, took over Hvammur after his brother, but by marrying Halldora, sister of Kolbeinn of Viðimyri, the *goði* of the Skagafjörður district, he gained a powerful ally in the north. Kolbeinn was the leader of the opposition to Bishop Guðmund of Hólar, and, after Kolbeinn was killed in 1208, Sighvat took over his role. In the next years the bishop's kinsmen in the Eyjafjörður region were outlawed and killed, and Sighvat was able to gain control of that district. In 1215 he moved to Grund near the head of the fjord.

Snorri had been sent as an infant by his father to be fostered by Jón Loftsson and was twenty years old when Jón died in 1197. Soon afterward, by marrying Herdis Bessadottir, he acquired the farm of Borg and the associated *goðorð*. He then obtained, by gift and purchase, most of the *goðorð* in that area, and as a result had extensive power in western Iceland, from

Hvalfjörður to Hunafjörður in the north. In 1206 he moved to Reykholt and began to play a leading role in Icelandic politics. He was elected lawman in 1215, went to Norway, and returned in 1220. By then he and his brothers were the most powerful chieftains in northwest Iceland. In 1222 he was again elected lawman and soon afterward married the richest woman in Iceland, Hallveig Ormsdottir of Breiðabolstaður in the south, who had been widowed in 1221. In this way he gained control of the Rangar district and many valuable farms in different parts of Iceland, including Bessastaðir, later the residence of the Norwegian (later Danish) king's governor (*hirðstjóri*) and now of Iceland's president. Snorri attempted to extend his power further by the marriages he arranged for his three daughters with some of the few remaining major Icelandic chieftains. Such an extension of power, especially in Iceland, naturally excited jealousy and incited some people to look for ways of checking Snorri's dominance. What followed is a good illustration of the limitations of such marriage alliances. Two of his sons-in-law divorced their wives, and one of them, Gizur Thorvaldsson, as a retainer of the Norwegian king, was commissioned to arrest Snorri and take him to Norway. He joined forces with Hallveig's sons by her first marriage (another hazard of marriage alliances) and, taking the law into his own hands, had Snorri killed.

Inheritance

Marriages were not only used to create social and political networks; they resulted in transfers of land, sometimes on a very large scale, in the form of dower and dowry. Their size was the subject of negotiation and could vary greatly. In order to achieve an advantageous match a father could, for example, in his lifetime give away such large marriage portions that there was relatively little left for the unmarried heirs. This freedom of action was limited, however, as a result of ecclesiastical and royal demands.

The church pressed the claim that Christ should be coheir in all inheritances, but as long as people could freely dispose of their property in their lifetimes, large amounts of land could be transferred to heirs without the church having a chance to claim its share. The church also urged everyone to make gifts in alms for the sake of their souls. It was therefore important that all should have a fair share of family property, but the shares could not be finally determined until the head of the family died. When that happened any children who had been given some of the family estate when they married could either be excluded from a further share or return what they had been given to the estate so that a new and just division could be made. For such a redistribution to be fair it was desirable that the amount each heir was entitled to should be fixed legally. It was in the interest of the church that the division should, if possible, be equal—the larger the amount that could then be claimed as Christ's portion, or expected as gifts in alms. It was also in the interest of the church and secular government that all heirs should have a right to a predetermined share of their family property so that they would better be able to pay any legal penalties that might be imposed (and so that the shares of their coheirs would be protected).

Inheritance in Theory

The Scandinavian laws reflect different stages in the transition from the relatively unrestricted division of inheritances to systems in which the shares were fixed for both men and women. The change was completed in Denmark by the beginning of the thirteenth century, and in Norway later in that century. In Sweden the change is reflected in most provincial laws of the early fourteenth century but was not effective in the kingdom as a whole until the acceptance of the landlaw, issued in about 1350. Earlier there had been great variations in the way heirs and heiresses were treated. In the provincial laws of Norway, the Icelandic *Grágás*, the Older Law of Västergötland, and the Law of Dalarna, it is assumed that a daughter would be provided with dowry, but the amount depended on her guardian (and on the negotiation preceding marriage). An unmarried daughter had no legal right to inherit as long as she had brothers. These laws applied what is known as the *gradual principle*, in which inheritance rights were determined by the degree of kinship, with men having priority. In the Danish and other Swedish provincial laws daughters have a right to inherit, but only half as much as their brothers. The rules for more distant kin varied, but in general these laws applied what is known as the *parentela principle*, namely that descendants have priority over other kin.

It has generally been supposed that women benefited when they were all given a legal right to inherit. That is questionable. The laws that allowed unmarried daughters to inherit only if they had no brothers assumed that those who married received dowry, which could have been significantly larger than what was left for their younger brothers, and which they were, before the legal change, entitled to keep. The law granting daughters half a "brother's share" certainly benefited those who did not marry, but the amount that could be given as dowry was also fixed (unless a special arrangement was made with the consent of all). There was another limitation: a daughter who married without the consent of her father or guardian lost her right to her share.

Inheritance in Practice

The division of inheritances specified in the laws was not necessarily that used in practice. Other arrangements could be made with the consent of those who were involved. In order to arrange a desirable marriage alliance, a father or brothers could give more than the half a "brother's lot" prescribed in the laws, but only if the other potential heirs agreed. They were sometimes prepared to do so in order to gain a valuable ally. Late medieval Swedish diplomas (1350–1500) show that sometimes brothers gave up part of their shares so that a sister could have as much as they did. The division prescribed in the laws applied only if there was no special agreement, or if the heirs disagreed (Gunneng, 83).

The legal limitations of women's inheritance rights that existed throughout the Middle Ages give a somewhat misleading impression of reality. In practice many women were the sole heirs, some of them of great wealth. This circumstance was partly because women tended to live longer than men, and many survived not only their husbands but also, because of the high rate of infant mortality, their children. What is more, in societies that practice monogamy, about 20 percent of all couples have only girls and another 20 percent have no children at all (Goody, 44). The runic inscriptions offer many examples of sole heiresses, including some mothers who inherited from their children. Gerlög of Hillersjö, whose inscription is illustrated in figure 8.2 and whose inheritance history is shown in figure 8.3, is the most remarkable example, but there are many others (B. Sawyer 1988, 1991b). Another illustration, from the end of this period, of the key role that women played in inheritance, is the fate of the huge estate owned by Magdalena, daughter of Karl Knutsson (see fig. 9.3).

Even newborn babies could have a role in the transmission of an inheritance. The law only demanded that a child must be born alive to inherit, and if the mother died when giving birth it was a matter of great importance to determine whether the child survived its mother. A dramatic example concerns the right of Bo Jonsson (Grip) to reverse inheritance. When his first wife, Margareta Porse, died in labor in 1360, he had her body opened and took those present as witnesses that the child was still alive. Although it died soon afterward, its brief life was sufficient for the property of the dead wife to pass via the baby to its father.[4] It is, of course, impossible to say whether such an event was rare or common, but the popularity of stories about evil relatives who had wax dolls baptized in order to keep an inheritance suggests that contemporaries would not have been astonished (Dahlerup, 113).

Inheritance was one of the best ways that some people—like Bo Jonsson

Figure 8.2. The Hillersjö inscription. This runic inscription (*SR*, Uppland, no. 29) is on a rock at Hillersjö on an island in Mälaren. It is one of the most elaborate and describes a complicated series of reverse inheritances that enabled Gerlög of Hillersjö to acquire the property of three families. Photograph by Bengt A. Lundberg. © Antikvarisk-topografiska arkivet, Stockholm.

```
Germund = ¹Gerlög² = Gudrik, of Hillersjö
         |                    |
        son                   |
                              |
        Ragnfast = ¹Inga² = Erik
     of Snottsta  |
                  |
                 son
```

Figure 8.3. The inheritances of Gerlög of Hillersjö. Gerlög first married Germund, and they had a son. Germund drowned, and his son inherited his property. When the son died, that inheritance passed to Gerlög, who later married Gudrik, the owner of Hillersjö. They had several children, but only one daughter, Inga, survived; she married Ragnfast, the owner of Snottsta, about nineteen miles northeast of Hillersjö. They had a son, who inherited Snottsta when Ragnfast died, and on his death Inga inherited from him. She also inherited from her father. When Inga died, her mother, Gerlög, inherited all she owned. Four rune-stones put up by Inga at Snottsta confirm and supplement the information in the Hillersjö inscription (*SR*, Uppland nos. 329–32).

(Grip)—acquired large estates or greatly increased them in a relatively short time; magnates with five hundred or more tenants were not uncommon in Denmark and Sweden in the late Middle Ages. The rules of inheritance could, however, have the opposite result and lead to the breakup of a large estate after one generation. Partible inheritance was the universal custom; the estate of a dead man or woman was divided between all the heirs with a legitimate claim. This could be a complicated matter and take a long time. The legal consequences of inheritance were, indeed, one of the main concerns of the aristocracy. The division of the estate of the Danish magnate Olof Axelsson (Tott) is a good illustration of the complications and delays that could, and often did, occur. The division of his cash fortune, excluding the land, took twenty years. This money was part of the jointly owned estate in which the widow, two sons, and five daughters had shares. Because in Denmark a widow inherited a son's share, which was double that of a daughter, the whole sum was divided into eleven equal parts, each amounting to 545.5 marks—one part for each daughter and two for each son and the widow. After one of the daughters died, her share was divided into ten parts and allocated to the surviving heirs, and when one of the sons died his double share was divided into eight parts and allocated similarly. The process was repeated when yet another daughter died, but after the death of the last son, the mother and three surviving daughters took equal shares, a quarter each (Dahlerup, 113–14).

It was almost impossible for a large estate to survive if there were many male heirs, and during the later Middle Ages numerous families were reduced from the high to the low aristocracy, or gentry. Some estates were preserved for several generations by careful planning and luck. One that survived for over 150 years was created toward the end of the thirteenth century by the marriage of Bjarne Erlingsson of Bjarköy in north Norway and Margareta Niklasdotter, sole heiress of Giske. This estate amounted to about 250 farms, approximately 10 percent of all land held by the secular Norwegian aristocracy at that time. It was inherited by Bjarne's nephew, Erling Vidkunnsson, whose daughter married the owner of Sörum in Romerike and seventy-eight other farms, thus making the estate even larger. It passed through three generations of daughters before being inherited by Sigurd Jonsson, who became regent in 1439. When his only son, Hans, died in 1466, the division of the inheritance took twenty-four years, and much of the Bjarköy, Giske, and Sörum property was inherited by Alf Knutsson, father of Knut who was killed in 1502 (Bagge and Mykland, 34–35).

Although the Scandinavian aristocracy, unlike that in most of western Europe, did not practice primogeniture, efforts were made to ensure that the eldest son inherited the main residence or traditional center of his family property. Some families could therefore be identified by their main residences (for example, Bjarköy or Sörum). In general the better land was reserved for sons. The integrity of a family property could be preserved for a while by postponing the division. In most cases it would then be managed by the eldest son. Alternatively, one heir, who would normally be the eldest son, could buy out the other heirs with money obtained by selling or mortgaging part of the property, but that was not a realistic solution for estates as large as Bjarköy and Giske. In practice smaller inheritances might therefore be managed, if not entirely owned, by the eldest son.

Although partible inheritance ensured the regular redistribution of property, the equal weight given to maternal and paternal kinship prevented the development of lineages of the kind familiar in other parts of Europe. There were no surnames; an individual was identified as the son or daughter normally of their father but sometimes of their mother. Early in the thirteenth century families began to be identified by their heraldic devices, such as Night and Day (*Natt och Dag*, referring to their black-and-white shield) or *Vasa*, "sheaf." It was not unusual for a man to adopt his mother's arms if she was considered to have higher status than his father, and these were often retained by his descendants.

Conclusion

The Scandinavian kinship system, from the earliest stage it can be traced in the rune-stones, was bilateral, and, thanks to the custom of reverse inheritance, much land was transferred from one family to another. But where a line of descent was unbroken, through both men and women, inheritance could be claimed from even distant ancestors. Some rune-stones name forefathers or foremothers; one or two stones name them for several generations. Because kinship was counted through both sexes, it is possible to speak of a cognatic lineage system, the existence of which has long been ignored—even denied—by many social anthropologists. The explanation is that cognatic lineages have seemed to have been so complicated and confusing that they have generally been considered characteristic of unilinear systems in dissolution. In fact, in many cognatic societies descent lines and kindreds exist side by side, each serving different purposes (Murray 1983, 3–7, 27–30, 111). In these, as in medieval Scandinavia, the kindred could be used for reciprocal help and revenge, and bilineal (cognatic) descent could be used to support claims to property, status, and other rights, including titles of rank and heraldic devices.

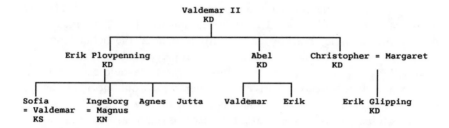

Figure 8.4. The daughters and brothers of Erik Plovpenning (KD = King of Denmark; KN = King of Norway; KS = King of Sweden).

There is nothing to support the belief that in Scandinavia an original, patrilinear system, supposedly common to all Germanic peoples, was changed into a bilateral system. The transition is, on the contrary, in the opposite direction, beginning in some of the aristocracies of western Europe in the eleventh century and observable in Scandinavia five hundred years later.

Appendix: The Daughters of Erik Plovpenning

The principle of primogeniture influenced the choice of Scandinavian kings, but it was not always accepted without question. The issue became acute in Denmark when Valdemar II died in 1241, leaving three legitimate sons, Erik, Abel, and Christopher. The Danes normally chose the eldest son of the dead king as his successor, and that happened in 1241. Erik had, in fact, been designated and crowned as Valdemar's successor in 1232. He was soon challenged by his brothers, and in 1250 he was killed by Abel's men, leaving four daughters but no son. The Danes then accepted Abel despite suspicions about his complicity in the murder. Abel's reign was short; he was killed campaigning against the Frisians in 1252. He had two sons, but in 1252 the elder was a prisoner of the archbishop of Cologne, and Abel's brother, Christopher, was proclaimed king. Christopher died in 1259 and was succeeded by his young son, Erik Glipping. For almost a century Danish politics was dominated by the rival claims of the descendants of Abel and Christopher. The claims of Erik's daughters were an additional complication. Their fate illustrates very well many of the issues discussed in this chapter.

Valdemar II's extensive properties were divided among his sons, and, as heirs to their father's third share, Erik's daughters—Sofia, Ingeborg,

Agnes, and Jutta—were very attractive as marriage partners who might also be the source of future claims to the Danish throne (fig. 8.4).[5] Two of them were already betrothed when Christopher died. He had needed the help of the Norwegian king Håkon and of the effective ruler of Sweden, Birger Jarl, and confirmed these alliances by arranging to marry Sofia to Birger's son, the Swedish king Valdemar, and Ingeborg to Håkon's son Magnus. After Christopher's death, his widow, Margaret, took control of the government on behalf of their young son, Erik, who had been chosen to succeed. She was also the guardian of the princesses and did her best to prevent these foreign marriages. She was unable to prevent Sofia's marriage, which was celebrated in 1260, but Erik's estate had not been divided between the girls, so Sofia's dowry was relatively small: gold and silver with the income of Malmö and Trelleborg. Margaret was equally unsuccessful in her attempt to stop Ingeborg's marriage (see "Nunneries" in chapter 9). Ingeborg was not provided with a dowry at her marriage, but her husband began demanding a settlement, and as a result in 1262 the Danes were forced, at last, to divide Erik's estate and give his daughters their shares. Valdemar and Magnus soon discovered, however, that although their wives were major landowners in Denmark, it profited them little. They were dependent on Danish stewards, and although some were loyal servants of their Norwegian and Swedish masters, most were not. The Danish government did nothing to help; on the contrary its attempts to tax these estates caused many conflicts.

The younger sisters, Agnes and Jutta, were prevented from marrying by being forced to enter the nunnery of Saint Agnete in Roskilde, endowed with their paternal inheritances (see "Nunneries" in chapter 9). After the girls escaped to their brother-in-law in Sweden, they lived as laity but never married. They did, though, treat their inheritance as if it had never been given to the nunnery, and a prolonged series of disputes resulted.

9

Women: Ideal and Reality

Until recently little attention has been paid to the different ways in which the sexes were affected by the religious, political, and cultural changes that occurred in Scandinavia during the early Middle Ages, and even now, despite the great advances that have been made in the past two decades in women's studies, the results that have been achieved have not been satisfactorily integrated with each other or with what is known about medieval Scandinavian society in general.

It has been generally supposed that in prehistoric Scandinavia women had a higher status, greater freedom, and fewer restraints on their activity than later. This view was already current in the nineteenth century and was closely related to the belief that the freedom and equality supposed to characterize Germanic society survived longer in Scandinavia than elsewhere (see chapter 10).[1] Few scholars still accept that interpretation of Germanic and Scandinavian society, but belief in free Nordic women has lasted better and continues to influence discussions of the period. It has therefore been necessary for modern students of women's history to consider how this idea originated and on what basis.

Literary Evidence

Early discussion of women's status made much use of Tacitus and of Icelandic sagas, which were believed to show that an early ideal of active and martial "shield-maidens" was replaced by the passive and submissive Madonna ideal favored by the church. Few, if any, scholars now believe that women warriors led war bands in prehistoric Scandinavia; the shield-maidens have been relegated to the world of Amazon myths. It is, however, commonly assumed that in the early Middle Ages housewives had a great deal of independence and authority, doing much of the work on their farms, and that they were entirely responsible for running them when their men were away on Viking expeditions. Support for this view has been found in Icelandic sagas about pagan times in which many, but not all, women are depicted as having full control of their lives, arranging their own betrothals and marriages, divorcing their husbands, and inciting their menfolk to revenge insults or injuries. Such dominant women are conspicuously absent from the sagas about contemporary events in thirteenth-century Iceland. In them the women are pale shadows of their predecessors: passive, submissive, and completely subordinate to their husbands and kinsmen. The same contrast between pagan and Christian women is found in the major histories that cover both periods, Saxo's *Gesta Danorum* and Snorri's *Heimskringla*.

It is obvious that conversion changed conditions for women as well as men, but it may be doubted whether the effect of Christianity was so sudden and complete as thirteenth-century authors make it appear. The reality of this contrast has recently been questioned for a number of other reasons. In the first place, literary texts are an untrustworthy guide to reality. Although there are different, sometimes contradictory interpretations of literary motifs, it is generally agreed that their relationship to the historical background is far more complicated than has formerly been recognized. Increased awareness of the limitations of our knowledge about the pagan past and of the complexity of medieval Europe, with great variations between different regions and different social levels, has made many scholars reluctant to generalize about either period or to treat women, or any other group, as homogenous.

For scholars who regard accounts of recent or contemporary events as "historical" but narratives about the past as "literature," the contrast is between fact and fiction. Thus *Sturlunga Saga* is supposed to describe the real condition of women in the twelfth and thirteenth centuries, while sagas about the pagan period that were written at the same time are considered to have no value as evidence. The powerful women in the latter have been interpreted as the romantic equivalent of the great figures of heroic poetry. An alternative explanation is that they were invested with their independent characteristics by clerical authors who hoped in this way to teach Christian values and raise moral standards. Thus the women who had a say in the choice of their husbands were exercising the right to consent that the church approved of, while women who practiced sorcery, fought, or urged men to take bloody revenge were intended to remind men that female power was dangerous, that women were indeed the root of all evil (Jochens 1986a, b).

The assumption that accounts of contemporary events are reliable is unsatisfactory. "Historical" sagas cannot be sharply distinguished from "fictional" ones. They are *all* literature in which fact and fiction are mixed. The contemporary sagas are just as likely as others to have features deliberately intended to serve the interests of the authors or their patrons. The depiction of women as powerless and submissive may have been a product of wishful thinking and may show what their role should be, not what it was. In other words, the descriptions of women in both the distant past and the present could have been part of the same educational campaign. Indeed, many of the women in the pagan sagas are as weak and passive as those in the contemporary narratives. This has been seen as an attempt to present women as they ought to be and as they really were; in Carol Clover's words, "the stories the sagas choose to tell of women repeatedly both illustrate and turn on the tension between theory and practice" (1988, 182).

The recognition that sagas and, indeed, all historical works written in the twelfth and thirteenth centuries were both fact and fiction means not only that the contemporary narratives should not be accepted as reliable, but also that those about the pagan past may have *some* historical elements. Several commentators have agreed that the motif of powerful women would not have figured so prominently in the pagan sagas without some basis in reality. It has, for example, been argued that the shield-maidens, although mythical, were a "collective fantasy" that can reveal much about tensions in the society in which they were produced. Carol Clover has pointed out that the stories about them have much in common with other medieval transvestite traditions—for example, those about Amazons and female monks—revealing "an underlying concern with the basic issue of where one sex stops and the other begins—not only psychosexually, but also socially" (1986b, 36). She sees the motif of the young, unmarried woman who carries arms and acts like a man as the literary expression of situations where, in the absence of a male heir, a daughter became the surrogate son responsible for what was normally man's business.

Another way in which women show their power in the pagan sagas and in Saxo's *Gesta* is by inciting their kinsmen to take revenge. Several explanations have been advanced for the emphasis on this role. One is that women, being by nature conservative and "less realistic in their outlook" more often "allowed their emotions to discount the overwhelming odds which frequently the men could foresee and assess" (Thomas 1946–53, 317). Another, more convincing, suggestion is that women continued to encourage the old custom of vengeance because they had no economic incentive to seek compensation. The attempts of churchmen to put an end to revenge killings and insist on the payment of compensation were vigorously resisted in Scandinavia; it was long considered shameful to "carry one's kinsmen in a purse," and, as Clover points out, "if legal revenge was second class revenge for men, it must have been no revenge at all for women" (1986a, 174–75). She has moreover suggested that women in early Iceland may have had advantages compared with their contemporaries in other parts of Scandinavia, because in a newly colonized land they were probably in short supply and were thus able to negotiate favorable terms for themselves. That, however, would not explain why Saxo contrasted women in the pagan and Christian period in much the same way as did thirteenth-century Icelandic authors. Their common approach is best understood as a literary convention reflecting current ecclesiastical ideas about the proper place of women in society.

Real Changes

It is possible that the status of women was adversely affected in Scandinavia as it was in other parts of Europe by demographic, economic, and political as well as religious changes that occurred in the eleventh and twelfth centuries. In England, for example, before the Norman Conquest of 1066, the fact that some women had a leading role in public affairs excited no particular comment from contemporaries, but twelfth-century historians of Anglo-Saxon England thought it was extraordinary. This change of attitude has been interpreted as a result of "the actual shrinking of opportunities for women to participate in the whole life of the community, as war and government left the home area and became genuinely 'public' activities, and also the extent to which the climate of opinion regarding the ideal or even possible role of women changed under the impact of such social changes and the development of the literary convention of courtly love" (Bandel, 114). Similar social and literary developments somewhat later also affected Scandinavia, and it is therefore worth considering whether they had the same kind of effect there.

It is a complication that, although Scandinavians had long been exposed to Christian influence, in the eleventh and twelfth centuries Christianity put down firm roots and began to affect Scandinavian society in fundamental ways. It is therefore difficult, if not impossible, to distinguish the direct effects of Christianization from the effects of other changes that happened at the same time. It is also obvious that any attempt to discover whether Scandinavian women did indeed have higher status and greater freedom of action before the twelfth century is hampered by the dearth of evidence. Fortunately some evidence is provided by poetry, runic inscriptions, and archaeological remains.

One change was demographic (see chapter 2). In the eleventh century women were tending to live longer than they had earlier, and they began to form a larger proportion of the whole population, which began to increase at that time (Sellevold 1989a, b). The evidence of graves, from the third or fourth centuries to the tenth or eleventh, when pagan burial customs ended in most parts of Scandinavia, show that some women, especially older ones, were treated with great respect. In Denmark the quantity and quality of the furnishing in men's graves decreased with the age of the dead man, but some of the richest burials were of women who were fifty years old or more. This contrast shows that the elaborateness of a burial was not determined by the status of the dead person's family. What it does suggest is that respect for women increased with age and was perhaps earned by the experience gained during a long life. In other parts of Scandinavia, too, many of the richest burials were of women. The most lavishly furnished burial known in Sweden, at Tuna in Badelunda near Västerås, is of a woman who was buried in the fourth century with an abundance of gold and imported goods. One of the richest Norwegian graves, the ninth-century ship burial at Oseberg, was also a woman's. In Norway in this period it was women above all who were buried in large and richly furnished long-barrows (Farbregd).

Pre-Christian Attitudes and Ideals

There are indications that some women in pre-Christian Scandinavia were highly regarded for religious reasons. Eddic poetry shows that in Nordic mythology knowledge of the past and of the unknown, especially the future, was associated with female beings, as were the arts of writing, poetry, and magic. The name given to this collection of poetry, *Edda*, may itself originally have meant "great-grandmother." If so, it underlines the role of women as transmitters of tradition, as do many of the poems (see further in Steinsland 1983; Mundal and Steinsland). In *Sigrdrífumál*, for example, when Sigurd asks the Valkyrie Sigerdriva to teach him wisdom, she does so by instructing him about victory runes, healing runes, and runes to protect the unborn. The collection begins with *Völuspá*, "Völva's prophecy." Völva, a sibyl, addresses Odin and describes creation, the golden age of the gods, and their corruption. In response to Odin's request for wisdom she prophesies Ragnarök, the destruction of the world of the old gods, and a new age with one powerful ruler, in which the innocent gods are resur-

Figure 9.1. The "Sigurd-carving" on Ramsundsberget. This runic inscription is part of an elaborate composition that includes scenes depicting some episodes from the *Völsunga-saga*, which was very popular in early medieval Scandinavia (*SR*, Södermanland no. 101). The king's son Sigurd is incited by his foster father, Regin the smith, to recover the large gold treasure that his brother Fafnir, in the shape of a dragon, is jealously safeguarding. With the help of a sword that Regin has forged, Sigurd kills the dragon, and in this carving we see him frying its heart. According to the saga he burns himself, and, when he puts his finger into his mouth, he suddenly understands the song of the birds. They tell him that Regin intends to deceive him and advise him to kill Regin. To the left we see the smith lying with his head cut off and with his tools beside him. To the right of Sigurd his horse stands loaded with the gold treasure. The inscription reads: "Sigrid, Alrik's mother, Orm's daughter, had this bridge built for the soul of her husband Holmger, Sigröd's father." We do not know how this inscription is related to the mythical scenes depicted with it. It has been suggested that it is simply the close similarity between the names Sigurd and Sigröd, but a deeper symbolism may lie behind it. If Sigrid's son Alrik is the same Alrik who had a stone erected nearby commemorating his father, a Viking chieftain (*SR*, Södermanland, no. 106), her inheritance after them may have consisted of riches plundered abroad, a "gold treasure" she used for a pious purpose, that is, to build a bridge close to this inscription for the sake of the soul of her second husband, the father of Sigröd. Photograph by Bengt A. Lundberg. © Antikvarisk-topografiska arkivet, Stockholm.

rected and righteous men live forever. The poem is clearly influenced by
Christian ideas, and its date (if it has one) is uncertain (see "The Oral Texts"
in chapter 1), but it is a vivid reminder of the close association of women
with wisdom and prophesy.

According to Snorri the gods known as Æsir learned wisdom from the
goddess Freyja, and it is even more significant that Odin is said to have
done so by becoming *argr*. That word had extremely offensive implications
and was used for men who took a passive—that is, female—role in homo-
sexual relations. To accuse a man of being *argr* was a grave insult, not so
much because of the homosexuality but because submission to another man
implied submissiveness in other ways, cowardice, and loss of honor; it
amounted to declaring that a man was no longer a worthy member of society (Sørensen 1980, 24–39). It has been suggested that such insults were
considered exceptionally serious in Iceland because, in the absence of a superior authority, social stability depended on the integrity of men.

The emphasis on masculine qualities is also reflected in heroic poetry and
tales by the common theme of women who were not only beautiful and
accomplished but also warriors. Heroes had to overcome such women in
their manly role in order to win and deserve them as partners; the proper
destiny of shield-maidens was marriage. Another aspect of this literature is
that proud and confident women were especially attractive and highly valued as wives, not only because of the prestige of winning them but also
because their sons could be expected to inherit the qualities of their mothers
as well as those of their fathers (Mundal 1988, 24).

Once married, a woman was expected to assume a completely feminine
role with her own well-defined responsibilities quite distinct from those of
her husband. In Icelandic law her duties were entirely confined to the farm,
where she had great authority, symbolized by the keys on her belt. She
could not represent the farm externally and was excluded from public life,
but she was involved in all family business. It was in her interest to see that
the honor of the family was upheld; as we have seen, the common theme
in sagas about early Iceland of women urging their menfolk to take revenge
probably had some basis in reality. In poetry, revenge appears to have been
above all the concern of women. Skalds who feared that their reputation
had been damaged because they had not taken revenge as they should have
done turned to women. Most examples of skalds addressing women are in
the family sagas. They are less common in the king's sagas, and such poems
are never in *drottkvætt*, the prestigious meter of court poetry. In general it
was when a skald was most concerned about himself that he turned to a
woman and spoke of his dreams and fears, or of his wounds and impending

death. The good opinion of women was valued. As Roberta Frank has put it: "What, after all, was the point of the institutionalized male violence celebrated by the skalds, those excessive vendettas and duels, that piracy and harrying, if women were not watching you, constantly comparing you to little Alf the Stout or to Snorre Gore-Fang?" (1990b, 78).

Most of the literature so far mentioned in this chapter was written in Iceland, where conditions were in some respects very different from Scandinavia. That the proportion of early medieval farms named after women was ten times greater in Iceland than in Norway may indicate that women had a higher status in the newly colonized land. It may also be significant that the most active volcanoes in Iceland all have female names (Frank 1973, 483). Archaeological evidence and runic inscriptions, however, suggest that women had much the same roles in other parts of Scandinavia as in Iceland and that at least some were highly regarded. One way of showing concern for the honor and reputation of a family in the late tenth and eleventh centuries was to erect a rune-stone, and it is significant that almost a quarter of them were sponsored by widows. Few are as explicit as the stone from Norra Härene in Västergötland—"Åsa honored her husband in a way that henceforth no woman will ever do" (*SR*, Västergötland, no. 59)—but they all show family pride. One woman in Uppland erected a stone in memory of a kinsman and named his killer, apparently to keep the memory of this shameful act alive and perhaps even as an incitement to revenge. There is another inscription at Bällsta in Uppland in which a widow says that she has had a lament made for her husband. These can be compared with Icelandic laments in which widows mourn and sometimes demand revenge (Clover 1986a, 146). Carol Clover has drawn attention to other cultures with the custom of blood feud in which women had a leading role in commemorating the dead and maintaining feud. That lamentation by women, often in poetic form, is a widespread feature of funeral rituals suggests that in Iceland women lamented in real life as well as in literature (Clover 1986a, 180–83).

In marriage the sexes had well-defined, distinct roles, but widows and women who were unmarried or had no near male kinsmen were able, or forced, to assume some of the responsibilities that were normally men's. Some women were clearly highly regarded, whether as representatives of powerful families, or for their age and wisdom. There is no hint that women's abilities were doubted in the pagan period, and their association with wisdom and magic is notable. Their links with both nature and the supernatural were a source of power. Conversion to Christianity meant that many earlier beliefs and customs were condemned, and this reversal obviously affected the attitude to women and their role in society. Christian authors regarded much magic as an evil to be eradicated, with the result that they tended to depict women of the pagan past in the mold of Eve, the root of all evil.

Pre-Christian Religious Beliefs

In Norse mythology females were abundant.[2] There were goddesses who were considered as holy and powerful as the gods: Dísir (singular *dís*, "woman"), whose cult was particularly important in Uppsala; sibyls, such as Thor's wife, Sif, and the prophetess of Völuspá; Valkyries, who conducted selected dead warriors to Valhalla; *fylgjur*, "accompaniers," spirits who were attached to particular families or individuals; demonic giantesses; and, especially significant, the Norns, supernatural women who determined the success or failure of both gods and men.

There were two groups or families of gods and goddesses, the Æsir and the Vanir. Conflict between them had been resolved, and later commentators could treat all these deities as Æsir, but they seem originally to have been associated with different cults. One was an essentially masculine warrior cult centered on Odin and his descendants, the Æsir; the other, in which women had a key role, worshiped the Vanir. The main Vanir deities were Niord, his wife Freyja, the guarantor of health, wealth, and fertility, and her brother Freyr, a pair whose names originally meant "lady" and "lord." The Vanir cult emphasized kinship and was celebrated both in the privacy of homes, where housewives seem to have had the main responsibility, and in larger family assemblies. In the latter, sacrifices were offered to the Dísir, the most important of whom was Freyja, known as Vanadis, "Lady of the Vanir," accompanied by her maidens. It has been suggested that the Dísir cult was connected with the worship of ancestral mothers of powerful families or clans. Women seem to have had a leading role in the worship, but not as priestesses, for there is no reliable evidence of priests in pagan Scandinavia. It is uncertain whether women could act publicly in cult celebrations or whether they were represented by men, as happened later with the legal and political responsibilities of a woman who inherited a *goðorð* in Iceland.

The Odin cult emphasized comradeship and loyalty, not kinship. Its dissociation from things female was demonstrated by the belief that Odin learned the magic known as *seiðr* (a ritual in which the sorcerer fell into a trance), which was supposed until then to have been the preserve of women. This then led Odin to become *argr*. Selected dead warriors were conducted by Valkyries to Valhall, "Hall of the Slain" and home of the gods. Valhall was a totally male world of feasting and fighting. Most of the dead, women and men who were not so chosen, were assigned to Helheim, ruled by the goddess Hel. They were not destined to spend eternity with the gods. For most people life after death was a family matter, for it was in the family that the dead, buried in the family cemetery, were best remembered by their descendants and kin.

Effects of Conversion

The acceptance of Christian ideas and values meant the abandonment of most such beliefs. The church prized chastity more than fertility; concern for the family was less significant than concern for the salvation of the individual soul; Christians were taught to be tolerant and merciful, not vengeful; humility was a greater virtue than honor; and the new cult was in the hands of a completely male priesthood—women could only participate passively.

Conversion thus meant many fundamental changes, but the revolution was not complete. Some features of the old religion survived, if in modified forms, partly because Scandinavian beliefs had been long influenced by Christianity. The church condemned many rituals and practices, but it had to accommodate some. The survival of magic in Christian form is well illustrated by the inscription on a Norwegian rune-stick: "Mary gave birth to Christ, Elizabeth gave birth to John the Baptist. Be delivered in their names. Come out child. The Lord is calling you into light!" (Jacobsen 1984, 104–5). The female helpers of pagan times were replaced by Christian saints, above all by the Virgin Mary.

Runic inscriptions show that the cult of Mary developed early in Svealand and was favored by women. Numerous inscriptions include the prayer "May God and God's mother help his soul"; almost half of the inscriptions were commissioned by women. These and other inscriptions suggest that women were among the first and most eager converts. That is not surprising. Much Christian teaching must have been particularly welcomed by women, a point obscured by the misogyny that colors so much medieval literature. They must have found the prospect of the Christian paradise far more attractive than the gloomy realm of Hel to which they had previously been consigned. Many must also have been glad to believe that in the sight of God they were men's equals and that their worth did not depend on their fertility, family, or social status; the community of Christians had room for all, including women who were barren or unmarried, as well as orphans and the poor. Christian teaching that all had an obligation to help those in need was especially welcome to women without near kinsfolk, for they had far more limited opportunities to support themselves than had men in a similar situation. It may also be supposed that many mothers were gladdened by the attempts of the Church to prohibit, or at least severely restrict, the custom of infanticide, despite the increased burden that this must often have imposed.

It can safely be assumed that in Scandinavia, as in other parts of Europe, women not only were among the earliest converts but also were generous donors to the infant church and active in the work of evangelism, encouraging their husbands to convert and teaching the new faith to their children. Normally it must have been the father who determined the religion of his family, but there were exceptions. A rune-stone at Enberga in Uppland, erected by two brothers in memory of their parents, implies that only their mother was Christian. It was erected in a pagan cemetery, and the inscription reads "Gisl and Ingemund, good 'drengs,' had this monument made after Halvdan, their father and after Ödis their mother. May God now help *her* soul well" (*SR*, Uppland, no. 808; emphasis added). It is also significant that most of the monuments commemorating deathbed converts were erected by women. Five of the six Uppland runic monuments to men who "died in white clothing," meaning that they had very recently been baptized, were erected by women—two mothers and one wife acting on their own and two mothers together with their husbands.

Monuments referring to the building of bridges are further proof of the leading role of women in the process of conversion. The missionaries taught that to build a bridge (the word could mean a causeway over marshy ground) was a meritorious act earning divine favor. A relatively large proportion of the approximately 120 inscriptions that mention the building of such a bridge were erected by, or were in memory of, a woman. Those commemorating women are especially significant, for whereas only 1 in 14 of all inscriptions are in memory of women, 1 in 4 of the bridge-stones are. Also, in an inscription in Uppland two daughters commemorate their father and record that he had built a "soul-house" (probably a resting place for Christian travelers) in memory of his wife (*SR*, Uppland, no. 996). It is also noteworthy that women were responsible for the two inscriptions that refer to pilgrimages. One reads: "Estrid had this stone raised after Östen, her husband, who went to Jerusalem and died away in Greece," and the other: "Ingerun, Hård's daughter, had these runes carved after herself. She wanted to go east and to Jerusalem" (*SR*, Uppland, nos. 136, 605). We do not know whether Ingerun's wish was granted, but that a woman could even *plan* such a pilgrimage at this early date is remarkable.

The inscriptions were predominantly Christian monuments, manifesting the acceptance of the new religion by the sponsors or the dead and implying a willingness to give the missionaries active support. It is therefore significant that almost a quarter of all inscriptions involved women as property owners. Most of them were widows who could expect support from churchmen who urged them not to remarry, presumably in the hope that at least part of their property would be given to them as an endowment for their churches.

It is no accident that one of the chapters in Rimbert's *Vita Anskarii* was devoted to the piety and steadfast devotion of Frideborg, a rich widow in Birka, and the care she took to ensure that her wealth would be distributed as alms in a suitable manner for the sake of her soul. She is said to have lived to a great age and always been a generous almsgiver. As death approached she enjoined her daughter Catla to distribute all that she possessed to the poor. According to Rimbert, she said, "Because there are here but few poor, at the first opportunity after my death, sell all that has not been given away and go with the money to Dorestad. There are there many churches, priests, and clergy and a multitude of poor people. On your arival seek out faithful persons who may teach you how to distribute this, and give away everything as alms for the benefit of my soul" (*VA* 20). Catla did so. Although there must have been many deserving poor in Birka and its neighborhood, Frideborg insisted that Catla go to Dorestad because she wanted the recipients to be Christians and the distribution to be under the guidance of clergy. She seems to have included among the poor the *pauperes Christi*, the servants of Christ who were vowed to poverty, and at the time of Frideborg's death there was only one priest in Birka. Another consideration was almost certainly that Frideborg feared that, after her death, Catla would be vulnerable to pressure from relatives who did not share her enthusiasm for the new religion and were, more likely, hostile to it. By going abroad Catla could fulfill her mother's wish without interference.

The generosity of women to churches was a common cause of family conflict in medieval Europe, and sometimes kinsmen took extreme measures to protect their claim to family property. This seems to have been the reason two twelfth-century Scandinavian women, conventionally remembered as pious and generous, were venerated as martyrs. Saint Helena of Skövde in Sweden and Saint Margaret of Roskilde in Denmark were both killed by their kinsmen. Their legends do not provide any further details, but it is more than likely that they were killed by kinsmen who were determined to prevent further alienations of family property.

Ecclesiastical Misogyny

As ecclesiastical influence grew, women were blamed for much that churchmen disapproved of. This happened even in Iceland, where misogynist attitudes were not so pronounced as they were in other parts of Europe—for example, in Saxo's *Gesta Danorum*. In the sagas most divorces were caused by women, and it was women who urged their menfolk to take revenge, while the men were said to be ready to negotiate and accept compensation for insult or injury. The diminished respect for women in Iceland is also evidenced by the bynames they were given. Before conversion these were often complimentary—for example "the wise" (*in spaka, in djúpúðga*), "the pride of the home[bench]" (*bekkjarbót*), or "the sun of the islands" (*hólmasól*)—but afterward pejorative bynames began to be given, such as "the mare of the farm" (*garðafylja*) and "the noisy" (*ysja*) (Frank 1973, 483).

Thirteenth-century Icelandic authors were, unlike Saxo, prepared to depict independent and active women with sympathy. Such favorable attitudes to women survived longer in Iceland than elsewhere, especially in literary genres that were most firmly rooted in oral culture. Women had a significant role in the preliterary culture of Scandinavia, but they had virtually no place in the literary culture brought by churchmen. In Iceland, as elsewhere, Christian literature was almost exclusively produced by men who had been educated in church schools, but much of what they wrote was based on oral traditions that had been shaped by women as well as men. Women are sometimes explicitly mentioned as sources of information—for example, by Ari—and there were some women skalds. It is also likely that women were at least partly responsible for stories in which the interest is focused on women. The different forms of the very common triangle motif in different genres are significant. In the so-called realistic sagas the normal pattern is that two men fight over a woman. In the heroic sagas, where the triangles tend to consist of two women and one man, the women are the center of interest. Heroic sagas were not the earliest to be written, but their substance and themes were drawn more directly from oral tradition, and in them female points of view are best represented and women tend to be described in positive terms, maintaining their rights and achieving their aims. Such favorable representations of women are much less common in contemporary sagas, because they tended to disappear when traditions were reshaped to meet the demands of literary culture (Mundal 1983, 22–23).

The relatively evenhanded treatment of women in much Icelandic literature may have occurred partly because most of that literature was written in the vernacular. Women were not authors, but they were in the audience. The sagas were intended to be read aloud, and the large number of surviving manuscripts suggests that there was a lively demand for them on the farms of medieval Iceland. They reached a much wider range of people than contemporary works in Latin; only a few highly educated people could read *Gesta Danorum* with any profit. This audience also explains why slaves, servants, old people, and children occur so much more frequently in the sagas than in most contemporary literature.

Saxo expressed his attitude to women much more explicitly than the Icelanders did. He left no room for doubt that he considered them the weaker sex, not so much physically or psychologically as morally. They were driven by passion and lust and were both inconstant and shameless, unreliable, unfaithful, cunning, and cruel. He interpreted the moral weakness of women as the source of their power, and for him their inconstancy and unreliability represented the unforeseen complications that threatened to undermine the proper ordering of the world (Strand 1980, 188).

Ideal Womanhood

Virgins are rare in the profane literature of thirteenth-century Scandinavia. Their absence may have been in part because of the great importance of marriage and marriage alliances in Scandinavia, especially in Iceland, where, in the absence of a superior authority, social stability largely depended on the links so formed between families. Another possible factor was that, although the church insisted that the clergy should be celibate, it encouraged the laity to marry (Nors). There are no holy virgins or nuns in the *Gesta Danorum*; the only women Saxo describes as chaste all their lives were pagan shield-maidens. The women he praised were those who subordinated themselves to their husbands. His message is clear: women were expected to marry. A woman's calling was to be a good wife, supporting and helping her husband and bearing his children. It is significant that the Scandinavian women who were venerated as saints had all been married, and at least some of them were regarded as martyrs apparently because they had been killed by relatives angered by their generosity to the church.

Icelandic authors also seem to have assumed that women were expected to marry. The family sagas have few who did not marry, and only six Icelandic nuns are mentioned before the end of the thirteenth century. The earliest, Gudrun in *Laxdæla saga*, had four husbands, a few lovers, and several children before taking vows late in life. Two others, who were also widows with children, belonged to clerical families; one was a bishop's daughter and the other the mother of a priest. According to the bishops' sagas two other nuns were celibate, but that did not ensure good health; one had poor eyesight and the other became mentally disturbed. In Iceland lifelong chastity was not considered an ideal either for men or women. Roberta Frank has pointed out that "in the family sagas . . . one way to find out who is the villain is to locate the nearest bachelor, if you can find one. He is usually an outlaw, a thug, a poet, or worse. . . . When there are two unmarried protagonists in a saga, on the one hand the man who openly declares that he wants nothing to do with women will be the greater scoundrel. On the other hand, the bachelor who demonstrates his heterosexual interests—however crudely—is judged redeemable" (1973, 481). The Icelandic attitude to the unmarried is well reflected in their language. The Icelandic for bachelor, *einhleypingr*, means "vagabond" or "scoundrel," and the word for spinster, *úgiptr*, also means "one who has bad luck."

By the thirteenth century court romances that had long been popular in other parts of Europe were being translated in Scandinavia and had begun to serve as models for sagas and poems in which the portrayal of women is colored by chivalrous ideals. This aristocratic literature also influenced the development of balladry, an art form that flourished in the later Middle Ages and afterward. Many types of women figure in the ballads, from viragos to the weak and often oppressed. The ballads do, however, take up an issue that is ignored by Saxo and the saga authors, namely the difficulty of preserving virginity before marriage, which is represented as a problem that all kinds of women might have to face.

Nunneries

In the early thirteenth century some unmarried Scandinavian women could hope to find safety in a nunnery. By then several of these religious communities had been founded and endowed by kings, members of royal families, prelates, and magnates, in the first place for their own and friends' kinswomen—unwanted daughters, or widows whose remarriage could have led to the dispersal of family property. Others might be admitted in return for a donation. Not all were voluntary recruits—some were in effect consigned to a nunnery by their kinsmen. Nuns, like monks, were expected, after a period of probation and preparation, to vow poverty, chastity, and obedience. This vow meant renouncing any hope of marriage, a promise many girls may have been glad to make, but in practice such vows could be broken; the spiritual family of a nunnery was rarely able to withstand pressure from the worldly families of its members.

The need for nunneries seems to have been most acute in Denmark, where by 1250 twenty-two had been established (nine of them were founded before 1175) together with two double houses with monks as well as nuns (Smith). There were thirty-one Danish monasteries, some of which were much larger and richer than any nunnery, but the proliferation of the latter is remarkable; there were more nunneries in Denmark than in the whole of the rest of Scandinavia. In Sweden the earliest religious community was a nunnery at Vreta, and by the mid-thirteenth century, when most religious communities other than mendicant friaries had been founded, there were equal numbers of nunneries and monasteries, six of each. In Norway and Iceland conditions seem to have been different. By 1250 there were only five nunneries but fourteen monasteries in Norway, while only one of Iceland's six religious communities was a nunnery—Kirjubær, founded in 1186.

In Sweden nunneries were not only as numerous as monasteries, they were hardly less wealthy, and most were founded and endowed by royalty or by families of the highest status. It is also noteworthy that several of the monasteries were founded or richly endowed by women. According to the early history of the Cistercian order the Swedish queen, who can be identified as Sverker's wife, Ulfhild, asked for the first two colonies of Cistercians to be sent. One of the monasteries they established, Alvastra, was later believed to have been built on land that Ulfhild had been given as her dower. The other, after an unsettled start, was given land at Varnhem by a woman called Sigrid, who was related to King Erik's queen. The earliest monastery in Svealand was richly endowed by a widow called Doter.

In other parts of Scandinavia some modest nunneries were founded by families that would later be classed as lower aristocracy or gentry, but the most important were, like the Swedish nunneries, founded and endowed by kings or powerful magnates, their wives, and other close relatives. From these families the communities recruited many of their members. Vadstena, founded for Birgitta by King Magnus Eriksson, is exceptional, for few of its nuns came from families with such high status as Birgitta herself.

Religious houses could also accommodate men and women who did not wish to take vows but, in return for a donation, could be assured of food and shelter in their old age. We do not know how common this custom was in the thirteenth century, but in late medieval Norway it was women in particular who took advantage of this opportunity.

The important role of nunneries in family and royal politics can be illustrated by three examples, one drawn from each kingdom. The first concerns the wife of the Swedish king Knut Eriksson.[3] He was betrothed to her in his father's lifetime. Although her name is not recorded, she was certainly a member of an exceptionally powerful family; it was later said that she did not have her like in the land. After Erik's death in 1160 Knut went into exile, and the woman was placed in a nunnery to avoid the risk that she would suffer violence. After Knut had overcome his enemies and was recognized as king she was taken from the nunnery; they married and had children, including a son who was recognized as heir by the magnates. When she was taken seriously ill and in fear of death, she promised that she would live a celibate life if restored to health. It is likely that she thought her illness a divine punishment for breaking her vows. Knut consented to her entering a nunnery, but after her recovery he appealed to the pope to release her from her vow and allow them to resume their married life. He gave as his reasons that he needed the support of his wife's relatives in his fight against "pagans," and that he also needed protection against the slanders of his enemies concerning his marriage. It was clearly vital for Knut to have his marriage declared legitimate to avoid a break with his wife's family, and to ensure that his heirs were legitimate. The pope commissioned the archbishop of Uppsala to investigate the matter, but the outcome is not known. That Knut was succeeded by a member of the rival dynasty, Sverker Karlsson, may mean that his wish was not granted. This remarkable affair is not only a good example of the use of a nunnery as a place of shelter, it also shows that ecclesiastical ideas about legitimacy were being used for political purposes very early in Sweden.

The second example is from Denmark, a century later. Erik Plovpenning died in 1250, leaving four daughters, and was succeeded in turn by his brothers Abel and Christopher. After Christopher's death in 1259 his widow Margaret was unable to prevent the marriage of the eldest daughter, Sofia, to Valdemar, king of Sweden, that Christopher had arranged. She did make a determined, although unsuccessful, effort to block Sofia's sister Ingeborg's marriage to Magnus, son of King Håkon of Norway, by confining her in a nunnery in Jutland. Norwegian agents succeeded in rescuing Ingeborg, and the marriage took place in 1261. Margaret was, however, able to stop the younger sisters from marrying. Agnes was given her share on condition that she use it to found a nunnery, Saint Agnete in Roskilde, which she joined. That the Danes produced no less than four documents to prove that she had taken her vows voluntarily suggests that she did not. The youngest daughter, Jutta, later joined her sister in the nunnery, and they were in turn its abbess, but in 1270 or 1271 they both escaped and lived abroad as laywomen (see "Appendix" in chapter 8).

These examples from Sweden and Denmark show how women of high status entered nunneries not for religious reasons, voluntarily, but because they were consigned to them by relatives for safety in time of war or to prevent the alienation of family property. There were other circumstances in which a woman could be urged, even forced, to remain chaste and join a religious community—for example, if her husband became a monk. That is what happened to a Norwegian woman called Ragna early in the fourteenth century.[4] When her husband, Torolv of Idse, became a monk in Lyse Abbey, Ragna was summoned to the vicarage and urged by the bishop, two canons from Bergen Cathedral, the local priest, and others to swear within three months (that is, by Christmas 1309) that she would remain chaste for the rest of her life. She did not do so and in the following February was summoned by the bishop to be confronted by an imposing array of notables; in addition to the bishop there were seven canons, the royal treasurer, a baron, and two monks from Lyse, one of them her husband. It was said to have been his urgent pleas that persuaded her to change her mind and promise to remain chaste and to live, at her own expense, in Nonneseter Nunnery and to live purely to the best of her ability—and the bishop promised that so long as she lived chastely and did not raise claims to her husband's or their children's property he would not force her to become a nun. No reasons were given for the great pressure on Ragna. She could not have remarried so long as Torolv lived, but his relatives may have feared that she would not act in the best interest of the children. The vow of chastity removed the risk that she might remarry if she outlived her husband, and the renunciation of any claim to Torolv's or their children's property meant that she could not challenge any donations they might make to Lyse Abbey or any other church.

Many women joined religious communities with more enthusiasm than did Agnes or Ragna, and there are numerous examples of women who were generous donors to churches of all kinds, beginning with a very large gift by Estrid, King Knut's sister, to Roskilde Cathedral in the mid-eleventh century. No systematic investigation has been made of the proportion of donations by women, or of the relative scale of their gifts, but a study of Danish wills has shown that half of those made by the laity between 1250 and 1350 were by women, while in the following hundred years that proportion dropped to a fifth (Jexlev). In Sweden about a third of the nonroyal donations to churches known before 1280 were by or for women. Church archaeology has also cast some light on the role of women as patrons. In the early Middle Ages some patrons enhanced their prestige by adding a tower to their church. In some of them a grave has been found, carefully placed in the middle. If, as seems likely, these were for the patrons themselves, it is significant that in four of the five Romanesque towers that have been excavated in Denmark, a woman was buried in the "patronal" grave (Stiesdahl).

The Influence of Women

Women made an important contribution to the development of the church in Scandinavia as donors, as patrons, and in religious communities, but they had little opportunity to mold doctrine or to take part in church administration. Even the nunneries were subject to supervision by bishops or the abbots of neighboring monasteries. The one woman who did wield great power in the church, and not only in Scandinavia, was Birgitta. She was born in 1303, the daughter of Birger Persson, lawman of Uppland, and at the age of thirteen she was married to Ulf Gudmarsson, later lawman of Östergötland; they had eight children. Her religious instructor and confessor was Master Mathew, a canon of Linköping Cathedral and Sweden's leading theologian, and he guided her reading of contemporary apocalyptic literature. Ulf died in 1344, a year after he and Birgitta returned from a prolonged pilgrimage to Santiago de Compostela, and soon afterward Birgitta received the first of her revelations, in which God called her to be his bride and spokeswoman. Thanks to her family connections and her high standing in the court of Magnus Eriksson and his queen, Blanche, she was well informed about contemporary politics not only in Sweden, where she soon allied with the aristocratic opposition to the king, but also in Europe, where she tried to reconcile England and France and to end the Babylonian captivity of the papacy in Avignon. In her *Revelationes* she reprimands kings and magnates, popes and bishops. Such boldness, extraordinary for a woman, was in part made possible by her high social status, but another consideration was that she was highly regarded by many throughout Europe as a remarkable religious leader, at once mystic, prophet, and theologian.

In 1346 Magnus and Blanche bequeathed a royal estate at Vadstena for the religious foundation that Birgitta was already then planning. Four years later she went to Rome in order to obtain approval for her new order and its rule; she never returned. She died there in 1373 shortly after returning from a pilgrimage to the Holy Land. Her remains were taken to Sweden a year later and interred at Vadstena. In 1391 she was canonized.

Vadstena was the only house of her order in Sweden, but many others were soon founded elsewhere; the final total was seventy-nine. Vadstena was an important educational center with a library of about 1,400 volumes, a third of which have survived. Birgitta hoped that the nuns, who were more numerous than monks in her house, would retain the leadership of the community, but they did not.

There has naturally been much discussion about Birgitta's attitude to women and their place in society. She does not seem to have considered that her sex made her in any way inferior, and she approved of marriage; for her, true virginity was a state of mind. Her ideal was the Virgin Mary, the good mother, symbolizing wisdom, strength, obedience, mildness, humility, and purity (Losman).

Economic and Legal Status

The kinship system in all parts of medieval Scandinavia was bilateral; women could, by means of their dowries, dower, or inheritance be land-owners (see chapter 8). There were two different principles determining women's inheritance rights. One of them allowed unmarried daughters to inherit only if they had no brothers; the other allowed both married and unmarried daughters half a "brother's lot." It is not possible to say which was the earliest, for the rune-stones suggest that both were to be found in different parts of Scandinavia in the late tenth and early eleventh centuries, but by the fourteenth century the latter principle prevailed everywhere. The families of husband and wife were expected to help set up their new household. In Norway there was a legally fixed relation between the size of the dowry provided by the woman's family and the dower given by the husband's family. In the Swedish landlaw of about 1350 both were graded according to social status. In Iceland, Norway, and Sweden both dowry and dower seem to have been regarded as the wife's own property, although administered by her husband, throughout the Middle Ages. If the couple died without children, the dower returned to the husband's family and the dowry to the wife's, but if there were children, both were treated as part of their maternal inheritance. In Denmark the laws do not mention dower, apparently because widows there were provided for by being given a full share (the same as a son's) in the jointly owned estate of the household.

As a widow a woman was responsible for her own property, and when the inheritance was divided after the death of her husband, she took her share of the jointly owned estate first. She was never completely independent, and according to most laws she could not remarry without the con-

Figure 9.2. Ivar Axelsson (Tott) and his wife, Magdalena, daughter of Karl Knutsson (Bonde). These are the earliest known Scandinavian portraits, and were originally part of an altar screen. They were painted in about 1475, probably on Gotland, which was then held by Ivar. Magdalena's heraldic symbol, a boat, is that of her family. Photograph from Gyldendals billedarkiv, Copenhagen.

sent of her relatives. In Denmark and Sweden a widow had to have a guardian, but she could in practice choose who that should be. In the laws of east Sweden a widow was allowed to decide about remarriage, and she could be the guardian of her own daughters. In Norway and Iceland widows had the greatest degree of independence and were responsible for their own property, as were unmarried women over the age of twenty.

Early Norwegian and Icelandic laws also differ from most laws in the rest of Scandinavia in treating unfaithfulness of both husbands and wives as a crime to be punished by a fine; in Denmark and Sweden only unfaithful wives were punished, and a husband had the right to kill the adulterer (and in some laws the wife as well) if he caught them in the act. In Denmark an adulteress forfeited all right to her property, but it is only the town laws that prescribed public punishment. The ecclesiastic demand that both husband and wife should be faithful first appeared in Sweden in the Law of Uppland of 1296, and Magnus Eriksson's landlaw prescribed the same punishment for adulterous husbands and wives. According to Christo-

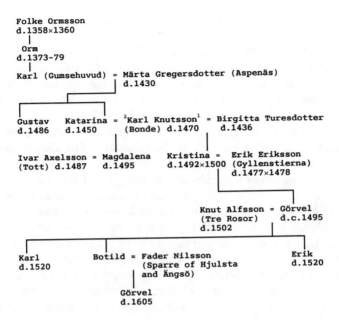

Figure 9.3. The inheritance of Magdalena Karlsdotter. Magdalena inherited a great deal of land in Sweden from her parents and her uncle, who died childless. As she had no children, on her death her property passed to Görvel, her father's granddaughter by his first marriage. After 1520 Görvel's daughter Botild was her sole heiress, and eventually the whole inheritance passed to Botild's daughter, also named Görvel. As she had no heir, she bequeathed all her Swedish property to the Danish king Christian IV, but on her death it was confiscated by the Swedish king Karl IX (B. and P. Sawyer 1985, 72–74).

pher's law of 1442 a man who eloped with another man's wife was to be hanged, and the runaway wife buried alive.

Legally a married woman was always under her husband's guardianship, but many diplomas show that, in practice, married women could enjoy a great degree of freedom. There are numerous indications that it was normal for husband and wife to make decisions about family property together, although it was in the interest of the wife's relatives that the law made the husband alone responsible; if the wife's property was diminished during the marriage, her family could require the husband or his relatives to make good the loss. Conditions were very different in towns than in the countryside, and women were generally given greater freedom to do business and to dispose of property in towns' laws than in the rural or landlaws.

Status in the Countryside

The nature of our sources means that we know most about Scandinavian women who belonged to landowning families. The laws tend to be most concerned with women who owned or had some claim to land. These same women figure most prominently in charters and official records, and the efforts of landowning men to retain control over kinswomen, made necessary by the laws of inheritance, have left their mark on much of the available evidence, narrative as well as documentary. The circumstances of women in landless familes were different and varied greatly.

The differentiation of the sexes that is thought to have characterized the division of labor in medieval society was not strictly observed in working households. It was probably clearest on the larger farms, where the master and his wife had well-defined and separate functions. Unmarried members of such households, children, and the old were not so limited in what they could or were expected to do (Österberg). On smaller farms, and in regions where fishing and handicrafts were important subsidiary occupations, many married women did men's work; the evidence of skeletons from medieval graves shows that some women did the heaviest kinds of work.

There was no legal obstacle to a widow's taking over her dead husband's tenancy and working the holding herself, with other members of her family, but despite the tendency of women to outlive men very few women tenants appear in medieval surveys and rentals. A survey of Roskilde Cathedral's estates in 1568 names 1,409 tenants, but only 15 were women. It has been suggested that the agrarian crisis of the fourteenth century made it easier for women to be tenants, but in a survey of the property of the bishop of Roskilde made in about 1370 only 2 percent of the tenants were women, even though 30 percent of the best land in Sjælland was then deserted. The explanation must be that most tenants were succeeded by a son, or, if there was none, the widow normally remarried (Nielsen, 6).

Unmarried daughters of both tenant farmers and small-scale landowners who were not needed at home had the choice of working on another farm or earning their living in towns. It is difficult to compare the wage rates of men and women, because the part that was paid in kind was rarely specified, but in the later Middle Ages women tended to be more poorly rewarded than men (Munktell, 25–28). As day workers, however, women had the advantage of being able to work all year, brewing, baking, spinning, and weaving indoors during the winter months; men, whose work was mostly outdoors, could not.

Status in Towns

Towns offered a wider range of employment for women than did the countryside, and those with some craft skill could gain a degree of economic independence that was virtually impossible in rural society. Nevertheless, their way to social advancement was the same in town and country—by inheritance or marriage. Many wives of craftmen and merchants took part in their husbands' businesses, and if widowed could continue it. Those who were wealthy enough could even become burgesses, but they had no part in urban government; their only responsibility was to "milk the maids who have let themselves be tempted"—that is, to check whether unmarried maids had secretly given birth by testing their breasts for milk. Such illegitimate mothers were punished and expelled from the town (Dahlbäck, 98–100).

One way of caring for poor female relatives was to hire them as servants; only burgesses were allowed to be unemployed. In Bergen female servants formed their own guild. This was a remarkable initiative, especially for women of such low status, and it is the only example of a female guild in medieval Scandinavia. It was clearly unwelcome to the town authorities, for it was banned in 1293 or 1294 (Helle 1982a, 463). Guilds did admit some women but not on the same terms as men. Those who had mastered a craft were generally paid less than their male counterparts, and this naturally caused resentment as unfair competition.

The trades women engaged in were mostly the traditional female tasks of washing, cleaning, brewing, and baking. Women made cloth and clothes, cared for the sick, and acted as midwives, but they could also work in the building trades, and some worked boats. They rarely had the more lucrative occupations, and most of those who paid taxes were in the lower reaches of the social scale (Österberg, 4).

A woman could also support herself as a prostitute. The profession was allowed but regulated. The Norwegian Hirdskrå warns against prostitutes and brothels, and in 1313 Håkon V ruled that prostitutes could not act as witnesses (Helle 1982a, 463). "Loose women" were supposed to dress more simply than honorable women, and in 1459 it was decreed in Stockholm that prostitutes were not allowed to wear expensive fur, silver, or gold, which suggests that the profession could be rewarding (Dahlbäck, 123–24). The presence in Bergen of a German colony that was exclusively male naturally led to increased prostitution in the town, but most customers were natives. A Bergen diarist noted in 1563 the death of "Katilbrog the old prostitute who had earlier served monks, canons, priests, courtiers and others"; her medieval predecessors certainly had similar clients (Helle 1982a, 464).

Prostitution began to be more strictly regulated toward the end of the Middle Ages. In 1496 Danish prostitutes were ordered to wear identifiable hoods colored red and black and to live in special districts. This more restrictive policy was in part due to the spread of venereal disease, but the later persecution of prostitutes owed more to the attitude of Luther and other reformers toward sexual matters. The Middle Ages had been more tolerant.

Conclusion

It is not possible to give a clear answer to the question posed at the beginning of this chapter regarding whether Scandinavian women had higher status and greater freedom of action in pre-Christian times than later. Many women were highly regarded in all periods. One significant change was that the importance of women as transmitters of tradition and knowledge was undermined by Christianity and the written culture that came with it. Women's freedom of action was both increased and reduced, and it is not possible to say whether overall their situation improved or deteriorated after conversion. The demand of the church for monogamy and the prohibition of divorce and concubinage worked to both the advantage and disadvantage of women. The church's teaching about the subordination of women could be taken as justifying laws that put women at a disadvantage compared with men, but we do not know how novel those laws were. The insistence of the church that all children should have a right to inherit a fixed share of their parents' property in particular benefited unmarried daughters. Nothing is known about the status of unmarried women in pagan Scandinavia, but in Christian Scandinavia such women could win respect as donors to or patrons of churches, and some could become members of privileged and prestigious communities by becoming nuns. In general it is clear that women, at least those belonging to the upper ranks of society, had a wider range of opportunities in the Middle Ages than after the Reformation. Church courts gave women, married or not, some protection against the arbitrary will of husbands and kinsmen. That many clerical authors were misogynists and treated women with hostility hardly proves that they were of no account, rather the opposite (the only other group treated with similar hostility in medieval literature, the clergy, were certainly not powerless). Such attitudes were to some degree balanced by the teaching that both men and women were equal in the sight of God.

In many respects the situation of women in Christian Scandinavia was much the same as in other parts of Europe in the Middle Ages. Improved diet and a reduction of arbitrary violence, however slight, benefited all, but especially women, who tended to live longer and to make up a larger proportion of the population, creating a surplus that was to some extent absorbed in religious communities and in towns, although in Scandinavia these were small and few.

It has been suggested by David Herlihy (1976) that the importance of women in the aristocracy declined after the eleventh century. His argument is that with the replacement of a bilateral with a patrilineal system of inheritance, in which women only counted if there were no male heirs, women lost their significance as "central signposts indicating kin" and as the "principal conduits in the flow of wealth down the generations." Another factor contributing to the change was, he argues, that the cost of setting up new homes was increasingly met by the families of brides, whereas earlier dowers contributed by husbands and their families were relatively more important, a change that he attributes to the surplus of women.

Herlihy's conclusions, whether or not they are correct for Europe as a whole, do not apply to Scandinavia. Throughout the Middle Ages kinship systems continued to be bilateral at all social levels, and normally the families of both partners in a marriage helped to endow the new family. There may have been some surplus of women in Scandinavia, but the imbalance is unlikely to have been as great as it may have been elsewhere. There were relatively few monasteries into which men could withdraw from the world. The proportion of men who were priests may have been much the same as in other parts of Christian Europe, but many priests did not obey the church law requiring them to be celibate, and as all sons inherited a share of their patrimony there were many more potential husbands with property than in societies where primogeniture was the rule.

Women played a leading role in Scandinavian politics throughout the Middle Ages, from Thyre in the tenth century to Queen Margaret in the fifteenth. It is true that more examples are known from the end of the period, but that is certainly a function of the availability of sources. Women were greatly affected by the changes brought about by the church, but most of these changes happened very slowly. The picture of sudden alteration in the role of women in Scandinavian society implied by thirteenth-century authors and discussed at the beginning of this chapter is a reflection not of reality but of the new attitudes that educated Scandinavians learned from their contacts with Europe and its literature.

10

Uses of the Past

In pre-Christian Scandinavia, as in all societies, the past was used for a variety of purposes: to provide models of conduct, to justify friendship or enmity between families, to legitimize authority, or to explain its loss. Genealogies furnished rulers with suitable ancestors, whose virtues or vices were commemorated in poetry and stories; legends about the origins of kingdoms served to explain their existence. Before conversion, and for some time afterward, ideas about the past were mainly transmitted by word of mouth. History was first written in Scandinavia by churchmen who initially had no use for the vernacular traditions about the pagan past. They set out, instead, to replace them with Christian traditions drawn from the Bible and lives of saints. It was also important for them to justify their claims to moral and religious authority in this newly converted region. Their view of Scandinavian history only reached back to the conversion, which explains why several of the earliest histories produced in Scandinavia begin with kings who were converted or who were benevolently disposed toward missionaries: Horic in the *Roskilde Chronicle* written in about 1140, Harald Finehair in Theodoricus's work and in *Ágrip* ("compendium") produced in Norway later in the century, and Olof Skötkonung in the earliest Swedish king list compiled in about 1250.[1]

The history of conversion was, however, not the first priority for clergy, who were trying to ensure the security of their churches and establish ecclesiastical organization. Their main concern was to enlarge and defend their own rights and to secure endowments and privileges for the churches they had been able to establish. Consequently the earliest histories they wrote or commissioned were concerned with particular churches, especially bishops' sees, and the saints associated with them—for example, Olav at Nidaros, Sunniva at Bergen, Knut at Odense, or Sigfrid at Växjö. The lives of these and other saints together with lists recording the succession of bishops are among the earliest accounts of the past that were produced in Scandinavia. Native Scandinavian saints and missionary martyrs had special appeal, but most important were the royal saints—Olav in Norway and Knut in Denmark—whose cults and legends served the interests of clergy and kings as they sought to extend their authority. Erik, the royal saint of Sweden, died later, in 1160; although his cult soon flourished, the legend was not produced until the end of the thirteenth century. Royal saints conferred an element of divine sanction on their dynasties, and the churchmen who encouraged the cults could hope in return for support from kings whose power was thus enhanced. Not only missionaries needed protection and support; for several generations their successors were faced with opposition that could be violent from laymen who resented the granting of privileges and land to churchmen, many of whom were foreigners, who challenged traditional values and customs.

The protection and support churchmen needed could, and was, provided by local chieftains and magnates, but kings were better patrons while they lived and could be patron saints later. Kings naturally had higher status than anyone else, and their power was, or could be represented as, greater and more extensive than that of magnates, however rich and influential they were. The remarkably quick recognition of both Olav and Knut as saints after their violent deaths was a result of their reputation as supporters of the church, but their efforts to extend and consolidate royal authority was another factor, for it greatly benefited the church and its organization. Norway was more effectively united under Olav than ever before; he summoned Mostering, the assembly in which Christianity was formally accepted for the whole kingdom, and he was credited, together with Bishop Grimkell, with the earliest Norwegian Christian laws. In Denmark Knut was remembered as a generous donor to Lund Cathedral, and his attempt to mobilize an army from the whole kingdom—apparently the first time this had been done—provoked the opposition that led to his death. Knut's posthumous fate is, indeed, a good example not only of the way such a cult grew but also of its importance for the development of written history.

The Beginnings of Written History

In 1086 the Danish king Knut was killed in Odense by magnates who were opposed to his innovations. They transferred their loyalty to his brother Olaf, who promised to maintain the traditional order. When, during Olaf's reign, the Danes suffered both famine and an epidemic, the clergy, who had been blamed for similar disasters a few years earlier, attempted to es-

cape renewed criticism by claiming that these misfortunes were divine punishment for the murder of Knut, thus shifting the blame to the king's
opponents. The clergy, especially those in Odense, began to press Knut's
claim to sanctity, and by the last year of Olaf's reign (1095) Knut's remains
were given a more worthy burial and were soon being credited with cures
and other miracles. Olaf's successor, Erik, invited a colony of English
monks to establish a priory in Odense, and it was largely thanks to them
that Knut's saintly reputation grew and spread. Erik enthusiastically encouraged the cult. He obtained papal canonization of Knut in 1099, and a
year later the saint's remains were translated to a new shrine on the altar of
the cathedral church, which was dedicated to him. Erik's purpose was not
simply to raise the status of the dynasty but to emphasize the divine roots
of kingship and to minimize the significance of election in provincial *things*.

Erik's brother Niels, who succeeded him in 1104, had the same ambition
and was the first Danish king to include the formula *rex gratia Dei* in his
title. During his reign, about 1120, one of the English monks in Odense,
Ælnoth, wrote a chronicle to show that Knut and his brothers were indeed
appointed by God as his earthly representatives. The implication that not
only Knut but also his brothers were beyond criticism posed a problem,
for Knut had been hated by many of his magnates and had been killed not
by pagans, but by his Christian subjects. What was more, the brothers had
not all been eager supporters of the church. Ælnoth's solution was to avoid
criticism and treat the election of these kings as part of God's plan for the
Danes, describing their history as a dramatic battle between supernatural
powers (God and the devil). By crediting Knut as he died with the last
words of Jesus on the cross, Ælnoth compared the martyrdom with
Christ's crucifixion. Just as Jesus had been sent by God to rule the Jews,
Knut's divine mission was to rule the Danes. When they resisted, God punished them, but thanks to Erik and Niels the divine plan to convert the
land was finally accomplished (Sørensen 1984).

Ælnoth's interpretation of Danish history was not accepted by all, and
about two decades later a very different version was given in the *Roskilde
Chronicle*. It has been supposed that this, "Denmark's first history," was
produced by someone in Archbishop Eskil's circle, but there is no hint that
the anonymous author shared Eskil's enthusiasm for reform. Whatever role
Eskil had in its composition, it is clear that the author's attitude was very
different from Ælnoth's. He was rather a conservative who advocated a
balance of power in the kingdom. He thought the king's main functions
were to see that justice was done and that, in particular, property rights
were protected, and to share power and wealth fairly between church leaders and lay magnates. Unlike Ælnoth, who deals with only two genera-

tions, the Roskilde chronicler attempted to cover the whole Christian history of Denmark, from Horik to the civil war of his own time. He seems to have been a pessimist with little hope for the future: King Niels had been killed, a victim of the strife that began with the battle of Fotevik in which his son Magnus and many bishops fell—for the author there was no end to the misery in sight. In such circumstances it is hardly surprising that Saint Knut's family no longer appeared to have been chosen by God to rule the Danes. The chronicler was cool toward Knut himself; his sanctity could not be denied but was said to have been earned by the manner of his death, not that of his life. The author also had a negative attitude to Erik, and he did not think much of King Niels. His judgments on kings do not seem to have been the expression of a considered ideology opposed to Ælnoth's; the criterion was rather the way the kings had treated Roskilde Cathedral, and the cursory treatment of Eskil, who belonged to a powerful Jutland family, may have been colored by the chronicler's local patriotism as a Sjællander (Gelting).

Church influence is also clear in one of the earliest Norwegian histories (perhaps the first), by Theodoricus, written in about 1180. Like the *Roskilde Chronicle* it is in Latin, with many citations and episodes from the Bible, and it begins with the first king who tolerated Christianity, Harald Finehair. In both Norway and Denmark other historians began their accounts much earlier, in pagan times, but only Saxo Grammaticus showed interest in pagan beliefs. In Iceland, too, history was written by men who had been educated in the church, but from the outset their works, mostly in the vernacular, were more secular in tone and exhibit a great interest in native, pre-Christian traditions.

The First Icelandic Historians

Written culture in Iceland was not so church oriented as in other parts of Scandinavia, because the church there remained under secular control to a greater degree than in most of Europe where, in the twelfth century, the reformers were gaining firm ground. Some *goðar* were ordained priests without giving up their chieftaincies, thus retaining the leading role in both religious and secular affairs that they had enjoyed before conversion. *Goðar* built churches and founded the bishops' sees and monasteries. They also established schools in which ecclesiastical literature was being translated into the vernacular by the twelfth century and members of Iceland's leading families began their education. Many of these men were deeply interested

in their Norwegian ancestors, which is one reason for the Icelandic enthusiasm for history and traditions.

The school founded by the first native bishop of Iceland, Ísleif, on
his farm at Skálholt was especially important. Its pupils included Jón
Ogmundarsson, the first bishop of Hólar, and Ísleif's own sons—Gizur,
his successor, and Teit, Ari's informant. Both Jón and Ari founded schools,
and Gizur made Skálholt the bishop's see. In Gizur's time, or soon after,
history began to be written in Iceland. The earliest example was a Latin
account of the Norwegian kings by Sæmund Sigfusson (1056–1133), which
has not survived but is mentioned by many later writers, most revealingly
in a late-twelfth-century poem about Norwegian kings, *Nóregs konunga tal.*
The following stanza comes after the description of the reign of Magnus
the Good, who died in 1047: "Now I have enumerated ten rulers, each
descended from Harald; I have rehearsed their lives as Sæmundr the wise
said" (cited by T. Andersson, 199). The first text that survives, but only in
later copies, is an account of Icelandic history from the settlement to about
1120, written in Norse by Ari (1067/8–1148). Much of the later history
produced in Iceland and Norway drew on the works of these two men.
They seem to represent two different attitudes, one stressing Norwegian
roots, the other written in the vernacular, emphasizing Icelandic independence and, as Theodore Andersson notes, "entitled, almost program-
matically, *Book of the Icelanders.*" He continues: "It may not be without significance that Ari was advised by the bishops Thorlak and Ketill to delete
the kings' lives and genealogies (with their Norwegian ancestries) from the
first version, thus making the book more Icelandic, more about the new
Iceland than the old Iceland with its Norwegian affiliations and family
roots" (225).

Despite the relatively secular character of the church in Iceland the history written there had the same point of departure as that produced in other
parts of Scandinavia, namely the ecclesiastical culture of eleventh- and
twelfth-century Europe, which was itself profoundly influenced by the
writings of classical antiquity. The Icelandic kings' sagas would not have
developed as they did without generations of contact with European
hagiography, historiography, and other literature that the church had made
available. From the classical authors used to teach Latin, lessons in rhetoric
could also be learned. Churchmen had adopted the paradigmatic technique
of Roman rhetoricians, for they recognized that their message could be
more effectively communicated by ideal or deterrent examples than by
rules and commands (K. Johannesson, 19–23). *Exempla* were useful for
moral and political, as well as religious, purposes, especially to historians
in their attempts to exhort and warn. When Icelanders wrote about Scan-

dinavian history, they did not try impartially to discover the truth; like other historians, their aim was to present a plausible account of the past that reinforced their own, or their patrons', ideas and values, in the process modifying or even inventing episodes. The Icelanders' mastery of the technique is shown clearly by the veritable spate of sagas that they began to produce in about 1190. Indeed, most surviving histories produced in Scandinavia in the twelfth and thirteenth centuries were written by Icelanders, and they initially tended to concentrate on Norwegian history.

The Heyday of History Writing

The interest in Norwegian kings shown by Sæmund may have been dampened by pride in "the new Iceland," but it was reawakened shortly before 1200. One sign of this is *Nóregs konunga tal*, which was composed in about 1190 in honor of Jón Loptsson following the recognition that his mother was an illegitimate daughter of Magnus Bareleg. Other Icelanders similarly traced their ancestry back to Norwegian kings, which was one reason so much attention was paid to them in Iceland. A more important factor was the subordination of the Icelandic church to the archbishop of Nidaros, who in 1190 began to reduce the ecclesiastical authority of the *goðar* by prohibiting their ordination. This new church order, enthusiastically supported by Thorlak, bishop of Skálholt, seems to have stimulated interest in Olav Tryggvason, the missionary king. A Latin saga about him was written in about 1190 by Odd Snorrason and translated into Norse about a decade later, around the same time another saga on him was produced by Gunnlaug Leifsson. The link with Nidaros may have encouraged interest in Saint Olav, about whom a saga was produced in about 1200, and before 1230 there were two others. At the same time as these sagas about Olav Tryggvason and Saint Olav were being written, Icelanders were also producing one devoted to King Sverri, *Sverris Saga*. It was begun at the king's initiative as propaganda for his cause but was not completed until about thirty years after his death. Icelandic interest in current events in Norway is evidenced by the *Böglunga Saga*, a contemporary account of the civil war after Sverri's death, and later by Sturla Thorðasson's saga on Håkon Håkonsson shortly after his death in 1263. Sturla also wrote one about Håkon's son Magnus "Lawmender," but only a fragment of it survives.

In the early thirteenth century Icelanders also wrote about earlier Norwegian kings and composed three works dealing with longer periods of Norwegian history. The first of these surveys, compiled in about 1220, only survives in a defective manuscript, whose physical character is reflected by its name, *Morkinskinna* ("rotten skin"). It begins with the death of Saint Olav and seems originally to have ended with the arrival of Sverri in 1177, although the last part is not preserved. A few years later another survey, known in contrast as *Fagrskinna* ("fine skin"), was produced by an Icelander, probably in Norway. It covers a longer period, from Halfdan the Black to 1177. The most elaborate collection of kings' sagas, produced between 1225 and 1235, is Snorri Sturluson's *Heimskringla*, which ends at the same time but begins with Odin and the Yngling kings of the Svear, who were supposedly the ancestors of the Norwegian royal dynasty.

Early sagas were also written about the jarls of Lade, including Håkon, who was Harald Bluetooth's ally and agent in Norway, and his grandson, also called Håkon, who supported Knut's claim to be king of Norway. Another saga written at about the same time was devoted to the Jómsvikings, a warrior band who were allies of Harald.

Icelanders thus seem to have produced histories as propaganda in the final stages of the Norwegian civil war. *Sverris Saga* was not the first to be written for partisan purposes—an account of the unsuccessful attempt of a pretender called Sigurd to win the kingship between 1136 and 1139 was written in about 1150—but it marked the beginning of a remarkable period of historical activity by Icelanders.

A few early sagas dealt with other parts of the Scandinavian world, but these are exceptions; almost all those written between 1190 and 1230 were about Norway, and some were written for Norwegian patrons. Apart from *Heimskringla, Böglunga Saga*, and *Sverris Saga* they deal with events between the mid-ninth century and 1177. The production of so many accounts of the same period and the same people (the lives of Olav Tryggvason and Saint Olav were each described five times) in a span of not more than forty years was obviously a response to the Norwegian civil war, which began with the death of Sigurd the Crusader in 1130. The wars were violent and disruptive from the outset, but with the arrival of Sverri and the death of Magnus Erlingsson the conflict began to be polarized between factions with very different ideals; Sverri claimed to have been chosen by God, while his opponents, including the archbishop, insisted that God's will could only be mediated by the church and that only the church could give legitimacy to a king. This development released the torrent of Icelandic historiography. The conflict directly affected Iceland, for many leading Icelanders were themselves involved and took sides, which naturally affected relations among them at home. The efforts of the archbishop to reform the Icelandic church were also a source of conflict. There were at the same time internal disputes in Iceland caused by the competition for power between *goðar*, which grew more intense in the course of the early thirteenth century. Snorri Sturluson was deeply involved in this power struggle, and it has been argued that his status as one of Iceland's most powerful chieftains determined his attitude to Norwegian history, which he tended to see in terms of the relationship between the king and Norway's leading aristocrats.[2] For him this process culminated in the election and coronation of Magnus Erlingsson, a chieftain's son.

The conflicts of thirteenth-century Iceland were the subject of sagas that were collected to form what is known as *Sturlunga Saga* (see "Icelandic Sagas" in chapter 1). The family sagas, dealing with an earlier Golden Age, can be seen as a reaction against the violence and disruption of the 1200s, describing a time when life was simpler and when, as George Thomas put it, "a bondi's allegiance had been first to his own, inherited notion of *drengskapr* (the Northern ideal of honor), then to his own kin (injury and insult to them was injury and insult to himself), and, finally, to the *goði* whose *thingman* he was and whose authority he accepted" (1970, 26–27).

The Norwegians only produced three slight accounts of their own history; they seem to have been content to rely on Icelanders. The claim that the *Historia Norwegiæ* was written in the 1170s has been questioned; it may have been written some decades later. There is, however, no doubt that Theodoricus wrote his *Historia de Antiquitate Regum Norwagensium* in about 1180, some ten years before the vernacular *Ágrip af Nóregs konunga sögum*. Norwegians thus began to write about their own past long after the Danes and Icelanders and did so at much the same time as the spate of Icelandic historical sagas. The same is true of Denmark, where the major medieval histories by Sven Aggesen and, on a far larger scale, Saxo Grammaticus were produced between 1170 and 1220. The early sections of later Danish chronicles were largely based on Saxo's *Gesta Danorum*, and a simplified compendium of it was produced in the fourteenth century, but no alternative version of early Danish history was produced before the Reformation.

Sweden did not contribute to this remarkably productive period of Scandinavian historiography. A legend of a Swedish saint, Sigfrid, may have been written toward the end of the twelfth century, but that version has not survived, and the earliest known historical compilation, apparently produced in the mid-thirteenth century, is a group of lists, with biographical details, of Swedish kings, beginning with Olof Skötkonung, and of contemporary bishops of Skara and lawmen of Västergötland. The first substantial history is *Erik's Chronicle*, composed in rhyme soon after the accession of Erik's infant son Magnus, describing the history of his family and of Sweden from the time of Erik's grandfather, Birger Jarl. It was another hundred years before Swedish history began to flourish in response to disputes over the Union.

Adam of Bremen

As already remarked, one of the principal concerns of the early Scandinavian historians was to explain how the conversion had happened. They could draw on traditions preserved in their church communities and elsewhere, but one of the most important sources of information was Adam of Bremen's *Gesta Hammaburgensis Ecclesiae Pontificum*, the original version of which was completed in about 1075. Adam's main purpose was to describe the history of the see until the death of Archbishop Adalbert in 1072, and to demonstrate the justice of his archbishop's claim to metropolitan authority over the church in Scandinavia. Adalbert had even hoped to be acknowledged as patriarch over the churches of northern Europe, but nothing came of this ambition, and in 1103 or 1104 Hamburg-Bremen's province was reduced by the creation of the archbishopric of Lund. The German archbishops did not abandon their claim to authority and used Adam's work as a quarry of evidence to support it.

Adam's history was known, directly or indirectly, by many Scandinavian historians, and for most of them his message was unwelcome. They were therefore unwilling to accept his account as it stood but changed it to suit their various purposes. Some of the kings Adam admired as supporters of his archbishopric were denigrated, while others he condemned were praised. This process of revision can be seen clearly in the work of the Danish historians Sven Aggesen and Saxo Grammaticus, who were writing when German imperialism, symbolized by Hamburg-Bremen's claims, was a serious threat to Danish independence. According to Adam Denmark had been converted and the first Danish sees established with bishops appointed by the German archbishop during the reign of Harald Bluetooth. This "just" king, whose claims to sanctity were urged by Adam, was overthrown in a rebellion Adam described as a pagan revolt, which was led by Harald's son Sven, who was said to be an apostate. The late-twelfth-century historians depict Harald very differently, as a weak and incompetent king whose actions threatened the security of the Danish kingdom. Sven Aggesen denied that Sven Forkbeard was an apostate, and Saxo ignored Harald's role in the conversion of the Danes and gave his son credit for the first Danish bishoprics. Saxo accepted that Sven was a pagan at the beginning of his reign but described him after his conversion as a "most religious king." By suggesting that Olof Skötkonung was converted by an English bishop who was buried in the church of Lund, Saxo cast doubt on Hamburg-Bremen's responsibility for establishing the church in Sweden and reinforced Lund's claim to primacy over it. The archbishop of Lund had indeed been given authority over the Swedish church when the archbishopric of Uppsala was established, but this move was resented, and in the thirteenth century it was widely believed in Sweden that Olof Skötkonung had been baptized and his people converted by Sigfrid, archbishop of York. The choice of York was significant, for its archbishops had struggled long against the claim of the archbishops of Canterbury to primacy over the whole English church.

According to Adam the first truly Christian king of Norway was Olav Haraldsson. His predecessor, Olav Tryggvason, who did not acknowledge Hamburg-Bremen's authority, was described as an untrustworthy and barbaric semipagan. Icelandic and Norwegian historians present Olav Tryggvason in a very different light, as a missionary king who began the process completed by his namesake. The revision owes much to Ari, who gave Olav Tryggvason credit for the conversion of both Norway and Iceland, although Ari was careful to emphasize that his efforts were successful in Iceland only after he had gained the support of some native chieftains. Olav Tryggvason was the subject of an Icelandic saga before Saint Olav was. That circumstance was doubtless largely a result of the knowledge, reported by Ari, that Iceland was converted in Olav Tryggvason's reign, but interest in the earlier king may have been at least partly a reaction against the attempts of the archbishop of Nidaros, the shrine of Saint Olav, to gain more effective control of the Icelandic church and to limit the traditional rights of the Icelandic chieftains in it. It is even possible that a negative view of Saint Olav was shared by some people in Tröndelag, for they were most vulnerable to the archbishop's demands; at least Olav Tryggvason, unlike Olav Haraldsson, was remembered as a friend of the Trönder. They recognized Sverri first and generally supported him in his struggle for power.

Adam's account of the conversion of Iceland was completely different. He asserted that it happened in 1056, when the first Icelandic bishop, Ísleif, was consecrated by Adalbert, a good example of his use of the word *conversio* to mean "conversion to our religion" (*nostra religio*), meaning submission to Hamburg-Bremen.

One thing Adam and most early historians of Scandinavia did agree on was the importance of kings in the process of conversion. For the church, the baptism of a king implied the conversion of his people. In fact missionaries must often have depended on the support and protection of chieftains and magnates, but most historians were concerned with the past of the kingdoms in which they lived and tended to focus their attention on kings, not only during the period of mission but at other times too. When they wrote, kingship was considered the central institution in society, and at least churchmen hoped it would guarantee the unity they needed. Those who, like Adam, were interested in the history of their own churches had an incentive to exaggerate the authority of royal converts and the extent of their kingdoms, for that could influence, even determine, the bounds of the bishoprics they founded. What is more, if the first Christian kings were represented as primarily responsible for the conversion and for establishing the church in their kingdoms, they could serve as symbols of that superiority of king over church that Sverri and many others demanded.

Iceland was exceptional. Its unity was expressed not by a king but by law. For Ari and his successors, the acceptance of Christian law marked the decisive step in the conversion, and in *Hungrvaka*, an account of the conversion written in the first years of the thirteenth century, native Icelanders are given all the credit; Olav Tryggvason is not even mentioned. This deliberate rewriting of history to deprive the Norwegian king of any part in the process may be seen as a reaction to the growing influence of Norway, represented at that stage by the archbishop. But, as the proliferation of sagas about both Olav Tryggvason and Saint Olav shows, some Icelanders were very interested in them, although they were sometimes described in unfavorable terms. Snorri Sturluson, for example, put great emphasis on the coercive violence of their missionary methods. It may be suggested that, by making the pagans spokesmen for common sense in contrast to the cruelty and impetuosity of the missionary kings, Snorri was commenting on the contemporary conflict between Icelandic chieftains and the Norwegian archbishop and king and indirectly criticizing the Norwegians for their disregard of traditional Icelandic customs.

Church Reform

Denmark was affected by the church reform movement much earlier than Iceland. Archbishop Eskil was its leading protagonist, and his dispute with Valdemar and its resolution are described in chapter 5. It has been generally accepted that the harmonious cooperation between king and archbishop, most dramatically displayed at Ringsted in 1170, continued under Eskil's successor, Absalon, and was one of the principal themes of Saxo's *Gesta Danorum*. A detailed analysis of Saxo's work, however, shows that he indirectly questioned and criticized royal policies, and that his message was rather that secular rulers ought to be instructed and guided by their spiritual advisers. His *Gesta* has many examples of weak kings and capable bishops, and Saxo called Archbishop Absalon, not the king, *pater patriae* ("father of the fatherland"). It is significant that for the greater part of the *Gesta* the division into books is determined by the reigns of kings, and only the last four focus on the archbishops; book 14 ends not with the death of Valdemar but with the election of Absalon as archbishop (B. Sawyer 1985).

Saxo devotes a great deal of space to Absalon, who was his patron. The description of him as a loyal and self-sacrificing servant performing heroic deeds for the Danish kingdom was partly intended to justify the leading role of the church. It also served to remind ungrateful contemporaries of his achievements; there are clear indications that one of Absalon's motives in commissioning the work was the fear that his preeminence in Valdemar's reign might be forgotten under Valdemar's son Knut (K. Johannesson, 329–32). It is, however, doubtful whether Saxo fulfilled Absalon's expectations. The archbishop died long before the work was finished, and Saxo had the opportunity to make alterations and additions without his patron's knowledge. His original commission was probably to give an account of recent history in order to record Absalon's version of events, but Saxo later extended the work back in time, and his implied criticisms of Absalon's ideals occur mainly in the prehistoric books, the last to be written.

Absalon, as portrayed by Saxo, appears to have been far too involved in secular affairs to be considered a Gregorian reformer, but his eagerness to uphold the privileges and authority of the church was hardly less than Eskil's. The crucial difference between them was that Absalon had the advantage of being a member of the family that helped Valdemar to win power, a relationship that greatly increased his influence and was largely responsible for the cooperation (which was not always harmonious) between king and church in his time. Contemporary tensions were caused not only by ideological conflicts but in large measure also by rivalry between magnates. This is shown very clearly by the contrast between Saxo's work and the Danish history written by his contemporary, Sven Aggesen. Sven's view was that kings ruled by the grace of God, while Saxo emphasized their dependence on the guidance of churchmen; Sven hardly mentions priests or bishops, while Saxo represents many bishops as more important than kings. Sven's indifference to Absalon and his limited interest in the clergy in general was certainly due to his own background. He belonged to the Thurgot family, based in Jutland, whose most important member was Archbishop Eskil. When Absalon succeeded Eskil, the Thurgots lost their influence in the Danish church to the Hvide family of Sjælland. These two histories reflect not only different ideologies but also the rival interests of the two most powerful Danish families. They both claimed to be official histories, but they were in reality partisan contributions to a contemporary political debate.

In Norway the church reform movement had some remarkable and early success during the reign of Magnus Erlingsson, but it was vigorously resisted by Sverri, and the consequent conflict is reflected in the historical works produced in Norway in his reign. Church reform also left its mark on some contemporary English chroniclers. Archbishop Øystein, who was exiled in England from 1180 to 1183, may have been responsible for the hostile attitude of William of Newborough and Roger Howden to Sverri. It is even more likely that he encouraged Theodoricus to write his *Historia de Antiquitate Regum Norwagensium*, which he dedicated to the archbishop. He comments unfavorably on the groups that supported Sverri; Øysten Møyla, Sverri's predecessor as "Birchleg" king, is called an unhappy tyrant (*infelix tyrannus*), and the Trönder are described as unreliable. Theodoricus's explanation for ending the work in 1130 is revealing: "It is not worth preserving for future generations the memory of the crimes, killings, perjuries, parricides, the profanation of holy places, the contempt of God, the plundering of both clergy and people and other abuses too tedious to relate that have poured as if into a ship's bilge since the death of Sigurd" (chapter 34, p. 67). These misfortunes were interpreted by Theodoric as divine punishment inflicted on the Norwegians because of their habit of opposing rightful kings.

Ágrip, which was written in the last decade of the twelfth century, presents a view of Norwegian history very different from Theodoricus's. It may possibly have been produced for Sverri to counter Theodoricus's clerical interpretation and to complement his own saga. It ends when *Sverris Saga* begins, and both of them are in Norse. *Ágrip*'s author, like Sverri, was particularly interested in the law and the way it functioned. Some scholars, for example Munch and Finnur Jónsson, argued that it was favorable to the Birchlegs, but others, including Paasche and Indrebø, deny this bias and point out that Sverri's father and brother were treated as tyrants. This disagreement is enough to show that the work has no consistent tendency; its author had an independent attitude to royal power and judged earlier kings by his own criteria. This does not exclude the possibility that Sverri commissioned the work; even in his own saga his opponents are sometimes presented in a more favorable light than the king himself.

Theodoricus, in contrast, is consistent in representing the ideals of the church reformers. As Sverre Bagge (1989b) has pointed out, his marked Gregorian attitude may even have led him to criticize Øystein for being too interested in secular affairs and seeking economic advantage from his alliance with Magnus Erlingsson. The criticism is made indirectly in two of the digressions. In the first an angel is said to have accused the German emperor Otto I of having poisoned the church by his generosity in giving it lordship over secular vassals. The other, concerning Charlemagne and the pope, underlined the need to keep spiritual and secular authority separate (Theodoricus, chapters 5, pp. 11–12, and 23, pp. 46–48).

It is remarkable that, although the Danes and Norwegians wrote far less history in the twelfth and thirteenth centuries than the Icelanders, two very different accounts of Danish and Norwegian history were written in each kingdom at much the same time. One important reason for the difference between the Norwegian pair is that they were written for different audiences. Theodoricus wrote in Latin, with quotations from classical authors and rhetorical flourishes. The book has a complex structure with allegorical digressions inserted in the narrative to reinforce his message. *Ágrip*, in contrast, is written in a lively saga style in the vernacular, very much like *Sverris Saga*, with which it has many verbal similarities. The authors of both works were churchmen but had very different attitudes. Theodoricus was manifestly clerical, interested in universal, not just Norwegian, history and showed only slight interest in secular politics. The other was no less obviously worldly and was largely concerned with the traditions, events, and people in Norway's past. *Ágrip* emphasizes the working of the law rather than divine intervention, a characteristic that it shares with the later kings' sagas.

The obvious contemporary relevance of many episodes in histories written in the twelfth and thirteenth centuries has encouraged some scholars to identify particular writers as representatives of different factions—in effect, as spokesmen for class or national interests. This tendency has perhaps been overdone; there was no simple class conflict, and even if an early form of nationalism can be recognized, there are many signs of local interests and loyalties in these works. Their authors did take sides, but in doing so and projecting current issues and conflicts into the past, they tend to obscure the fact that the groupings both of their own time and earlier were mainly around rulers, rivals who challenged them, and magnates. Until the latter part of the twelfth century these competing factions seem largely to have accepted the same ideals and values; the disputes in which rivals exchanged places were much like the shifting overlordships of Dark Age Europe, and this is particularly true of the disputes over succession between members of royal families. The twelfth century was, however, a time of structural change effected by the church and growing royal power. The church was responsible for some of the most fundamental developments, and many struggles of the period were over the rights of the clergy and their churches or were provoked by new rules they sought to impose. These conflicts have left their mark on much of the history written then. Theodoricus, for example, showed by his treatment of Jarl Håkon's overthrow by Olav Tryggvason that he was very conscious of the clash between Christian and pagan values, and Saxo ostentatiously emphasized the leading role of the secular clergy. Saxo had little time for monasticism; he only mentions one monk and then only to cast suspicion on him for having poisoned Valdemar. The generosity of women to the church was considered by some to threaten stability by depriving families of their inheritances, and Saxo shows clearly that he did not think that women should have the right to inherit land.

Another cause of fundamental change was the growth of royal power, which was thought by some to be a challenge to the traditional order. This view is reflected in histories written at the time, most clearly in those written by Icelanders. Much of the history they wrote after about 1220 was influenced by the growing Norwegian threat to Icelandic independence. One very well known illustration of their response is the accusation, made by Snorri Sturluson and others, but not before the thirteenth century, that Harald Finehair deprived all men of their right to inherit land.

Any explanation for the production of so much history in Denmark, Norway, and Iceland in a short period of time must take account of other purposes it was made to serve, for the past was used to criticize, support, or merely comment on other contemporary issues as well as ideological and political conflicts. There was, for example, a need to strengthen the sense of unity as kingdoms grew larger, to encourage respect for new laws, or to instill the moral values taught by the church. One way of making such changes acceptable was to show that they were not complete novelties but were rooted in the past—a task for historians.

Attitudes to Paganism

A problem faced by any who wrote about the time before conversion was, obviously, how to make paganism relevant. One solution was to treat it as a form of natural religion, imperfectly foreshadowing Christianity. Adam of Bremen's comment that before their conversion the Icelanders had a "natural faith which did not differ very much from our own religion" (4.36) shows that he was prepared to adopt that attitude. Moreover, the Icelanders endowed the heroes in their sagas with such Christian virtues as mercy, compassion, or a sense of justice. Such "noble heathens" were unwilling to take revenge and avoided sorcery and idolatry, and the belief in him "who created the sun and who rules everything," which some are said to have had, was clearly intended to prepare the way for Christian monotheism. Some of these noble heathens are, indeed, compared favorably with Christians who did not practice what they preached. In this way the pagan past could be made to provide ethical models for contemporaries (L. Lönnroth 1969, 5). Theodore Andersson has analyzed "the ethical temper" of ten family sagas that are mostly about the period before conversion and concluded that they are characterized by a sense of proportion and moderation, stressing the dangers of self-seeking, passion, and ambition and the benefits of moderation and forbearance. Andersson points out that moderation is not necessarily Christian and that "what we probably have in the sagas is not so much a replacement of a pagan ideal with a Christian ideal as the replacement of a warrior ideal with a social ideal" (592).

The family sagas do, however, show the influence of one Christian ideal, for they depict the Icelanders as monogamous and faithful. The church made many demands affecting the status and rights of women, and their relations with men, that met stiff resistance, and the varied responses of the historians and of the authors of sagas that are only vaguely historical are discussed in chapter 8. It is relevant here to note that the saga authors in general display little interest in religion, religious experiences, or the notion of divine justice. Their secular spirit has been explained as a reaction to the extreme clerical claims that were made in thirteenth-century Iceland: "People could not avoid being brought face to face with the choice posed by the claims of Bishop Thorlakr and Bishop Gudmund for clerical supremacy. . . . Certainly, a human worldly response was likely, a tendency to concentrate on secular values in everyday life, a reluctance or refusal to accept the reality of religious sanctions in ordinary dealings" (Foote 1984, 45).

Saxo's attitude to the pagan past was very different from the Icelanders'. He treated it as an imperfect and barbaric time, the prevailing chaos being well illustrated by many examples of women's evil influence and ill-fated actions. Christianity brought divine order, which meant, among other things, the subordination of women to men. It did, though, suit his purpose to acknowledge that some noble qualities—bravery, fidelity, a sense of honor—were evidenced in pagan times by Danes, not by Norwegians or Swedes. Unlike the Icelanders, who had a positive interest in the pagan gods, Saxo treated them with contempt. He shared the Icelanders' euhemeristic interpretation of the gods as real people whose achievements were so exceptional that they were worshiped, but by placing their home in Sweden, more specifically in Uppsala, he distanced his countrymen from their contaminating influence. Saxo also used the pagan period to comment on some current concerns, including the threat posed by the Germans. This was a delicate matter, for Knut was married to a German, the daughter of Henry the Lion, Duke of Saxony. Another topic that was treated obliquely was of particular interest to Saxo personally. He described many episodes, in recent as well as pagan times, demonstrating that eloquence, intelligence, and general ability were qualities the fatherland needed, thus stressing the point that a man's career should not be determined by birth alone. Saxo was arguing on behalf of educated men of relatively humble origins, like himself, in the service of churchmen or kings.

History Writing as a Crisis Symptom

Historians are inevitably influenced by their contemporary circumstances, consciously or not, and their interpretations of the past can cast light on their own times. We have noted some of the ways in which the early Scandinavian historians used the past to comment on current issues. What is surprising and has not attracted much attention is that so many accounts of the same period were produced in Denmark, Norway, and Iceland in the sixty years after 1170. A few were written before or after that period, but the overwhelming majority of histories written in those parts of Scandinavia were produced in those decades. It may be tempting to suppose that the Scandinavian historians were simply following the lead given elsewhere in Europe, and that the fashion reached this peripheral and backward region relatively late. Doubt is cast on that explanation by the very uneven distribution of history writing in Scandinavia. The absence of such texts from Sweden can hardly be explained by assuming that the Swedish clergy were so much less well educated and out of touch than their contemporaries in Iceland. What is more, a delayed reaction hardly explains why, even in Iceland, interest in early Norwegian history diminished so dramatically after about 1230.

That the wave of historical writing began at much the same time in both Denmark and Norway, in the reigns of Valdemar I and Sverri, suggests that the initial stimulus was the need to legitimize the rule of these kings after a prolonged period of civil war in each land. Sven Aggesen's chronicle and *Sverris Saga* were both written in the royal interest, and Sverri's was manifestly intended by the king to present him as the legitimate ruler of the Norwegians who, despite doubts about his birth, had been chosen by God. Most of the other histories produced before 1230 were also about kings, but they are not so royalistic as those two works. Theodoricus and Saxo wrote in support of the church, while Snorri and perhaps also the *Historia Norwegiæ* reflect rather the interests of the aristocracy. They were all in some measure written in response to the changes that were occurring then, in particular the creation of new and more effective forms of kingship. That was the reason no history was written in Denmark after Valdemar II consolidated his power. The later decline of Danish royal authority stimulated no renewed interest in the past. Most of the histories written in Norway or for Norwegians were produced at a time of intense conflict. After the civil wars ended, the only new contributions to Norwegian history were *Håkon Håkonssons Saga*, which was commissioned by his son and successor, Magnus, and a saga on Magnus himself by the same author, only a small part of which has survived.

The conflicts in Norway were also partly responsible for awakening historical interest in Iceland, but this interest was sustained by the growing authority of archbishops and kings and the resistance they provoked, as well as by the internal conflicts that disrupted Icelandic society in the thirteenth century. The last major historical saga that survives, Håkon Håkonsson's, written after Iceland had submitted to the Norwegian crown, was, although official history, hardly a panegyric on the king, who was regarded as an enemy by many Icelanders, including some of the author's own family. Another response, represented by the family sagas, was to look back to the good old days before kings and archbishops challenged the traditional interests of the aristocracy.

It was obviously risky to criticize kings, archbishops, or other powerful men openly. Both Snorri and Saxo were careful to express any negative opinions obliquely, by implication, with such success that there is little agreement about their own views. They both exploited ambiguity, but in different ways. Snorri used a deceptively objective style, expressing no opinions directly, apparently leaving his audience to draw their own conclusions, but conveying his own attitude by the actions and words of his characters. Saxo, in contrast, offered many explicit judgments but skillfully implied his own, often very different, opinion. So, for example, Saxo emphasized the unity of the Danish kingdom under the Valdemars, but he referred to the untrustworthy Jutlanders and cowardly Skanians while praising the men from his own island, Sjælland, suggesting that the unity was little more than a veneer.

One of his most important tasks was to legitimize the rule of the Valdemarian dynasty, but he described many episodes and actions that cast doubt on its worthiness, on occasion even making its members appear ridiculous. The *Gesta* ends in 1185 in the reign of Knut but was completed when his brother Valdemar was king. In the preface Saxo addresses the king and praises him for enlarging the kingdom and "overleaping the reputation of his predecessors." This eulogy is introduced by a significant passage in which Saxo appeals to the king to look kindly on the way he has described his illustrious descent and continues, "for I fear that I shall be shackled by the weight of my subject and, far from properly depicting your lineage, I shall only reveal my lack of aptitude and meager talents" (preface, i.6). Such humility was a familiar rhetorical device, but it had some substance. Saxo had good reason to fear that some of his readers might think that he had done much less than justice to the king's grandfather, father, and brother.

Sweden

That no history of Sweden was produced in the twelfth and thirteenth centuries (apart from some meager lists of kings, bishops, and lawmen) is consistent with the suggestion made here that interest in the past was aroused by the increased effectiveness of royal power. The Götar and Svear were not permanently united until the middle of the twelfth century, and for the next hundred years Swedish kings were relatively weak. It was not until the fourteenth century that histories of the Swedish kingdom began to be written, many of them in the form of rhyming chronicles in Swedish.

The first was *Erik's Chronicle*, written soon after Magnus Eriksson was elected king. It deals with the period 1230–1319 and draws on traditions that were current among the companions of the king's father, Duke Erik. It is addressed to the young king and reminds him not only of the achievements of his forefathers but also that he owes his throne to God and the men of Uppland. This metrical chronicle was written for the entertainment and instruction of courtiers and magnates and is in a suitably courtly and polished style. Its author approves of the existing order, extols chivalrous virtues, and supports the royal policy of expansion by conquest on the far side of the Baltic. The later metrical chronicles about Engelbrekt, Karl Knutsson, and others were intended for a wider audience that included burgesses, miners, and minor landowners and are very different from *Erik's Chronicle* in both style and content. They are doggerel, full of burlesque humor and crude expressions, and are openly hostile to the Danes.

These differences illustrate very clearly the changed political situation in Sweden. Until the early years of the fifteenth century Swedish politics were a matter for the aristocracy and higher clergy, but after Engelbrekt's rebellion in 1434 other groups had increased political significance in the traditional *things* and assemblies held in connection with the great fairs. The rebellion was not directed against the Union, but it was at just that time that the first signs of incipient nationalism are evident in some circles. Indeed, in 1434 at the Council of Basle, Nicolaus Ragvaldi (later archbishop of Uppsala) praised the achievements of the Goths and claimed that they were the ancestors of the Swedes. This was the first sign of Gothicism, the romantic dream of the former greatness of the Swedes that soon became a significant element in Karl Knutsson's propaganda.

A series of chronicles were produced in Karl's chancery that were designed to gain support for his policies. The most important of them, *Karl's Chronicle*, was in fact an attempt to counter the fierce criticism expressed in 1447 in a pamphlet that accused him of being a traitor and oath breaker. It is not known how widely copies of this pamphlet were distributed, but the production of *Karl's Chronicle* implies that the views expressed in it were considered a serious threat by Karl and his supporters. The pamphlet also influenced the only major medieval Swedish history written in Latin, the *Chronica Regni Gothorum* that Ericus Olai completed in about 1470.

For long sections Ericus Olai followed *Karl's Chronicle* fairly closely, but for his account of the years 1436–39 he was greatly influenced by the criticism voiced in 1447. Moreover, it is clear that Ericus had more sympathy for Archbishop Jöns Bengtsson than for Karl, and his view that secular rulers should be subordinate to spiritual leaders echoes the attitude of the twelfth-century archbishops Eskil, Absalon, and Øystein.

This ambiguity seems to have been necessary because Ericus wrote at a time when Karl Knutsson could not be criticized openly. His attacks were therefore oblique rather than direct (E. Lönnroth 1964). His situation was very much like Saxo's three centuries earlier, and their techniques were similar. Their works had to be acceptable to secular rulers and to their ecclesiastic superiors, and if possible reflect the values and purposes of both. In times of rapid political change and uncertainty historians could not speak only for one group and have in consequence posed problems for historical scholarship in modern times. Ericus Olai had little influence on later interpretations of late medieval Swedish history. That is not surprising, for it was Gustav Vasa's view that prevailed, and he favored the interpretation associated with Karl Knutsson.

Gustav Vasa's respect for history as a way of shaping opinion is shown by the efforts he made to control what was written about himself and the past and by his treatment of one historian in particular, Olaus Petri.[3] Olaus had been one of most active supporters of Gustav and his policy of Lutheran reform, but on New Year's Eve 1539 Olaus was condemned to death for having failed to expose a conspiracy against the king, and because he had encouraged rebellion not only by his preaching but also by his history of Sweden. His life was spared, but the extreme sentence shows what weight Gustav put on the use of the past. Olaus objected to the loss of the church's independence and the confiscation of its property, and in *En swensk crönika* he indirectly criticized the king. It is, in fact, an angry denunciation of earlier Swedish tyrants, who all suspiciously resembled Gustav Vasa. They debased the coinage, granted provinces as duchies to their sons, and welcomed Germans who plagued the unfortunate Swedes and drove them to justifiable rebellion. This criticism of royal policies was bad enough, but Gustav Vasa was further angered by the way this once eager reformer treated the early bishops and their privileges with much more sympathy than he showed the kings and secular magnates. To crown everything, among the magnates "dishonored" by Olaus were Sten Sture the elder and younger. This was particularly offensive, for Gustav put great weight on his kinship with them in order to enlarge his aristocratic connections and strengthen his right to rule.

Olaus Petri was silenced, and his chronicle was not printed (until 1818), but many copies were made and spread secretly. Gustav Vasa blamed the bishops for this and for distributing other "damaging" works. He made great efforts to stop this distribution; searches were organized, and some bishops were tried and imprisoned. Gustav reacted so vigorously because he feared that the bishops might provoke people to rebel, and that fear was all the greater after 1554, when a new history of Sweden was published in Rome by Johannes Magnus, the Catholic archbishop of Uppsala, who had been driven into exile by Gustav. In his *Historia de omnibus Gothorum Sueonumque regibus* Johannes, like Olaus Petri, obviously alluded to Gustav Vasa in his descriptions of early tyrants who plundered their subjects and temples. The book was an immediate success in Europe and was widely read and quoted with respect. Gustav could do nothing about that, but he was able to mount a counterattack of propaganda. He chose Peder Svart, bishop of Västerås, to write the official account of his own life. This work, full of vivid illustrations of the love and loyalty of the Swedish people for the father of their land, has been the basis for the classic view of the king. It was also important to rewrite earlier history to harmonize with the king's policies, and before 1560 this had been done in a chronicle attributed to Archbishop Laurentius Petri, brother of Olaus, giving a Lutheran interpretation of Swedish history. Laurentius deplored that Olof Skötkonung was persuaded to pay tax to Rome by foreign priests; praised Saint Erik for his piety and justice, not as a saint; suggested that Magnus Birgersson should have endowed schools and hospitals instead of an abbey; and accused Birgitta of inventing her revelations and pretending to hear heavenly voices. The work is colored by Gustav Vasa's own concept of the sanctity of kingship: when native kings are killed or exiled or blamed for evil acts, the blame is put on false friends or rebellious subjects.

There were two main themes in this royal propaganda: the terrible sufferings of the Swedish people under the Danish king Christian II, the Tyrant, and the irreparable damage that power-hungry and treacherous bishops had inflicted on the country. The alliance between the Swedish archbishop Gustav Trolle and Christian II provided Gustav Vasa with a good argument in his conflict with the church. He also made good use of Lutheran criticisms of the Catholic church, but even after the leading Catholic bishops had been forced into exile, he still needed the image of greedy and overweening bishops to justify the confiscation of church property and institutions. At the same time he suspected that the Lutherans themselves wanted bishops to be independent enough to be able to rebuke the king. Gustav Vasa's reaction to the appearance of Johannes Magnus's Swedish history in 1554 shows that he still found it necessary to fight on two fronts against Catholics and Lutherans, for in both camps there were bishops who, like their predecessors, thought the king was a tyrant.

Gustav Vasa was willing to make use of his opponents' works when it suited his purpose. According to Johannes Magnus, the Swedish princes were descendants of Noah's grandson, Magog, the progenitor of the Goths, and it was not long before the Gothic ancestry was dogma in the royal court. Johannes Magnus's history was especially useful in the growing tension with Denmark. In 1558 Gustav Vasa sent to his trusted men a copy of the speech against the Danes that Johannes put into the mouth of Bishop Hemming Gadh. In this the Danes are described as cruel, spewing curses continuously and speaking in a barbaric manner as though coughing out words between twisted lips. Danish "officials, warriors, monks, and whores who have always infested our land" are accused of having sown hatred and discord among the unsuspecting Swedes with cunning and lies.

Gustav Vasa's picture of the Middle Ages—and himself—has been remarkably influential in Sweden down to modern times. There was little to oppose it; the works of Ericus Olai and Johannes Magnus were in Latin, not Swedish, and Olaus Petri's chronicle was not printed. The use the king made of history is a good illustration of the need to reinterpret the past after periods of conflict and revolutionary change. There was at that time no comparable outburst of history writing in Denmark—only an attempt to counter the Swedish offensive. In using history for their propaganda, Gustav Vasa and his opponents were following a long tradition. There were, however, two significant new features. First, printing now made it possible to spread such propaganda more quickly and widely than before. Second, the church, which had enjoyed a virtual monopoly of history writing, had been brought under the firm control of the king, who could now take advantage of its very efficient system of communications.

Medieval Scandinavia since the Sixteenth Century

Scandinavia has often been regarded as the region in which Germanic society remained uncontaminated by Christianity and other alien influences longer than anywhere else. This picture has answered different needs at different times, has been used for a variety of ideological purposes inside and outside Scandinavia, and still has great influence on medieval research. It is the result of several centuries of development and reflects many different currents of thought, from sixteenth-century humanism to the democratic ideals of modern times. It was in reaction to the Italian humanists' glorification of their inheritance from ancient Rome that some learned Scandinavians were led to discover their own glorious and native past. In other parts of Europe scholars began to take an interest in early Scandinavia as a fascinating and distinct society. Saxo's work, which began to be widely known after it was printed in Paris in 1514, was a rich quarry of vivid details on which a picture of primitive Scandinavia could be based; the printing of some Icelandic sagas in the seventeenth century provided more material. Ideas about Scandinavia were also affected by Protestant attitudes to the medieval centuries as a time of oppressive bishops and corrupting alien influences. Scandinavia provided a contrast where primitive Nordic culture, uncontaminated by alien influence, was cherished by strong and just men who loved freedom.

The Enlightenment—with its interest in origins, the natural, and the primitive—and romanticism made their own contribution to an idealized picture of early Scandinavia, but the evolutionary concept of history, with Germanists in the lead, was especially influential. They saw in pre-Christian Scandinavia primitive Germanic society in a virtually pure state. More recently early Scandinavia has been believed to be an ideal democratic society, based on free and independent landowners. It has also been claimed that women had a higher status in that society than elsewhere; even today "a Germanic-Nordic model of independent womanhood is contrasted with a patriarchal and dependent model found in Mediterranean Europe" (Jochens 1986b, 35–37).

A central theme of European history has been the development of Christian kingdoms. Scandinavian sources have figured prominently in the search for the Germanic component. The concept of the Free Germans, which owed much to Tacitus's idealized account of them, has had great influence on the interpretation of the Germanic laws. Montesquieu's picture of Germanic society in *De l'ésprit des lois* was particularly influential. He claimed that it comprised equal clans with no superior authority and therefore no courts of law. Penal laws were not needed because disputes were settled either by reconciliation or duel. Punishment and processes to determine the truth were introduced into Germanic law by the church. Montesquieu tried to show that absolute kingship was un-Germanic and that Christianity had had a negative effect. In the nineteenth century, after the French Revolution, attitudes changed. The contribution of the church was rated more highly, and true history was thought to begin with rise of the Christian states. Until that happened the Germans had lived a life of barbarism, revengeful, bloodthirsty, and ruled by kin groups. It was Christian civilization that opposed the blood feud and insisted on individual responsibility.

Outside observers have tended to treat early Scandinavia, especially before the conversion, as a unity, paying particular attention to common features. Within Scandinavia there is more emphasis on the differences, partly because of various interests and past conflicts. The significance of the medieval centuries for the national identity differs among the countries. Norway lost its independence in the fourteenth century and did not recover it until 1905. The later Middle Ages have, as a result, been neglected in comparison with the earlier period of Norwegian greatness. In Iceland attention has been concentrated on the period before 1262 for a similar reason. The source of national inspiration in Sweden was found not in the early or even high Middle Ages, but in the fifteenth century, the period of resistance to the Union; and despite Saint Erik, the ruler generally thought of as the founder of the nation is Gustav Vasa, at once freedom fighter and father of the country. Finland was part of Sweden from the thirteenth century to 1809, and it is therefore not surprising that Finnish nationalism has drawn no inspiration from the period of Swedish domination. Instead national identity has been found in the Finnish traditions about the period before Swedish conquest that were the basis of Elias Lönnrot's poem *Kalevala* (34,873 lines, published in 1839–49). In the parts of Finland where Swedish has, until recently, been commonly spoken there has been more interest in medieval history, and for the national consciousness of the Ålanders that period is crucial, justifying their claim to autonomy. It may be noted in conclusion that national feelings in Norway, Iceland, and Sweden have been encouraged by the emphasis placed, especially by earlier generations of historians, on opposition to Denmark, which dominated Scandinavia for much of the Middle Ages.

Talk of national symbols and periods of national greatness may be considered anachronistic with no significance for modern historical scholarship, but they have played a key role in determining what periods of medieval history have interested modern Scandinavians most. The obscurity of the early medieval centuries in Sweden and Finland compared with the rest of Scandinavia is a consequence not only of the uneven distribution of sources but of the slight attention paid to the period in teaching and textbooks, which reflects the view that it has no relevance for the understanding of modern society. On the contrary, as we have tried to show, it is in that period that we can begin to trace the roots of later developments in all parts of Scandinavia.

Notes

1. Sources

1. The Scandinavian runic inscriptions are published in *Danmarks Runeindskrifter, Norges Innskrifter med de Yngre Runer*, and *Sveriges Runinskrifter*. See also Moltke and Jansson.

2. For a preliminary report of such a study, see B. Sawyer 1988, 1991b.

3. *Kulturhistorisk Leksikon for nordisk middelalder (KHL)* gives detailed information about the laws, with full bibliographies.

4. The leading exponent of this view was Konrad Maurer. See also Kern.

5. For a survey of the discussion, see Norseng.

6. For an up-to-date survey of saga research, see Clover and Lindow.

7. The translation is from Page, 169.

8. The exception is a stanza on the rune-stone at Karlevi, Öland (*Danmarks Runeindskrifter*, no. 411). See Jansson, 134–35.

2. Lands and Peoples

1. Sömme is an authoritative account of the geography of the Scandinavian world.

2. Citations to Adam throughout the text are to book and chapter.

3. Recent general surveys of Scandinavian activity abroad in the Viking Age are Roesdahl 1991 and P. Sawyer 1982.

3. Political History

The political history of the Scandinavian kingdoms is described in detail in the general works cited in the "Note on General Reading" that precedes "Works Cited." In this chapter we refer only to some recent publications, in particular those that offer new interpretations.

1. For early Swedish history, see P. Sawyer 1991b.

2. Roesdahl 1982, 147–55. For Trelleborg in Skåne, see Jacobsson 1990.

3. This marriage has been represented as a sign of the superiority of the Svear, but it is rather the opposite and may be compared with the marriage of Sven's son Knut to the widow of the English king Æthelred after Knut conquered England.

4. This paragraph and figure 3.8 are based on John Lind's elucidation of the treaty (see Gallén and Lind).

4. *Things* and Kings

1. Ian Wood makes this point in his forthcoming book on the Merovingian Franks.

5. Christianization and Church Organization

1. For the first part of this chapter, see Sawyer and Wood 1987; for a general introduction to the European background, see Southern 1970.

6. Landowners and Tenants

1. The first section of this chapter is based on *KHL*, s.v. "Jordejendom," corrected with the help of Knut Helle and Erik Ulsig.
2. For this section, see *KHL*, s.v. "Fæste," "Jordleige," "Landbo," and "Leiglending."

7. Trade and Towns

1. Ian Wood in his forthcoming book on the Merovingian Franks emphasizes the significance of the Frankish civil war and discusses its effects.
2. Clarke and Ambrosiani provide a useful survey of early towns and trading places in the Viking world.
3. There is a brief account, with references, of early Scandinavian activity in Russia in P. Sawyer 1982, 113–26.
4. See the discussion between Brita Malmer and Kenneth Johsson in *Nordisk Numismatisk Unions Medlemsblad*, 1982, 62–72.
5. For medieval Scandinavian towns in general, see Blom, and for Danish towns, Andrén. Swedish towns have all been treated in separate reports by *Medeltidsstaden*, a project published by Riksantikvarieämbetet and Statens Historiska Museer. An English summary edited by Hans Andersson is in preparation.
6. A good general survey of the activity of German merchants in the Baltic region and Scandinavia is Dollinger; see also Christiansen.
7. For trade with Norway, see Nedkvitne 1983.
8. Helle 1982a is a very full study of Bergen's medieval history.
9. Nedkvitne 1983, chapter 1, traces in detail the exclusion of Scandinavian merchants from most overseas trade.

8. Family and Inheritance

1. For a general discussion of these rights, see Sjöholm 1978, 244–464; 1988, chapters 8, 13.
2. This paragraph is based on Gunnes 1982.
3. This section on Snorri is based on Thorsteinsson, 66–67, 69–85; and on J. Johannesson, 226–56.
4. See an unpublished document dated 15 March 1361 in Riksarkivet, Stockholm.
5. This section on Valdemar II's properties is based on Rasmussen and on Hørby 1989, 115–17.

9. Women

1. For a survey of studies along this line of women's freedom, see Jochens 1986b, 36 n. 4.

2. This section is based on Steinsland 1979, 1983.

3. This paragraph is based on *Svenskt biografiskt lexikon*, s.v. "Knut Eriksson."

4. This paragraph is based on Tryti, 196.

10. Uses of the Past

1. Editions, translations, and commentaries on the works mentioned in this chapter are noted in the relevant articles in *KHL*, where there is also a long article on "Historieskrivning." For the works produced in the twelfth and thirteenth centuries, further details are noted in B. and P. Sawyer (1992).

2. See, for example, Sandvik, 56, 98. For another view, see Bagge 1991, e.g., 65–75, 237–51, which rejects the theory that the main theme in Snorri's work is the conflict between the king and the aristocracy. Bagge sees the conflicts not in "constitutional" terms but as "feuds," i.e., conflicts between individuals (75).

3. This paragraph is based on K. Johannesson 1982, 270–76; 1987, 140–58.

A Note on General Reading

Most publications on medieval Scandinavia are, naturally, in Scandinavian languages. The best introduction to Norwegian history is Helle (1991). More detailed general surveys of the period before 1319 are Andersen and Helle (1974). An old but very good account of the late Middle Ages is Taranger, but for an excellent, short, and up-to-date introduction to the period during which Norway and Denmark were united see Bagge and Mykland. There are two recent general histories of Denmark. The first two volumes of *Danmarkshistorie* (ed. Christensen et al.) cover the period to 1648, and volumes 3–7 (ed. Olsen) deal with the period 700–1600. The most substantial survey of Swedish history is Rosén. The best recent general account of Icelandic history is Thorsteinsson, but J. Jóhannesson and Byock are useful discussions, in English, of the period before Norwegian rule.

The articles in *KHL* are invaluable, but we have only given references where the key word is not obvious; we have, for example, not referred to the articles on "Distingen" or "Heimskringla." The only comprehensive account of the period in a non-Scandinavian language that we know of is Musset. General works in English include, for the early period, Foote and Wilson and, for the late Middle Ages, Bolin (1966) and E. Lönnroth (1963). Several periodicals publish articles on the subject in English. The *Scandinavian Journal of History* is particularly useful. Others are *Medieval Scandinavia*, *Scandinavian Studies*, and the *Saga-Book of the Viking Society*.

Works Cited

In citing works in the text, a few abbreviations have been used for works frequently cited.

Adam of Bremen   *Gesta Hammaburgensis ecclesiae Pontificum*. Reference is to book and chapter.

DD   *Diplomatarium Danicum*, 1st series

KHL   *Kulturhistorisk Leksikon for nordisk middelalder*

SR   *Sveriges Runinskrifter*

VA   Rimbert's *Vita Anskarii*. Reference is to chapter.

Adam of Bremen. 1961. *Gesta Hammaburgensis ecclesiae Pontificum*. In Trillmich and Buchner, 135–503, with a parallel German translation. English translation in F. J. Tschan, *History of the Archbishops of Hamburg-Bremen by Adam of Bremen* (New York: Columbia University Press, 1959).

Ælnoths Krønike. 1984. Trans. and commentary by Erling Albrectsen; afterword by Preben Meulengracht Sørensen. Odense, Denmark: Odense Universitetsforlag.

Ahnlund, Nils. 1922. "Svinnegarns Källa." *Rig* 5, 59–76.

Äldre Västgötalagen. 1979. In Holmbäck and Wessén, part 5.

Ambrosiani, Björn. 1983. "Background to the Boat-graves of the Mälaren Valley." In *Vendel Period Studies*, ed. J. P. Lamm and H.-Å. Nordström, 23–30. Stockholm: Statens Historiska Museum.

Ambrosiani, Kristina. 1981. *Viking Age Combs, Comb Making, and Comb Makers in the Light of Finds from Birka and Ribe*. Stockholm: University of Stockholm.

Andersen, Per Sveaas. 1977. *Samlingen av Norge og kristningen av landet 800–1130*. Bergen, Oslo, and Tromsø: Universitetsforlaget.

Anderson, Perry. 1978. *Passages from Antiquity to Feudalism*. London: Verso.

Andersson, Ingvar. 1965. "Det lundensiska Primatet över Sverige." *Historisk Tidskrift* (Stockholm) 28, 324–28.

Andersson, Theodore M. 1967. *The Icelandic Family Saga: An Analytical Reading*. Harvard Studies in Comparative Literature 28. Cambridge, Mass.: Harvard University Press.

————. 1970. "The Displacement of the Heroic Ideal in the Family Sagas." *Speculum* 45, 575–93.

————. 1985. "Kings' Sagas (Konungasögur)." In Clover and Lindow, 197–238.

Andrén, Anders. 1985. *Den urbana scenen. Städer och samhälle i det medeltida Danmark.* Malmö: Gleerup.

Aspects of Female Existence: Proceedings from the St. Gertrud Symposium, "Women in the Middle Ages," Copenhagen, September 1978. 1980. Ed. Birte Carlé, Nanna Damsholt, Karen Gletbe, and Eva Trein Nielsen. Copenhagen: Gyldendal.

Bagge, Sverre. 1975. "Samkongedømme og enekongedømme." *Historisk Tidsskrift* (Oslo), 239–73.

————. 1984. "Nordic Students at Foreign Universities until 1660." *Scandinavian Journal of History* 9, 1–29.

————. 1986. "Borgerkrig og statsutvikling i Norge i middelalderen." *Historisk Tidsskrift* (Oslo), 145–97.

————. 1987. *The Political Thought of the King's Mirror.* Odense, Denmark: Odense University Press.

————. 1989a. Review of Sjöholm 1988. *Historisk Tidsskrift* (Oslo), 500–507.

————. 1989b. "Theodoricus Monachus—Clerical Historiography in Twelfth Century Norway." *Scandinavian Journal of History* 14, 113–33.

————. 1991. *Society and Politics in Snorri Sturluson's* Heimskringla. Berkeley and Los Angeles: University of California Press.

————, and Mykland, Knut. 1987. *Norge i dansketiden.* Copenhagen: Politiken.

Bandel, Betty. 1955. "The English Chroniclers' Attitude toward Women." *Journal of the History of Ideas* 16, 113–18.

Beckman, Lars. 1959. *A Contribution to the Physical Anthropology and Population Genetics of Sweden.* Ph.D. diss., Uppsala University.

Bendixen, Kirsten. 1967. *Denmark's Money.* Copenhagen: National Museum.

————. 1992. "Coin-circulation, coin-policy, and the function of coins in Denmark, from around 1050 to around 1241." In Jensen et al. 1:154–56; Danish text with notes, 87–92.

Benedictow, Ole J. 1990. "The Great Pestilence in Norway: An Epidemiological Study," *Collegium Medievale* 3, 19–58.

————; Dahlerup, Troels; Lundholm, Kjell-Gunnar; and Eriksson, Jerker A. 1971. *Den nordiske Adel i Senmiddelalderen.* Rapporter til det Nordiske Historikermøde i København 1971, Copenhagen.

Blackburn, Mark. 1990. "Do Cnut the Great's First Coins as King of Denmark Date from before 1018?" In Jonsson and Malmer, 55–68.

————, and Metcalf, Michael, eds. 1981. *Viking-Age Coinage in the Northern Lands.* BAR International Series 122. Oxford: BAR.

Blom, Grethe Authén, ed. 1977. *Urbaniseringsprosessen i Norden,* vol. 1 of *Middelaldersteder.* Bergen, Oslo, and Trømso: Universitetsforlaget.

————. 1990. "Women and Justice in Norway c.1300–1600." In *People and Places in Northern Europe, 500–1600; Essays in Honour of Peter Hayes Sawyer,* ed. Ian Wood and Niels Lund, 225–36. Woodbridge, England: Boydell.

Bolin, Sture. 1931. *Om Nordens äldsta historieforskning.* Lunds Universitets Årsskrift n.s. 27 (sec. 1), no. 3.

————. 1966. "Medieval Agrarian Society in Its Prime: Scandinavia." In *The Cambridge Economic History of Europe,* 2d ed. 1:633–59. Cambridge: Cambridge University Press.

Byock, Jesse L. 1988. *Medieval Iceland. Society, Sagas, and Power.* Berkeley and Los Angeles: University of California Press.

Campbell, Alistair. 1949. *Encomium Emmae Reginae*. Royal Historical Society, Camden, 3d series, no. 72. London: Royal Historical Society.

Christensen, Aksel E., H. P. Clausen, Svend Ellehøj, and Søren Mørch. eds. *Danmarkshistorie*. 1977–80. 2 vols. Copenhagen: Gyldendal.

Christensen, C. A. 1950. "Estrids og dronning Margaretes gaver." *Historisk Tidsskrift* (Copenhagen), 450–62.

Christensen, Vibeke, and Sørensen, John Kousgård. 1972. *Stednavneforskning*. Vol. 1. Copenhagen: Universitetsforlaget.

Christiansen, Erik. 1980. *The Northern Crusades: The Baltic and the Catholic Frontier, 1100–1525*. London: Macmillan.

Clarke, Helen, ed. 1979. *Iron and Man in Prehistoric Sweden*. Stockholm: Jernkontoret.

———, and Ambrosiani, Björn. 1991. *Towns in the Viking Age*. Leicester: Leicester University Press.

Clover, Carol. 1985. "Icelandic Family Sagas (Islendingasögur)." In Clover and Lindow, 239–315.

———. 1986a. "Hildigunnr's Lament." In *Structure and Meaning in Old Norse Literature; New Approaches to Textual Analysis and Literary Criticism*, 141–83. Odense, Denmark: Odense University Press.

———. 1986b. "Maiden Warriors and Other Sons." *Journal of English and Germanic Philology* 85, 35–49.

———. 1988. "The Politics of Scarcity; Notes on the Sex Role in Early Scandinavia." *Scandinavian Studies*, 147–88.

———, and Lindow, John, eds. 1985. *Old Norse-Icelandic Literature: A Critical Guide*. Ithaca, N.Y.: Cornell University Press.

Crumlin-Pedersen, Ole, and Hansen, Kjeld. 1990. *Aspects of Maritime Scandinavia, A.D. 200–1200*. Roskilde, Denmark: Vikingeskibshallen.

Dahlbäck, Göran. 1987. *I medeltidens Stockholm*. Stockholm: Medeltidsmuseum.

Dahlerup, Troels. 1989. *De frie stænder; 1400–1500*, vol. 6 of *Danmarkshistorie*, ed. Olsen.

Dalalagen. 1979. In Holmbäck and Wessén, part 2.

Dalberg, Vibeke, and Sørensen, John Kousgård. 1979. *Stednavneforskning 2*. Copenhagen: Akademisk forlag.

Diplomatarium Danicum. 1975, 1963. 1st series. Vol. 1, *Regester 789–1052*, ed. C. A. Christensen and Herluf Nielsen (Copenhagen: C. A. Reitzel); vol. 2, *1053–1169*, ed. Lauritz Weibull with Niels Skyum-Nielsen. Copenhagen: Ejnar Munksgaards Forlag.

Dollinger, Philippe. 1970. *The German Hansa*. London: Macmillan.

Farbregd, Oddmunn. 1988. "Kvinneliv i vikingtid; kven var kvinnene som ligg i langhaugar?" *Kvinner i arkeologi i Norge (K.A.N.)*, 3–23.

Faulkes, Anthony. 1987. *Snorri Sturluson Edda*, translation and introduction. London: Dent.

Fell, Christine. 1983. "Unfrið: An Approach to a Definition." *Saga-Book of the Viking Society* 21, 85–100.

Female Power in the Middle Ages: Proceedings from the Second St. Gertrud Symposium, Copenhagen, August 1986. 1989. Ed. Karen Glente and Lise Winther-Jensen. Copenhagen: C. A. Reitzel.

Fidjestøl, Bjarne. 1982. *Det norrøne fyrstediktet*. Øvre Ervik: Alvheim and Eide.

Foote, Peter. 1984. *Aurvandilsta: Norse Studies*. Odense, Denmark: Odense University Press.

———, and Wilson, David. 1970. *The Viking Achievement*. London: Sidgwick and Jackson.

Förändringar i kvinnors villkor under medeltiden: uppsatser framlagda vid ett kvinnohistoriskt symposium i Skálholt, Island, 22.-25. juni 1981. 1983. Ed. Silja Aðalsteinsdóttir and Helgi Thorláksson. Reykjavík: Sagnfræðistofnun Háskóla Íslands.

Frank, Roberta. 1973. "Marriage in Twelfth- and Thirteenth-Century Iceland." *Viator* 4, 473–84.
————. 1981. "Snorri and the Mead of Poetry." *Speculum Norroenum, Norse Studies in Memory of Gabriel Turville-Petre*, ed. Ursula Dronke, Guðrún P. Helgadóttir, Gerd W. Weber, and Hans Bekker-Nielsen, 155–70. Odense, Denmark: Odense University Press.
————. 1985. "Skaldic Poetry." In Clover and Lindow, 157–96.
————. 1990a. "Ornithology and the Interpretation of Skaldic Verse." *Saga-Book of the Viking Society* 23, 81–3.
————. 1990b. "Why Skalds Address Women." In *Atti del 12 Congresso internazionale di studi sull'alto medioevo*, Spoleto, Italy, 4–10 September 1988, 67–83.
Gallén, Jarl, and Lind, John. 1991. *Nöteborgsfreden och Finlands Medeltida Östgräns*, andra delen (Skrifter utgivna av Svenska Litteratursällskapet i Finland no. 427:2).
Gelting, Michael. 1979. See *Roskildekrøniken*.
Gissel, Svend; Jutikkala, Eino; Österberg, Eva; Sandnes, Jørn; and Teitsson, Björn. 1981. *Desertion and Land Colonization in the Nordic Countries c. 1300–1600*. Stockholm: Almqvist & Wiksell International.
Gjerløw, Lilli. 1974. "Missaler brukt i Oslo bispedømme fra misjonstiden til Nidarosordinariet." In *Oslo bispedømme 900 år*, ed. Fridtjov Birkeli, Arne Odd Johnsen, and Einar Molland, 73–142. Oslo, Bergen, and Tromsø: Universitetsforlaget.
Goody, Jack. 1983. *The Development of the Family and Marriage in Europe*. Cambridge: Cambridge University Press.
Götlind, Anna. 1990. *The Messengers of Medieval Technology? Cistercians and Technology in Medieval Scandinavia*. Alingsås, Sweden: Viktoria Bokförlag.
Gräslund, Anne-Sofie. 1987. "Runstenar, bygd och gravar." *Tor* 21, 241–62.
Grøngaard-Jeppesen, T. 1981. *Middelalderlandbyens opståen. Kontinuitet og brud i den fynske agrarbebyggelse mellem yngre jernalder og tidlig middelalder*. Fynske studier 11. Odense, Denmark: Odense bys museer.
Gunneng, Hedda. 1987. "Kvinnlig arvsrätt under svensk medeltid; en forskningsrapport." In *Manliga strukturer*, 79–90.
Gunnes, Erik. 1982. "Prester og deier—sølibatet i norsk middelalder." *Hamarspor; eit festskrift til Lars Hamre 1912–23. januar-1982*, ed. Steinar Imsen and Gudmund Sandvik, 22–44. Bergen, Oslo, and Tromsø: Universitetsforlaget.
————. 1987. "Klosterlivet i Norge. Tilblivelse—økonomi—avvikling." *Forening til Norske Fortidsminnesmerkers Bevaring, Årbok* 1987, 49–84.
————. 1989. *Regesta Norvegica*, 1:822–1263. Oslo: Norsk Historisk Kjeldeskrift-Institutt.
Hårdh, Birgitta. 1978. "Trade and Money in Scandinavia in the Viking Age." *Meddelanden från Lunds universitets historiska museum*, n.s. 2, 157–71.
Harmer, F. E. 1950. "*Chipping* and *Market*. A Lexicographical Investigation." In *Early Cultures of North-West Europe*, ed. Cyril Fox and B. Dickens, 335–57. Cambridge: Cambridge University Press.
Harris, Joseph. 1985. "Eddic Poetry." In Clover and Lindow, 68–156.
Helgadóttir, Gudrún. 1985. "Kvinner og legekunst i den norrøne litteratur." In *Kvinnearbeid i Norden*, 17–30.
Helland, Amund. 1908. *Norges Land og Folk*. Vol. 18, *Nordlands Amt*, part 2, 865–908. Kristiania, Norway: Aschehoug.
Hellberg, Staffan. 1980. "Vikingatidens *vikingar*." *Arkiv för nordisk filologi* 95, 25–88.
————. 1986. "Tysk eller Engelsk Mission? Om det tidiga Kristna låneorden." *Maal og Minne*, 42–49.

Helle, Knut. 1972. *Konge og gode menn i Norsk riksstyring ca. 1150–1319.* Bergen, Oslo, and Tromsø: Universitetsforlaget.

———. 1974. *Norge blir en stat 1130–1319.* Bergen, Oslo, and Tromsø: Universitetsforlaget.

———. 1981. "Norway in the High Middle Ages. Recent Views on the Structure of Society." *Scandinavian Journal of History* 6, 161–89.

———. 1982a. *Bergen bys historie.* Vol. 1, *Kongsete og kjøpstad: Fra ophavet til 1536.* Bergen, Oslo, and Tromsø: Universitetsforlaget.

———. 1982b. "The Germans in Bergen in the Middle Ages." In *Bryggen: The Hanseatic Settlement in Bergen.* Det Hanseatiske Museums Skrifter, no. 24, 12–26. Bergen: Det Hanseatiske Museum.

———. 1990. "Norwegian Foreign Policy and the Maid of Norway." *Scottish Historical Review* 69, 142–56.

———. 1991. "Tiden fram til 1536." In *Grunntrekk i norsk historie fra vikingtid til våre dager,* ed. Rolf Danielsen, Ståle Dyrvik, Tore Grønlie, Knut Helle, and Edgar Hovland. Oslo: Universitetsforlaget.

Herlihy, David. 1976. "Land, Family, and Women in Continental Europe, 701–1200." In *Women in Medieval Society,* ed. Susan Mosher Stuard, 13–45. Philadelphia: University of Pennsylvania Press.

Hildebrandt, Margareta. 1985. "En kyrka byggd på hednisk grund?" *Populär arkeologi* 3, 9–13.

Historia Norwegiae. 1880. In Storm, 71–124.

Hødnebø, Finn. 1987. "Who Were the First Vikings?" In *Proceedings of the Tenth Viking Congress,* 43–54.

Högberg, Folke. 1965. "Medeltida Absidkyrkor i Norden." *Västergötlands Forminnesföreningens Tidskrift* 6(5):5–231.

Holmbäck, Åke, and Wessén, Elias. 1979. *Svenska Landskapslagar.* 5 parts. Stockholm: AWE/Gebers.

Hørby, Kai. 1966. "Øresundstolden og den skånske skibstold. Spørgsmålet om kontinuitet." In *Middelalderstudier tilegnede Aksel E. Christensen på treårsdagen 11. September 1966,* ed. Tage E. Christiansen, Svend Ellehøj, and Erling Ladewig Petersen, 245–72. Copenhagen: Munksgaard.

———. 1979. "The Fate of the Descendants of Christoffer I. Aspects of Danish Politics, 1252–1319." *Scandinavian Journal of History* 4, 207–29.

———. 1989. *Velstands krise og tudsind bakhold.* Vol. 5 of *Danmarkshistorie,* ed. Olsen.

Hvass, Steen. 1983. "Viking Age Villages in Denmark—New Investigations." In *Society and Trade in the Baltic during the Viking Age,* ed. Sven-Olof Lindquist (*Acta Visbyensia* no. 7), 211–28. Visby: Gotlands Fornsal.

———. 1984. "Wikingerzeitliche Siedlungen in Vorbasse." *Offa* 41, 97–112.

Imsen, Steinar. 1990. *Norsk bondekommunalisme fra Magnus Lagabøte til Kristian Kvart.* Part 1, *Middelalderen.* Trondheim, Norway: Tapir Forlag.

Jacobsen, Grethe. 1983. "Ændrede kvinders stilling sig ved overgangen til kristendom i Norden?" In *Förändringar i kvinnors villkor under medeltiden,* 26–40.

———. 1984. "Pregnancy and Childbirth in the Medieval North: A Topology of Sources and a Preliminary Study." *Scandinavian Journal of History* 9, 91–111.

———. 1985. "Kvinder arbejde i det danske bysamfund 1400–1550." In *Kvinnearbeid i Norden,* 7–16.

Jacobsen, L., and Moltke, E., eds. 1942. *Danmarks Runeindskrifter.* 1942. Copenhagen: Ejnar Munksgaards Forlag.

Jacobsson, Bengt. 1990. "Visst har det funnits en borg i Trelleborg!" *Populär arkeologi* 8, 7–10.

Jansson, Sven B. F. 1987. *Runes in Sweden*. Stockholm: Gidlunds.

Jensen, Jørgen Steen. 1992. "Coin Circulation in Denmark ca. 1241–1550, as Illustrated by Treasure Hoards and Other Types of Finds." In Jensen et al. 1:156–60; Danish text with notes, 93–104.

——, Kirsten Bendixen, Niels-Knud Liebgott, and Fritze Lindahl. 1992. *Danmarks middelalderlige skattefund c. 1050-c. 1550*. Nordiske Fortidsminder, series B, 12. 2 vols. Copenhagen: Kongelige Nordiske Oldskrift-selskab.

Jensen, Stig. 1991. *The Vikings of Ribe*. Ribe, Denmark: Den antikvariske Samling.

Jexlev, Thelma. 1980. "Wills, Deeds, and Charters as Sources for the History of Medieval Women." In *Aspects of Female Existence*, 28–40.

Jochens, Jenny M. 1980. "The Church and Sexuality in Medieval Iceland." *Journal of Medieval History* 6, 377–92.

——. 1985. "En Islande médiévale: à la recherche de la famille nucléaire." *Annales Economies Sociétés Civilisations* 40, 95–112.

——. 1986a. "Consent in Marriage: Old Norse Law, Life, and Literature." *Scandinavian Studies* 58, 142–76.

——. 1986b. "The Medieval Icelandic Heroine: Fact or Fiction?" *Viator* 17, 35–50.

——. 1987. "The Female Inciter in the Kings' Sagas." *Arkiv för Nordisk Filologi* 102, 100–121.

Jóhannesson, Jón. 1974. *A History of the Old Icelandic Commonwealth*. Manitoba: University of Manitoba Press.

Johannesson, Kurt. 1978. *Saxo Grammaticus; komposition och världsbild i Gesta Danorum*. Stockholm: Lärdoms historiska Samfundet.

——. 1982. *Gotisk renässans; Johannes och Olaus Magnus som politiker och historiker*. Stockholm: Almqvist & Wiksell International.

——. 1987. "Ordets stridsmän under Gustav Vasa." In *Den svenska litteraturen; från forntid till frihetstid*, ed. L. Lönnroth and S. Delblanc, 140–58. Stockholm: Bonniers.

Jonsson, Kenneth, and Malmer, Brita, eds. 1990. *Sigtuna Papers*. Stockholm: Kungl. Vitterhets Historie och Antikvitets Akademien.

Kalinke, Marianne. 1985. "Norse Romance (*Riddarasögur*)." In Clover and Lindow, 316–63.

Karras, Ruth Mazo. 1988. *Slavery and Society in Medieval Scandinavia*. New Haven, Conn.: Yale University Press.

Kern, F. 1939. *Kingship and Law in the Middle Ages*. Oxford: Blackwell.

Kilderne til den tidlige middelalders historie; Rapporter til den XX nordiske historikerkongress. 1987. Vol. 1, ed. Gunnar Karlsson. Reykjavík: Sagnfræðistofnun Háskóla Íslands.

Klackenberg, Henrik. 1992. *Moneta nostra: Monetarisering i medeltidens Sverige*. Lund Studies in Medieval Archaeology 10. Stockholm: Almqvist & Wiksell International.

Knudsen, Anders Leegaard. 1988. "Den Danske Konges Gods i Højmiddelalderen: en historiografiske undersøgelse af begreberne *Kongelev* og *Patrimonium*." *Historisk Tidsskrift* (Copenhagen) 88, 213–28.

Krag, Claus. 1989. "Norge som odel i Harald Hårfagres ætt." *Historisk Tidsskrift* (Oslo), 288–302.

Kulturhistorisk Leksikon for nordisk middelalder. 1956–78. 22 vols. Copenhagen: Rosenkilde og Bagger.

Kumlien, Kjell. 1962. "Sveriges kristnande i slutskedet-spörsmål om vittnesbörd och verklighet." *Historisk Tidsskrift* (Stockholm) 82, 249–94.

Kvinder i middelalderen; symposieforedrag, Københavns Universitet, 1982. 1983. Copenhagen: Den Danske Historiske Forening.

Kvinnans ekonomiska ställning under nordisk medeltid; uppsatser framlagda vid ett kvinnohistoriskt symposium i Kungälv 8–12 oktober 1979. 1981. Ed. Hedda Gunneng and Birgit Strand. Gothenburg: Kvinnohistoriskt arkiv 19.

Kvinnearbeid i Norden fra vikingtiden til reformasjonen; foredrag fra et nordisk kvinnehistorisk seminar i Bergen, augusti 1983. 1985. Ed. Randi Andersen, Liv Helga Dommasnes, Magnús Stefánsson, and Ingvild Øye. Bergen: Alvheim & Eide.

Kvinnors Rosengård; föredrag från nordiska tvärvetenskapliga symposier i Århus aug. 1985 och Visby sept. 1987. 1989. Ed. Hedda Gunneng, Beata Losman, Bodil M. Knudsen, and Helle Reinholdt (Skriftserie från Centrum för kvinnoforskning vid Stockholms Universitet, no. 1).

Lagerqvist, Lars O. 1970. *Svenska mynt under vikingatid och medeltid.* Stockholm: Numismatiska Bokforlag.

———. 1985. "Kring trekronorsvapnet på svenska 1300-tals mynt." *Hikuin,* 261–66.

Larsen, J. H. 1980. "Vikingtids handelsplass i Valle, Setesdal." *Universitetets Oldsaksamling Skrifter* n.s. 3, 143–8.

Lindkvist, Thomas. 1979. *Landborna i Norden under äldre medeltid.* Uppsala, Sweden: Historiska Institutionen, Uppsala University.

Lindquist, Ivar. 1941. *Västgötalagens Litterära Bilagor.* Lund, Sweden: Skrifter utgivna av Vetenskaps-Societeten i Lund 26.

Lönnroth, Erik. 1963. "The Economic Policies of Governments: The Baltic Countries." In *The Cambridge Economic History of Europe,* 3:361–96. Cambridge: Cambridge University Press.

———. 1964. "Ericus Olai som politiker." In Erik Lönnroth, *Från svensk medeltid,* 127–42. Stockholm: Bonniers.

Lönnroth, Lars. 1969. "The Noble Heathen: A Theme in the Sagas." *Scandinavian Studies* 41, 1–29.

———. 1984. "Studier i Olaf Tryggvasons saga." *Samlaren,* 54–94.

Losman, Beata. 1983. "Birgitta, en kvinnlig väckelsepredikant." In *Förändringar i kvinnors villkor under medeltiden,* 82–104.

Lund, Niels, ed. 1984. *Two Voyagers at the Court of King Alfred.* York: William Sessions.

Lundahl, Ivar. 1961. *Det Medeltida Västergötland.* Uppsala, Sweden: Nomina Germanica 12.

Lundström, Lillemor. 1973. *Bitsilver och betalningsringar. Studier i svenska depåfynd från vikingatiden påträffade mellan 1900–1970.* Ph.D. diss., Stockholm University.

Malmer, Brita. 1981. "Monetary Circulation in South-eastern Sweden c. 1350–1500 in the Light of Three Major Church-finds." *Nordisk numismatisk årsskrift,* 147–59.

———, and Rispling, Gert. 1981. "Om importen av islamiska mynt till Gotland under vikingatiden." *Nordisk Numismatisk Unions Medlemsblad,* 154–58.

Manliga strukturer och kvinnliga strategier; en bok till Gunhild Kyle. 1987. Ed. Birgit Sawyer and Anita Göransson. Göteborg: Historiska institutionen, Meddelanden 33.

Martens, Irmelin. 1987. "Iron Extraction, Settlement, and Trade in the Viking and Early Middle Ages in South Norway." In *Proceedings of the Tenth Viking Congress,* 69–80.

Moltke, Erik. 1985. *Runes and Their Origin; Denmark and Elsewhere.* Copenhagen: National Museum.

Mundal, Else. 1983. "Kvinner og dikting; overgangen frå munnleg til skriftleg kultur— ei ulukke for kvinnene?" In *Förändringar i kvinnors villkor under medeltiden,* 11–25.

———. 1988. "Forholdet mellom born og foreldre i det norrøne kjeldematerialet." *Collegium Medievale,* 9–26.

————. 1989. "Barneutbering." In *Kvinnors Rosengård*, 122–34.

————, and Steinsland, Gro. 1989. "Kvinner og medisinsk magi." In *Kvinnors Rosengård*, 97–121.

Munktell, Ing-Marie. 1981. "Landbokvinna-Frälsekvinna; en studie i kvinnors ekonomiska villkor under senmedeltiden, belysta med hjälp av jordeböcker och räkenskaper." In *Kvinnans ekonomiska ställning under nordisk medeltid*, 14–40.

Murray, Alexander C. 1983. *Germanic Kinship Structure; Studies in Law and Society in Antiquity and the Early Middle Ages*. Toronto: Pontifical Institute of Medieval Studies.

————. 1988. "From Roman to Frankish Gaul: 'Centenarii' and 'Centenae' in the Administration of the Merovingian Kingdom." *Traditio* 44, 59–100.

Musset, Lucien. 1951. *Les peuples Scandinaves au Moyen Age*. Paris: Presses Universitaires de France.

Myrvoll, Siri. 1986. "Skien og Telemark—naturresurser, produkter og kontakter i sen vikingtid og tidlig middelalder." *Viking* 1985/86, 161–80.

Nedkvitne, Arnved. 1977. "Handelssjøfarten mellom Norge og England i høymiddelalderen." *Sjøfartshistorisk Årbok 1976*, 7–254.

————. 1983. *Utenrikshandelen fra det Vestafjelske Norge 1100–1600*. Bergen.

Nielsen, Eva Trein. 1983. "Kvindearbejdes art, vilkår og muligheder i Danmark, ca. 1300–1650." In *Kvinder i middelalderen*, 3–10.

Norges Innskrifter med de Yngre Runer. 1941–. Ed. M. Olsen and A. Liestøl. Oslo: Norsk Historisk Kjeldeskrift Institutt.

Nørlund, Poul. 1924. "Klostret og dets Gods." In M. Mackeprang, *Sorø. Klostret, Skolen, Akademiet gennem Tiderne*. Vol. 1, *Tiden før 1737*, 53–131. Copenhagen: J. Frimodt.

Nors, Thyre. 1987. "Kampen om ægteskabet; en konfliktfyldt historie om kirkens forsøg på at genne lægfolk ind i den hellige ægtestand." *Den Jyske Historiker* 42, 28–46.

Norseng, Per. 1987. "Lovmaterialet som kilde til tidlig nordisk middelalder." In *Kilderne til den tidlige middelalders historie*, 48–77.

Ólason, Vésteinn. 1987. "Norrøn litteratur som historisk kildemateriale." In *Kilderne til den tidlige middelalders historie*, 30–47.

Olsen, Olaf. 1966. *Hørg, Hof og Kirke*. Copenhagen: G. E. C. Gad.

————, ed. 1988–91. *Danmarkshistorie*. 16 vols. Copenhagen: Gyldendal and Politiken.

Olsen, Rikke Agnete. 1986. *Borge i Danmark*. Copenhagen: Centrum.

Olsson, Gunnar. 1953. "Sverige och landet vid Göta Älvs mynning under medeltiden." *Göteborgs Högskolas Årsskrift* 59, 3.

Österberg, Eva. 1981. "Svenska kvinnors ekonomiska ställning under medeltiden." In *Kvinnans ekonomiska ställning under nordisk medeltid*, 1–13.

Östgötalagen. 1979. In Holmbäck and Wessén, part 1.

Page, R. I. 1980. "Rune-masters and Skalds." In *The Viking World*, ed. James Graham-Campbell, 154–71. London: Frances Lincoln.

Poulsen, Bjørn. 1985. "Mønter i den senmiddelalderlige danske agrarekonomi." *Hikuin* 11, 227–36.

Proceedings of the Tenth Viking Congress: Larkollen, Norway, 1985. 1987. Ed. James E. Knirk. Oslo: Universitetets Oldsaksamlings Skrifter, n.s. 9.

Procopius. 1919. *History of the Wars*. Vol. 3. Ed. and trans. H. B. Dewing. Cambridge, Mass.: Harvard University Press.

Rafnsson, Sveinbjörn. 1990. *Byggðaleifar i Hrafnkelsdal og á Brúardölum*. Reykjavík: Íslenska fornleifafélag.

Rasmussen, Kristen J. 1987. "Kong Eriks Døtre." *Den Jyske Historiker* 42, 47–67.

Refskou, Niels. 1986. "Det retslige indhold af de ottonske diplomer til de danske bispe-dømmer." *Scandia* 53, 167–210.

Resi, Heid Gjøstein. 1987. "Reflections on Viking Age Local Trade in Stone Products." In *Proceedings of the Tenth Viking Congress*, 95–102.

Rimbert. 1961. *Vita Anskarii.* In Trillmich and Buchner, 1–133. English translation by C. H. Robinson, *Anskar, the Apostle of the North* (London: Society for the Propagation of the Gospel in Foreign Parts, 1921).

Robberstad, Knut. 1981. *Gulatingslovi.* 4th ed. Oslo: Det Norske Samlaget.

Roesdahl, Else. 1982. *Viking-Age Denmark.* London: British Museum.

———. 1991. *The Vikings.* London: Allen Lane.

Rosén, Jerker. 1962. *Svensk historia: Tiden före 1718.* Stockholm: Svenska Bokförlaget.

Roskildekrøniken. 1979. Trans. and commentary by Michael H. Gelting. Wormianum.

Ruong, Israel. 1975. *Samerna.* Stockholm: Bonniers.

Sandvik, Gudmund. 1955. *Høvding og konge i Heimskringla.* Oslo: Universitetets Historiske Seminar.

Sawyer, Birgit. 1985. "Valdemar, Absalon, and Saxo. Historiography and Politics in Medieval Denmark." *Revue Belge de Philologie et d'Histoire* 63, 685–705.

———. 1987. "Scandinavian Conversion Histories." In B. and P. Sawyer and Wood, 88–110.

———. 1988. *Property and Inheritance in Viking Scandinavia: The Runic Evidence.* Alingsås, Sweden: Viktoria Bokförlag.

———. 1989. "Women as Landholders and Alienators of Property in Early Medieval Scandinavia." In *Female Power in the Middle Ages*, 156–171.

———. 1990. "Women and the Conversion of Scandinavia." In *Frauen in Spätantike und Frühmittelalter; Lebensbedingungen, Lebensnormen, Lebensformen*, ed. Werner Affeldt, 263–81. Sigmaringen, Germany: Jan Thorbecke Verlag.

———. 1991a. "Viking-Age Rune-Stones as a Crisis Symptom." *Norwegian Archaeological Review* 24(2):97–112.

———. 1991b. "Women as Bridge-builders: The Role of Women in Viking-age Scandinavia." In *People and Places in Northern Europe, 500–1600; Essays in Honour of Peter Hayes Sawyer*, ed. Ian Wood and Niels Lund, 211–24. Woodbridge, England: Boydell.

Sawyer, Birgit and Peter. 1985. *Innan Alingsås blev stad.* Alingsås, Sweden: Viktoria Bokförlag.

———. 1992. "Adam and the Eve of Scandinavian History." In *The Perception of the Past in Twelfth-Century Europe*, ed. Paul Madagliano. 37–51. London: Hambledon.

Sawyer, Birgit and Peter, and Wood, Ian, eds. 1987. *The Christianization of Scandinavia. A Symposium Report.* Alingsås, Sweden: Viktoria Bokförlag.

Sawyer, Peter. 1982. *Kings and Vikings.* London: Methuen.

———. 1986a. "Anglo-Scandinavian Trade in the Viking Age and After." In *Anglo-Saxon Monetary History: Essays in Memory of Michael Dolley*, ed. M. A. S. Blackburn, 185–199. Leicester: Leicester University Press.

———. 1986b. "Early Fairs and Markets in England and Scandinavia." In *The Market in History*, ed. B. L. Anderson and A. J. H. Latham, 59–77. London: Croom Helm.

———. 1988a. *Da Danmark blev Danmark.* Vol. 3 of *Danmarkshistorie*, ed. Olsen.

———. 1988b. "Dioceses and Parishes in Twelfth-Century Scandinavia." In *St Magnus Cathedral and Orkney's Twelfth-Century Renaissance*, ed. Barbara E. Crawford, 25–35. Aberdeen: Aberdeen University Press.

———. 1991a. "Kings and Royal Power." In *Høvdingesamfund og Kongemakt*, ed. Peder Mortensen and Birgit M. Rasmussen (*Jysk Arkæologisk Selskabs Skrifter* 22:2), 282–88. Højbjerg.

————. 1991b. *När Sverige blev Sverige*. Alingsås, Sweden: Viktoria Bokförlag.

————. 1991c. "Svein Forkbeard and the Historians." In *Church and Chronicle in the Middle Ages: Essays Presented to John Taylor*, ed. Ian Wood and G. A. Loud, 27–40. London: Hambledon.

Saxo, *Saxonis Gesta Danorum*. 1932. Vol. 1. Ed. J. Olrik and H. Ræder. Copenhagen: Munksgaard. English translation of books 1–9 by Peter Fisher, *Saxo Grammaticus History of the Danes*, vol. 1 (Cambridge: D. S. Brewer, 1979); of books 10–16 by Eric Christiansen, *Saxo Grammaticus Books X–XVI* (BAR International Series 84, 118, Oxford: BAR, 1980).

Schück, Herman. 1987. "Sweden's Early Parliamentary Institutions from the Thirteenth Century to 1611." In *The Riksdag: A History of the Swedish Parliament*, ed. Michael F. Metcalf, 5–60. New York: St. Martin's.

Sellevold, Berit Jansen. 1989a. "Fødsel og død; kvinners dødelighet i forbindelse med svangerskap og fødsel i forhistorisk tid og middelalder, belyst ut fra studier av skjelettmaterialer." In *Kvinnors Rosengård*, 79–96.

————. 1989b. "Fokus på kvinner. Kvinners helse i middelalderen belyst gjennem skjelett-studier." In *Kvinnors Rosengård*, 59–78.

Sigurðsson, Jón Viðar. 1989. *Fra goðorðum til ríkja: throun goðavaldes á 12. og 13. öld*. Reykjavík: Bókaútgáfa Menningarsjóðs.

Sjöholm, Elsa. 1978. "Rättshistorisk metod och teoribildning." *Scandia* 44, 229–56.

————. 1988. *Sveriges medeltidslagar; europeisk rättstradition i politisk omvandling*, Lund, Sweden: Rättshistoriskt Bibliotek.

Skyum-Nielsen, Niels. 1963. *Kirkekampen i Danmark 1241–1290, Jacob Erlandsen, samtid og eftertid*. Copenhagen: Munksgaard.

————. 1971. *Kvinde og slave; Danmarkshistorie uden retouche*. Copenhagen: Munksgaard.

Smith, Gina. 1973. "De danske nonneklostre indtil ca. 1250." *Kirkehistoriske samlinger*, 1–45.

Snorri Sturluson. 1977. *Heimskringla*. 3 vols. Ed. Bjarni Aðalbjarnarson (Íslenzk Fornrit 26–8). Reykjavík: Hið Íslenzka Fornritafélag, 1941–51; translated with introd. and notes by Lee M. Hollander (Austin: University of Texas Press, 1977).

Sølvberg, Ingvild Øye. 1976. *Driftsmåter i vestnorsk jordbruk ca 600–1350*. Bergen, Oslo, and Tromsø: Universitetsforlaget.

Sömme, A., ed. 1960. *The Geography of Norden*. Stockholm. Also published as *A Geography of Norden*, 1961, New York: Wiley.

Sørensen, Preben Meulengracht. 1977. *Saga och samfund*. Copenhagen: Berlingske Forlag.

————. 1980. *Norrønt nid*. Odense, Denmark: Odense Universitetsforlag.

————. 1984. See *Ælnoths Krønike*, 115–139.

Southern, Richard W. 1970. *Western Society and the Church in the Middle Ages*. Harmondsworth, England: Penguin.

Steinsland, Gro. 1979. "Den gamle religion." In *Norges kulturhistorie*, vol. 1, ed. Ingrid Semmingsen, 129–62. Oslo: Aschehoug.

————. 1983. "Kvinner og kult i vikingetid." In *Kvinnearbeid i Norden*, 31–42.

Stiesdahl, Hans. 1983. "Grave i tidlige vesttårne." *Hikuin* 9, 7–26.

Storm, Gustav. 1880. *Monumenta Historica Norvegiæ*. Kristiania, Norway: By official order.

Strand [now Sawyer], Birgit. 1980. *Kvinnor och män i Gesta Danorum*. Göteborg, Sweden: Kvinnohistoriskarkiv 18.

————. 1981. "Saxo's Description of Women Compared with Snorre's" and "Thyre Danebod in Gesta Danorum." In *Saxo Grammaticus: A Medieval Author between Norse and Latin Cultures*, ed. K. Friis-Jensen, 135–51, 152–67. Copenhagen: Museum Tusculanum Press.

Sveriges Runinskrifter. 1911–. Stockholm: Kungl. Vitterhets Historie och Antikvitetsakademien.

Taranger, Absalon. 1915–17. *Norges Historie, 1319–1537*. 2 vols. Kristiania, Norway: H. Aschehoug.

Theodoricus Monachus. 1880. *Historia de Antiquitate Regum Norwagensium*. In Storm, 1–68.

Thomas, George. 1946–53. "Some Exceptional Women in the Sagas." In *Saga-Book of the Viking Society* 13, 307–27.

————. 1970. "Introduction." In *Sturlunga Saga*, vol. 1, trans. Julia H. McGrew. New York: Twayne and the American-Scandinavian Foundation.

Thorsteinsson, Björn. 1985. *Island*. Copenhagen: Politiken.

Trillmich, Werner, and Buchner, Rudolf. 1961. *Quellen des 9. und 11. Jahrhunderts zur Geschichte der hamburgischen Kirche und des Reiches*. Berlin: Rutten & Loening.

Tryti, Anna Elisa. 1987. "Kvinnenes stilling i klostervesenet." In *Foreningen til norske fortidsminnesmerkers bevaring, Årbok 1987*, 187–208.

Ullén, Marian. 1979. *Södra Råda gamla kyrka* (Svenska Fornminnesplatser 4). Stockholm: Riksantikvarieämbetet.

Ulsig, Erik. 1968. *Danske Adelsgodser i Middelalderen*. Copenhagen: Gyldendal.

————. 1991. "Pest og befolkningsnedgang i Danmark i det 14. århundrede." *Historisk Tidsskrift* (Copenhagen) 91, 21–43.

Weibull, Curt. 1966. "Lübecks sjöfart och handel på de nordiska rikena 1368 och 1398–1400. Studier i Lübecks pundtullböcker." *Scandia* 32, 1–123.

Weibull, Lauritz. 1923. *Lunds Domkyrkas Nekrologium*. Lund, Sweden: Berlingska Boktryckeriet.

Winberg, Christer. 1985. *Grenverket; studier rörande jord, släktskapssystem och ståndsprivilegier*. Stockholm: Rättshistoriskt Bibliotek.

Wittendorff, Alex. 1989. *På Guds og Herskabs nåde, 1500–1600*. Vol. 7 of *Danmarkshistorie*, ed. Olsen.

Wood, Ian. 1987. "Christians and Pagans in Ninth-Century Scandinavia." In Sawyer and Wood, 36–67.

Index

Persons with the same name are listed, if necessary, in the following order: royalty, ecclesiastics, others. Kings with the same name are listed chronologically by kingdoms in the order Denmark, Norway, Sweden (KD, KN, KS). The letters D, F, I, N, and S used to locate places refer to the modern countries; see p. x of the preface.

Birgit Sawyer is an associate professor in the Institute of History, Gothenburg University. She is one of the founders of the biennial interdisciplinary conferences on Women in Medieval Scandinavia.

Peter Sawyer is retired and was a professor of history at the University of Leeds. He was also a visiting professor at the University of California-Berkeley and the University of Minnesota. His previous books include *Kings and Vikings* and *The Age of the Vikings*.